THE INTERNATIONAL COLOR GUIDE TO WORLD COOKERY

THE INTERNATIONAL COLOR GUIDE TO WORLD COOKERY

Edited by
Marie-Christine Comte

CRESCENT BOOKS
NEW YORK

Copyright © 1970 by Istituto Geografico de Agostini, Novara
This edition © 1976 by Orbis Publishing Limited, London
Library of Congress Catalog card number: 76-27146
All rights reserved
This edition is published by Crescent Books
a division of Crown Publishers Inc.
by arrangement with Orbis Publishing Limited
a b c d e f g h
Photographs by C. Mariorossi; edited by Marie-Christine Comte
Manufactured in England by Jarrold & Sons Ltd, Norwich

CONTENTS

Soups & Starters

1

2

3

Chicken Consommé

Prepare a small chicken for cooking, slicing and reserving the heart and liver. If possible, brown it in the oven in a little butter. Place in a large pan with the reserved heart and liver, 3 quarts water, and salt to taste. Bring slowly to a boil, skimming the scum as it forms on surface. Add 1 carrot, peeled, 1 leek, cleaned, and 1 small onion, quartered, and bring to a boil. Cook the chicken, covered, over low heat for 1½–2 hours. Remove and discard vegetables and strain broth through a sieve covered with a cloth soaked in water and wrung dry. Serve very hot, preferably in small bowls or cups.

Broths and Consommés

Meat Consommé

Ingredients: ¾ lb stewing beef · ¾ lb stewing veal · 1 beef bone · 1 veal knuckle · chicken neck and bones, if desired · 3½ quarts water · salt · 3 peppercorns · 1 carrot, peeled · 1 onion, peeled and stuck with 1 clove · 1 bouquet garni of parsley and celery

To clarify: 1 egg white

Put the meats, bone and knuckle, and chicken neck and bones, if using, in a large pan with the water, salt and peppercorns, and bring very slowly to a boil, skimming the scum as it forms on the surface (step 1). Add the vegetables and bouquet garni (steps 2 and 3), and bring to a boil. Cook, covered, over low heat for 3 hours. Strain through a sieve, reserving the meats for other uses, and discard fat from surface, if soup is to be served immediately. (The broth can be left to stand until cold, and fat can then be removed from surface.)

To clarify: put 1 quart cold broth in a pan with 1 egg white and bring to a boil, beating constantly with a wire whisk. Simmer, covered, over very low heat for ½ hour and strain through a sieve covered with a cloth.

1

2

3

Classic Consommé

Ingredients: *2 quarts warm broth, prepared with beef, chicken and vegetables · ½ lb lean beef · 1 small carrot and 1 leek, both thinly sliced · 1 egg white*

Clean the meat, removing all fat, and chop it. In a pan beat the meat and carrot, leek and egg white with a wire whisk (step 1). Beating constantly, add the broth a little at a time (step 2). Bring the mixture slowly to a boil, stirring constantly, and cook, covered, over very low heat for about 1 hour. Strain through a fine cloth, soaked in lukewarm water and wrung dry (step 3), then bring to a boil. The consommé should be perfectly clear. Serve in small bowls or cups.

Consommé Fantasia

Beat 3 eggs with a little salt until light and foamy, and stir in a generous handful of fresh spinach, chopped, 1 tablespoon Italian prosciutto, chopped, and 2 tablespoons grated Parmesan cheese. Cook the mixture on both sides as you would a frittata and cut it into thin strips. Divide the strips equally between 4 bowls or cups and pour in boiling consommé. Serve immediately.

Chicken Consommé with Marsala

Prepare chicken broth, leave to cool and remove the fat from the surface. Return to the heat, stir in 1 egg white and bring to a boil, beating constantly with a wire whisk. Strain the consommé through 2 or 3 fine cloths or through cheesecloth. Return to the heat, stir in 1 glass dry Marsala for each quart of consommé, and bring to a boil. Serve immediately in small bowls or cups.

Cock-a-Leekie Soup

Ingredients: *one 2-lb lean chicken ·
the white parts of 6 leeks, thinly sliced ·
2 quarts veal stock · 1 small carrot ·
1 small onion, peeled · 1 celery stalk · salt ·
2 tablespoons butter*

To serve: *16 prunes, cooked and pitted
(optional)*

Put the chicken and stock in a pan and bring
to a boil. Skim the scum as it forms on the
surface, add the carrot, onion, celery, and salt
to taste, and cook, covered, over low heat for
about 1½ hours. Put chicken on a chopping
board, remove and discard skin and bones and
cut flesh into thin strips (step 1). Cook the
leeks in the butter and a little salt (step 2).
Remove fat from chicken broth and strain
through a sieve. Return the chicken and leeks
to the broth (step 3), and serve very hot.
Prunes are traditionally served separately.
Serves 4–6.

Mulligatawny Soup

Sauté one 2-lb chicken, cut into pieces, in
1 tablespoon butter until golden on all sides.
Add 1 green apple, 1 green pepper and 1 carrot,
all chopped, and cook for a few minutes.
Sprinkle with 1 tablespoon flour, mixed with
½ tablespoon curry powder, and stir in 3 quarts
hot water, a little at a time, ½ tablespoon
parsley, chopped, 1 clove, 1 pinch of pepper
and ½ tablespoon each of salt and sugar. Cover
pan and cook over low heat for 1½ hours.
Half an hour before the end of the cooking
time, add ½ cup tomatoes, worked through a
food chopper or sieve, and continue cooking
the mixture until chicken is tender. Remove
the chicken from pan, discard skin and bones
and cube the flesh. Strain the broth through a
sieve and return the broth and chicken to the
heat for a few minutes. Serve immediately in
warm soup dishes, with boiled rice, in a separate platter.

1 2 3

Cream Soups

Cream of Artichoke Soup

Ingredients: *4 large artichokes · lemon juice ·
3 tablespoons butter · ¼ cup flour ·
1¾ cups milk · salt · grated nutmeg ·
3 cups stock*

To finish: *parsley, finely chopped ·
bread croûtons, toasted or sautéed in butter
until golden on all sides · grated cheese*

Clean the artichokes, halve them, discard the
chokes and let stand in water with lemon juice
to prevent discoloration. Cut in quarters and
sauté over low heat in 1 tablespoon butter for
10–15 minutes (step 1). Prepare a béchamel
sauce with the butter, flour, milk and salt and

grated nutmeg to taste. Work the artichokes
through a food chopper or sieve (step 2), add
to the béchamel sauce and return pan to heat
for 10 minutes. Add the stock and bring
mixture to a boil. Add a generous amount of
parsley. Serve with croûtons (step 3) and
grated cheese.

Cream of Lentil Soup

Put ¾ cup dried lentils in cold water to cover
with 1 clove of garlic, 1 carrot and 1 onion,
all peeled, and a bouquet garni. Bring to a boil,
skim off the scum and cook for about 1½ hours.
Remove and discard vegetables and bouquet
garni and work lentils and their liquid through
a food chopper or sieve. Prepare croûtons as
for above recipe. Stir 1 tablespoon butter and
½ cup cream into the sieved lentils, reheat
gently and serve immediately. Serve the
croûtons separately.

Cream of Carrot Soup
(Potage Crécy)

Put ½ lb carrots, peeled, 3½ tablespoons rice,
1 onion, peeled, 1 bouquet garni, 1 leek,
cleaned, and 1 quart water in a pan. Bring to
a boil and cook over low heat for about 45
minutes. Remove and discard the bouquet
garni and work the mixture through a food
chopper or sieve. Prepare bread croûtons to
taste. Stir 1 tablespoon butter and ½ cup
cream into the sieved vegetables, reheat gently
and serve immediately. Serve the croûtons
separately.

1   2   3

Cream of Mushroom Soup

Ingredients: *1¼ cups fresh mushrooms or 2 tablespoons dried mushrooms, soaked in lukewarm water, squeezed dry and sliced · 3¼ tablespoons butter · 3 cups stock · ¼ cup flour · 1¾ cups milk · salt · grated nutmeg*

To finish: *parsley, chopped · croûtons*

Clean and trim fresh mushrooms (if using) and slice them finely (step 1). Heat 1 tablespoon butter in a small pan, add the mushrooms and sauté for a few minutes. Add ¼ cup stock and cook, covered, over very low heat for about 15 minutes. Prepare a béchamel sauce with remaining butter, the flour, milk and salt and grated nutmeg to taste (step 2). Work mushrooms through a food chopper (step 3), add them to the béchamel sauce and cook over moderate heat for 10 minutes. Add remaining stock, bring to a boil and stir in the parsley. Serve with croûtons separately.

Cream of Pea Soup

Cover 1¼ cups dried split peas with cold water and let stand for 1 hour. Drain, put in a pan with cold water to cover and a little salt and bring to a boil. Skim the scum from the surface, cover pan and cook over low heat for about ½ hour.

In another pan cook ½ onion, finely chopped, in 2 tablespoons butter until golden, add 1 carrot, peeled, the green part of 2 leeks, cleaned, a few chopped lettuce or spinach leaves and ¼ bay leaf and cook for a few minutes. Add the peas and their cooking water and cook, covered, over low heat for about 1 hour. Work through a food chopper or sieve and return to the heat and reheat gently. Add salt to taste, 2 tablespoons butter and a few tablespoons cream, if desired. Serve with 3½ tablespoons diced ham, croûtons and a generous amount of grated Parmesan cheese.

Cream of Tomato Soup

Cook 1½ lb tomatoes, peeled and chopped, 1 medium onion, sliced, ½ teaspoon sugar and a pinch of salt for ½ hour. Work the mixture through a food chopper or sieve and keep warm. In another pan heat 4 tablespoons butter, add 4 tablespoons flour and cook, stirring constantly, until well blended. Stir in 1 quart cold milk and a pinch of salt and cook over low heat for about 20 minutes. Put a pinch of sodium bicarbonate in a soup tureen, pour in the tomato mixture and stir in the hot milk mixture. Mix well and serve with croûtons.

Potage Santé (Vichyssoise)

Ingredients: *2–3 leeks, depending on size ·*
3 tablespoons butter · 1 lb potatoes, peeled and
quartered · water · salt · hot milk ·
3½ oz sorrel leaves, chopped and cooked in
1 tablespoon butter · 1–2 egg yolks ·
a few tablespoons cream · ½ teaspoon chervil

To finish: *croûtons*

Slice the white parts of the leeks finely and cook
in 1 tablespoon of the butter for a few minutes
(step 1). Add the potatoes, 6 cups water and a
little salt to taste, and cook until potatoes are
tender. Work mixture through a food chopper
or sieve (step 2), and thin the soup if necessary, with a little water and hot milk. Add the
sorrel leaves and pour soup into a tureen
(step 3). Stir in the egg yolks, mixed with the
cream, the remaining butter and the chervil.
Serve with fried or toasted croûtons in a
separate dish.

Cream of Vegetable Soup

Clean and trim 1 small Savoy cabbage, slice
finely, cover with boiling water and leave to
stand. Finely slice 2 carrots, 2 potatoes, 1 tur-
nip and the white part of 2 leeks, and cook
over moderate heat in 1 tablespoon butter for
a few minutes. Add 6 cups boiling stock and
cook over low heat for 1 hour. Drain the
cabbage and add to the mixture with 1 clove
of garlic, peeled and crushed, and cook for 25
minutes. Work through a food chopper or
sieve and add enough hot stock to obtain 1
quart liquid. Reheat. Put 1–2 slices fried bread
in each plate and pour the soup over.

Potage Dubarry

In a pan, cook 1 cauliflower, 1 onion, and 1 bay
leaf in boiling salted water until cauliflower is
tender.

Prepare a roux: in a small pan heat 3 tablespoons butter, add 3 tablespoons flour and
cook mixture, stirring constantly, adding a
few tablespoons cooking water from the
cauliflower, until well blended and golden.
Work the cauliflower and its cooking liquid
through a food chopper or sieve, return to heat
and stir in the roux, 2 egg yolks and ½ cup
cream, without letting the mixture boil. Serve
the soup immediately with crusty bread
served separately.

Cream of Watercress Soup

Cook ¾ lb potatoes, peeled, and 1 bunch
watercress, washed and trimmed, in boiling
salted water for ½ hour. Work through a food
chopper or sieve and add 2 tablespoons butter
and ½ cup cream. Reheat gently and serve the
soup immediately with croûtons in a separate
dish.

1

2

3

Thick Soups

Zucchini and Tomato Soup

Ingredients: *4 zucchini · 1 or more tomatoes, depending on size · 1 tablespoon butter · 1 clove of garlic, peeled · 5 cups stock · ½ cup rice*

To finish: *grated Parmesan cheese*

Melt the butter in a large pan, add the garlic, cook for a few minutes then discard. Dice the zucchini (step 1) and sauté until golden (step 2). Chop the tomato and add to mixture. Cook for a few minutes, add the stock (step 3) and bring to a boil. Stir in the rice and cook until *al dente*. Serve with grated Parmesan cheese.

Pistou

Wash 2 leeks, dry them and slice finely. Dip 4 tomatoes in boiling water and peel. Wash and peel 6 oz potatoes and dice them. Put the leeks, 2 chopped tomatoes, the potatoes, ¾ cup green beans and ½ cup kidney beans in a large pan with 2 quarts water. Add salt and pepper to taste and cook for 15 minutes. Add 3 oz vermicelli and cook for 15 minutes. Chop 3 cloves of garlic, the remaining 2 tomatoes and a generous amount of basil very finely, and stir in 4 tablespoons olive oil and 3½ tablespoons grated Gruyère cheese. Put garlic mixture in the bottom of a soup tureen and pour in soup.

Leek and Rice Soup

Heat 2 tablespoons butter in a pan, add ¾ lb leeks, washed, dried and thinly sliced, and cook for a few minutes. Add 1 teaspoon tomato paste and 6 cups stock and cook for about 20 minutes. Add ¾ cup rice and cook until rice is *al dente*. Add parsley, finely chopped, and serve with grated Parmesan cheese.

Greek Vegetable Soup

Bring about 5 cups chicken stock to a boil, add about ¾ cup rice and cook until rice is *al dente*. In a soup tureen beat 2 egg yolks with the juice of 1 or 2 lemons and add ½ cup warm stock, stirring constantly. Add the rice and stock and serve immediately.

Onion Soup

Ingredients: *6 oz onions, thinly sliced ·
2 tablespoons butter · 2 level tablespoons flour ·
5 cups stock · salt · pepper · thin slices of bread ·
5 tablespoons grated Gruyère cheese*

Sauté the onions in the butter for a moment,
sprinkle them with the flour (step 1) and, as
soon as they start to brown, stir in the stock.
Add salt and pepper to taste and cook for about
20 minutes. Place thin slices of bread in the
bottom of a soup tureen, sprinkle with grated
Gruyère cheese (step 2) and pour the soup
over (step 3). Let stand for 10 minutes before
serving, or sprinkle with more Gruyère cheese
and put in a hot oven (400°F) until golden
and crusty on top.

Lentil Soup

Soak 2 cups dried lentils in lukewarm water
for 12 hours, drain and put in a pan with
cold water to cover. Cook, covered, for 2–3
hours, then work through a food chopper or
sieve. In a small pan, heat 2 tablespoons
butter, add a mixture of onion, celery, garlic
and sage leaves, all chopped, and sauté for a
few minutes. Stir the mixture into the lentils,
add 2 stock cubes, salt and pepper to taste,
and return the soup to the heat. Bring to a
boil, remove from heat and serve with slices
of bread fried in butter and a generous amount
of grated Parmesan cheese.

Spinach Soup

Clean and wash 1½ lb fresh spinach, cook
without water and chop coarsely. Sauté quickly
in 1 tablespoon butter and leave to cool. In a
bowl beat 2 eggs with 2 tablespoons grated
Parmesan cheese, and salt and grated nutmeg
to taste, and stir into the spinach. Pour spinach
into 5 cups boiling stock, return to heat and
bring to a boil. Place 2 toasted bread slices in
each plate, add soup and a generous amount
of grated Parmesan cheese and serve immediately.

Auvergne Soup

In a large pan put 2 quarts water, 4 carrots and
2 turnips, both sliced, one 2-lb cabbage,
quartered, and 1 clove of garlic, peeled and
crushed. Bring to a boil and simmer for about
10 minutes. Add 4 small potatoes, peeled and
sliced, salt and pepper to taste, and cook for
10 minutes. Fry 4 tablespoons diced lean bacon
in a skillet, drain and add to the soup.
Simmer for 5 minutes. Place a slice of French
bread in each plate and pour the soup over
them. Serves 6–8.

Bean and Noodle Soup

Ingredients: *¾ cup dried red or kidney beans, soaked in cold water for 12 hours and drained · 3½ tablespoons bacon fat, 1 celery stalk, 1 small onion, 1 clove of garlic, parsley, basil, 6 tablespoons canned peeled tomatoes, all chopped · 2 quarts cold water · 2 stock cubes · salt · pepper · 1 tablespoon oil · ¾ cup short noodles or macaroni*

Put the beans in a large pan (step 1), with the bacon fat, celery, onion, garlic, parsley, basil, tomatoes, and the water. Bring the mixture to a boil, add the stock cubes, salt and pepper to taste, and cook, covered, over low heat for about 1½ hours. Work ½ the beans through a sieve (step 2), and return to the pan. Raise the heat, add the noodles (step 3), and cook until noodles are *al dente*. Remove soup from the heat and let stand for a few minutes. Stir in the oil and serve immediately.

Potée Savoyarde

In a saucepan sauté 6 tablespoons chopped salt pork, for a few minutes, add 2 leeks and 1 onion, both sliced, and sauté for a few minutes. Add 1 celery stalk and 1¼ cups potatoes, peeled and sliced, and 1 quart water and bring the mixture to a boil. Cook over medium heat for 30 minutes then stir in 2 cups milk. Bring to a boil and cook over high heat for a few minutes, adding salt and pepper to taste. Grate 3 oz Gruyère cheese, sprinkle on slices of crusty bread, and toast in the oven until golden. Serve with the soup.

Brussels Sprouts Soup

Wash and trim 2 cups Brussels sprouts and cook in boiling salted water with ½ bay leaf, ½ onion, thinly sliced, ¼ clove of garlic and a few parsley sprigs until tender. Drain and work through a food chopper. Add salt, pepper and grated nutmeg to taste, and 1 quart stock, and bring to a boil. Serve with croûtons.

1

2

3

Cold Hors d'Oeuvres

Avocados with Shrimps

Ingredients: *2 avocados · 1 tablespoon vinegar, preferably tarragon vinegar · ⅓ cup olive oil · ⅓ cup lemon juice · 1 teaspoon Worcestershire · salt · pepper · cayenne pepper · ⅓ cup heavy cream · about 30 shrimps, cooked, shelled and deveined · homemade (see p.50) or commercial gelatin*

Halve the avocados lengthwise, discard the seeds and scoop out the pulp, keeping shells intact (steps 1, 2 and 3). Work the pulp through a sieve (always use silver, stainless steel or nylon utensils or the avocado pulp will turn black). Add the vinegar and oil,

Worcestershire, salt, pepper and cayenne pepper to taste. Add the cream, whipped until it holds its shape, and mix gently. Fill the avocado shells with the mixture, place them on a serving platter and garnish each shell with shrimps brushed with cold but still liquid gelatin. Decorate the platter to taste and chill.

Stuffed Avocados

Halve 2 avocados lengthwise, discard the seeds and sprinkle the halves with lemon juice and salt. Mix 1 can tuna fish and its oil with 3–4 celery stalks and 1 cucumber, both chopped,

2–3 tablespoons mayonnaise, lemon juice to taste and salt. Fill the avocado shells with the mixture and place them on a serving platter.

Grapefruit and Crab Cocktail

Peel 2 ripe grapefruit, chilled, and cut them in pieces. Combine together with 1 can crabmeat, drained and cleaned, and 1 cup mayonnaise mixed with 1 teaspoon each of lemon juice and vinegar and a few drops Tabasco. Spoon into 4 sherbet glasses. Chill.

Avocado Dip

Halve 1 or more avocados lengthwise, scoop out the pulp, keeping 1 shell for each avocado used, and mash it with a fork. Mix with 1 small onion, finely chopped, lemon juice to taste, a few drops Worcestershire, mayonnaise and salt. Pile the mixture into the shell, chill and serve on a platter surrounded by potato chips.

Italian Hors d'Oeuvre

Ingredients: ¼ lb Italian prosciutto · ¼ lb each of ham, Italian salami, mortadella and smoked tongue · butter · ¼ cup green olives · 3 oz artichoke hearts in olive oil

Place a ring or decorative mold upside down in the center of a serving platter (step 1), cover it with aluminum foil (step 2) and with the prosciutto slices, putting one slice in the form of a flower in the middle (step 3). Place the other cold meats around the mold and garnish them with butter curls, olives and artichoke hearts. The last two ingredients can also be served separately, with olives, mushrooms and onions in olive oil, and gherkins.

To make a more complete hors d'oeuvre, add sardines, anchovies in olive oil and chopped parsley, tuna fish in olive oil, eggplant slices, white bean salad with onion slices, grated carrots with mayonnaise and cream dressing, stuffed hard-boiled eggs, frankfurter (or beef sausage) salad dressed with mayonnaise, beet and endive salad, all on different platters.

Do not add cold meats to hors d'oeuvres until the last minute, to keep them fresh.

Eggplant Slices

Peel 1 large eggplant and cut it into ½-inch slices. Put the slices in an oven-proof dish and cover them with olive oil and 1 clove of garlic, thinly sliced. Marinate the eggplant slices for about 1 hour, drain them and discard the garlic. Broil the slices until golden brown. Let them cool and sprinkle them with chopped parsley.

Ligurian Anchovies

Soak anchovy fillets in an equal mixture of water and vinegar for about 3 hours, or until desalted. Drain and rinse the fillets. Place them on a serving platter, surrounded by sliced ripe tomatoes, and sprinkle them with olive oil, finely chopped garlic and oregano to taste.

Celery Hors d'Oeuvre

Clean 3 or 4 celery stalks and marinate them in white wine vinegar for at least 12 hours. Drain them and cut them thinly lengthwise. Dress the celery with homemade or commercial mayonnaise and chill in refrigerator before serving.

Broiled Peppers

Cook 1 yellow pepper and 1 red pepper, or 2 green peppers, under the broiler or directly on the flame (using a long-handled fork in the latter case), and peel and seed them. Cut each pepper in eighths and place them in a deep platter. Add olive oil, salt and chopped parsley, and, to make the dish more appetizing, pressed garlic to taste. The peppers can be cooked days in advance as they keep very well as long as they are covered with olive oil. They go well with anchovies in olive oil.

Kaleidoscope of Appetizers

Ingredients: *1 cauliflower · sliced white bread · salami · cheese · shrimps · artichokes in olive oil · frankfurters · gherkins · hard-boiled eggs · olives*

Clean the cauliflower, place it on a serving platter and garnish it with appetizers (step 1) prepared with the above ingredients, sliced and imaginatively arranged on cocktail picks. Garnish the platter with sliced hard-boiled egg. Grapefruit and watermelon are equally decorative and can be substituted for the cauliflower when in season.

Cheese Appetizers

Cut an assortment of cheeses, such as Gruyère, Emmenthal, Bel Paese, Cheddar and cacciotta, into cubes and arrange them on cocktail picks. Set the picks on a serving platter and surround them with an assortment of crackers.

Shrimp Appetizers

Shell and devein 2 lb cooked shrimps and chill them. Pierce the shrimps with cocktail picks and place them on a serving platter around a small bowl of mayonnaise (see p.48).

1 2 3

Club Sandwich

Ingredients for each sandwich: *3 slices of fresh bread · lettuce · ham · mayonnaise · sliced cheese, either Gruyère or Emmenthal · tomato · chicken meat · butter · oil · vinegar · salt*

To garnish: *tomato · 1 black olive*

Toast and butter each slice of bread (step 1). Put some lettuce, dressed with oil, vinegar and salt, on the first slice of bread, add a slice of ham, brushed with mayonnaise, and a slice of cheese (step 2). Add the second slice of bread, some more lettuce and tomato slices, also dressed, and the chicken meat, cubed and mixed with mayonnaise. Add the last slice of bread (step 3), brush it with mayonnaise and add a slice of cheese, a tomato quarter and a black olive. Decorate by piping mayonnaise in a border on top.

These sandwiches also make an ideal light lunch or snack.

Ham and Egg Sandwiches

Butter 8 slices of whole-wheat or rye bread. On 4 slices put gherkins and 2 hard-boiled eggs, both sliced, and 4 slices of ham. Add 2 hard-boiled eggs and gherkins, both sliced, and close the sandwiches with the remaining slices of buttered bread.

Sardine and Egg Sandwiches

Butter 8 slices of whole-wheat or rye bread. On 4 slices put sardines, drained, and 3 sliced hard-boiled eggs, and brush generously with mustard. Close the sandwiches with the remaining slices of bread.

Radish Canapés

Toast 4 slices of white or rye bread and spread them with mayonnaise. Add radishes and gherkins, both sliced.

Smoked Eel Canapés

Spread 4 slices of black bread with mayonnaise, sprinkle with dill and add smoked eel pieces.

1   2   3

Shrimp Cocktail

Ingredients: *1¼ lb small fresh or frozen shrimps · mayonnaise made with 2 eggs (see p.48) · 2 or 3 tablespoons ketchup · 1 teaspoon Worcestershire · 2 teaspoons brandy · salt · paprika · 2 or 3 tablespoons heavy cream · 1 lettuce heart*

To serve: *lemon wedges*

Wash the shrimps, cook them in boiling salted water for 5 minutes, drain, shell and devein them. Mix the mayonnaise together with the ketchup, Worcestershire, brandy, salt, paprika and heavy cream. Put lettuce leaves, sliced lengthwise, in the bottom of 4 crystal goblets or sherbet glasses (step 1), add the shrimps, putting 24 aside to use as decoration. Pour the mixture over the shrimps (step 2), and garnish each goblet with shrimps set around the rim of the crystal and one whole lettuce leaf on one side (step 3). The goblets can be served as they are or set in crushed ice on a silver platter.

Canadian Herring Salad

Broil smoked herring directly on the flame, skin, remove bones and cut flesh in cubes. Add an equal quantity of potatoes, boiled and peeled, and cored green apples, both cut in cubes, minced chives and parsley, and fennel seed to taste. Dress the salad with oil, vinegar, salt and pepper.

Mussels in Piquant Sauce

Clean thoroughly 3¼ lb mussels in cold running water, drain and dry them. Cook 1 clove of garlic in 2 tablespoons olive oil until golden and discard garlic. Add the mussels to the pan with 2 anchovies, desalted and mashed to a paste, and 1 cup each of vinegar and dry white wine. Cover the pan and cook the mixture over high heat until mussels open. Remove mussels and continue cooking the stock over high heat until it is reduced by half. Shell the mussels, put them in a covered earthenware dish, sprinkle with chopped parsley and pepper and add the stock. Chill 2−3 days before serving.

How to Serve Caviar and Smoked Salmon

Ingredients: *1 small can caviar or salmon roe ·
¾ lb smoked salmon, very thinly sliced · lemons ·
butter · pepper · parsley, preferably Italian
parsley · black bread · white bread*

Keep the caviar in the refrigerator until serving
time. Serve it in its can or in a small crystal
dish, set in a bigger dish on crushed ice, with
lemon quarters, sliced black bread and butter
curls. In Russia it is traditional for caviar to
be served with hot blini, melted butter, sour
cream and vodka.

    Put the smoked salmon on a serving platter,
garnished with black olives, parsley or lettuce
leaves. Serve it with toasted white bread slices
covered with a napkin (to keep them warm),
butter curls and lemon halves on separate
platters. Add a pepper mill so that each person
can grind his own pepper at the last moment.

Russian Blini

Ingredients: *1 cup flour · 1 teaspoon each of
sugar and double-acting baking powder ·
1½ cups milk · 2 eggs · 1 cup sour cream*

Sift the flour into a bowl and add the sugar
and baking powder. Make a well in the center
and pour in the milk. Blend with the fingers
until all ingredients are incorporated. Break
the eggs in a separate bowl, beat them hard
and blend them into the dough with 3
tablespoons sour cream. Beat the batter lightly
but thoroughly and add milk and sour cream
until it is the consistency of thick cream. Cover
and let stand at room temperature for 20
minutes. Heat a little butter in a very small
frying pan, add a small amount of batter and
fry quickly until golden on both sides. Repeat

with remaining batter, keeping blini in a hot
oven. Serve very hot.

Caviar Canapés

Trim the crusts off slices of white bread and
cut bread into quarters. Spread with butter.
Put caviar on one half of each bread quarter
so that it is diagonally covered and spread the
other corner with white and yolk of hard-
boiled eggs, mashed separately. Garnish the
platter with lemon quarters and sprigs of
parsley, if liked.

1   2   3

Crudités

Crudités, or raw vegetables, make a very healthy hors d'oeuvre. Various raw vegetables are cleaned and cut into fairly large pieces to be dipped into a vinaigrette sauce, made of oil, vinegar, salt and pepper. As guests may like to season their own crudités, it is best to serve the vinaigrette separately.

Artichokes: discard the stems and hard outer leaves; cut the softer leaves to $\frac{3}{4}$ of their height, quarter the artichokes and discard the chokes; sprinkle them with lemon juice (step 1) and keep them in cold water to prevent discoloration until serving time.

Carrots: scrape and wash young carrots (step 2) and slice them lengthwise in 4 or more pieces.

Fennel: discard the outer leaves and each end of the fennel bulbs (step 3). Quarter bulbs and wash them very carefully.

Peppers: wash them and discard the stems. Quarter peppers and discard the seeds and white membranes.

Radishes: wash them, trim the ends and scrape them lightly.

Celery: use only the hearts of the celery. Wash well and remove the bigger leaves.

Creamed Cucumbers

Peel 4 cucumbers and slice them thinly. Add salt, pepper and 4 or more tablespoons vinegar. Whip 1 cup heavy cream until slightly thickened and mix it gently with the cucumbers. Chill.

Artichoke Salad

Discard the stems and hard outer leaves of 3–4 tender artichokes. Starting from the bottom and using a very sharp knife, slice the artichokes very thinly and discard the chokes. Put the slices in cold water seasoned with lemon juice to prevent discoloration. Drain and dry them and season with 3 tablespoons oil, salt, pepper and lemon juice.

Carrot Salad

Scrape young carrots and grate them. Season with oil, lemon, salt and pepper, or with salt, pepper, mayonnaise and whipped cream. Chill before serving.

Mushroom Salad

Slice mushrooms very thinly and mix with an equal proportion of fresh Parmesan or Gruyère cheese, cut in thin strips. Add a few paper-thin slices of white truffle if available, oil, lemon juice, salt and white pepper.

1

2

3

Salad Niçoise

Ingredients: *potatoes · green beans · oil ·*
vinegar · salt · pepper · tomatoes · parsley ·
anchovy fillets · black olives · capers

Cook the potatoes and green beans separately
in boiling salted water until tender, drain
them and let cool. Cut the potatoes in cubes
and slice the beans (step 1). Season them with
oil, vinegar, salt and pepper, and pile them in
a salad bowl (step 2). Add tomatoes, quartered
and sprinkled with chopped parsley, and
decorate with desalted anchovy fillets, olives
and capers (step 3). Serve with lemon wedges.
This salad is good with grilled meats.

Fish and Potato Salad

Mix gently 2 cups cooked white fish, cleaned
and flaked, with 2 cups cooked potatoes, cubed,
½ cup thinly sliced celery, 1 tablespoon chopped
onion, salt, pepper, oil and lemon. Put the
salad on a serving platter and garnish with
mayonnaise. Chill. Sprinkle with chopped
parsley just before serving.

Spring Salad

Cook separately 1 cup each of asparagus tips,
green beans and small peas, and 3 artichoke

hearts (optional) in boiling salted water until
tender. Cook 2 eggs in boiling salted water
for 9 minutes. Mix a dash of pepper with ½
teaspoon each of salt and English powdered
mustard, 5–6 tablespoons olive oil and about
2 tablespoons vinegar in a salad bowl. Add
the cooked vegetables, the hard-boiled eggs,
coarsely chopped, 5–6 thinly sliced radishes
and chopped parsley, basil and chives to taste.
Mix lightly and chill for about 1 hour. Add
4 or more tablespoons homemade mayonnaise
(see p.48), mix gently and serve.

Russian Salad with Ham Rolls

Ingredients: *1½ cups potatoes · ½ cup each of carrots, green beans and fresh or frozen peas · 2 tablespoons pickled vegetables · 1 cup home-made (see p.50) or commercial gelatin · oil · vinegar · salt · pepper · mayonnaise made with 1 egg (see p.48), 1 teaspoon mustard, juice of 1 lemon · 6 slices ham · ¾ cup homemade (see p.31) or bought liver mousse*

To garnish: *1 hard-boiled egg · 1 tomato (optional)*

Wash, prepare and cook the raw vegetables separately in boiling salted water. Drain them, let them cool, and cut potatoes, carrots and green beans into cubes. Put the vegetables in a bowl, add the pickled vegetables and season with a little oil, vinegar, salt and pepper. Add the cool but still liquid gelatin in small amounts to the mayonnaise, reserving 2–3 tablespoons. Add the seasoned vegetables, mustard and lemon juice, and pour the mixture in a lightly oiled ring mold (step 1). Chill for about 2 hours. Make a roll of each ham slice and, using a pastry bag fitted with a large star tube, fill them with liver mousse. Unmold the Russian salad on a serving platter (step 2), place the ham rolls sunburst-fashion and brush them with the reserved liquid gelatin. Put the hard-boiled egg, topped with liver mousse, or a small stuffed tomato in the center. Chill before serving. Serves 6.

Red Cabbage Salad

Trim and wash 1 small red cabbage and slice it finely. Put it in a bowl, sprinkle generously with vinegar and sugar and marinate for 4 hours. Add 1 minced onion, and season the salad with mustard, oil, vinegar, salt and pepper. Garnish with 12 black olives, chopped parsley and chervil, and other herbs, if liked. Serves 6.

Salad Marly

In a salad bowl combine ¾ cup cold roast beef, cut in thin strips, with 2 potatoes, boiled and cubed, ½ cup cooked green beans, cut in pieces, 3 or 4 radishes, sliced, and 1 small onion, thinly sliced. Mix 2 tablespoons mayonnaise with oil, vinegar, a few drops of Worcestershire, salt and pepper. Pour the dressing on the salad and mix gently. Sprinkle with finely chopped parsley and basil, and other herbs, if liked, just before you serve the salad.

Stuffed Tomatoes

Ingredients: *¾ cup rice · ⅓ cup mushrooms · juice of 1 lemon · 4 tomatoes · 1 tablespoon tomato paste · 3–4 tablespoons mayonnaise · tarragon · salt · white pepper*

Cook the rice in boiling salted water. Wipe and trim the mushrooms, slice thinly and sprinkle with lemon juice to prevent discoloration. Wash the tomatoes, cut a thick slice from the top of each and reserve. Press the tomatoes gently to extract the water and seeds and salt them lightly. Mix the rice with the mushrooms, tomato paste and mayonnaise. Fill the tomatoes with the mixture, sprinkle with tarragon, season and replace the tops.

1

2

3

1 2 3

Oysters

Ingredients: *32 oysters · lemons · sauce made with minced shallots, vinegar, salt and ground pepper; or sauce made with 2 tablespoons tomato ketchup, 1 teaspoon each of chilli sauce, mayonnaise and horseradish, and salt and pepper · freshly ground pepper · buttered rye or white bread slices*

Open the oysters just before serving as shown in step 1. They may also be opened 2 hours before and kept in the refrigerator until serving time. Fill each plate with crushed ice and place 8 oysters on each; decorate with lemon quarters. A small container of the chosen sauce can be placed in the center or served separately. Ground pepper, extra lemon quarters and slices of bread are served separately. Clams and mussels can also be served in this manner (steps 2 and 3).

Mussels

Scrub and wash fresh mussels thoroughly, discarding the beards. Just before serving, insert the point of a small knife between the two shells and move it round, being careful not to go in too deeply. Serve the mussels on crushed ice with lemon quarters and freshly ground pepper.

Sea Urchins

Hold the sea urchin in the left hand in a heavy folded cloth. Insert the tip of scissors in the soft part of the shell (about ¾ of the way up) and cut all around, discarding the liquid and digestive tube. To eat scoop out the fleshy part with a teaspoon or with bread, as with a boiled egg. Season with lemon juice.

Shellfish Salad

Clean ¾ cup fresh or frozen small cuttlefish, wash and drain them and cook in boiling salted water for 10 minutes. Add ¾ cup shelled shrimps and continue cooking for 10 minutes. Drain the shellfish and let cool. Scrub and wash 1¼ lb mussels thoroughly, discarding the beards. Heat 1 tablespoon oil in a pan, add the mussels and cook them over high heat, stirring occasionally, until all the shells are open. Let cool and discard the shells. Combine with cuttlefish and shrimps on a serving platter and season the salad with oil, salt, pepper and a generous amount of chopped parsley.

27

pepper and mixed herbs. Roll out ⅔ of the dough on a floured board into a rectangle, reserving remaining dough for cover. Lightly oil a 9-inch loaf pan and line it with the dough, leaving an extra inch all around (step 1). Add ¾ of the veal and pork mixture, a layer of veal strips and a layer of ham strips (⅔ of the two ingredients). Add the hard-boiled eggs, the veal and truffle mixture (step 2), and the remaining veal and ham strips with the remaining marinade. Cover with the remaining veal and pork mixture and a few bay leaves. Fold the extra dough toward the center, brush with beaten egg yolk and cover with reserved dough rolled out into a rectangle. Roll out any remaining dough to make a border and leaves or other decoration to put on top of the pie. Brush top with beaten egg. Make a hole in the center and put in a double roll of aluminum foil to make a funnel (step 3) so that the steam can escape during cooking. Bake the pie in a moderate oven (350°F) for about 2 hours. Remove the pie from the oven and, using the roll of aluminum foil, pour in, a little at a time, enough cool but still liquid gelatin to fill the mold (step 4).

When pie is cool, refrigerate for a few hours until cold and then turn out on a serving platter. Serves 8.

Garnish with remaining gelatin, diced, if liked.

Individual Pies

Prepare flaky pastry as for Barquettes (p.38) or use frozen puff pastry. In a mortar pound 6 drained and desalted anchovy fillets with 1 piece of onion and 1 clove of garlic, both minced, and 3–4 peppercorns. Add 2 teaspoons oil (the oil from the anchovy fillets will do very well) and 1 tablespoon brandy. Let the mixture stand for ½ hour. Add 1 egg yolk, 1 knob softened butter and about ¾ cup finely chopped ham.

Roll out the dough on a floured board and cut it into 4-inch rounds. Put 1 tablespoon of the mixture in the center of each round, dampen the edges and fold over the dough, pressing the edges tightly together. Brush the pies with beaten egg white and cook them in a moderate oven (350°F) for 35–40 minutes.

Serve immediately while still hot. Garnish with a little chopped parsley, if liked.

Veal, Ham and Pork Pie

Ingredients: for the pastry, *2 cups flour · 1 teaspoon salt · ½ cup butter or margarine · 2 eggs, whipped with 2 tablespoons cold water*

For the filling: *½ lb lean veal · ¾ lb ham in one piece · 1 glass brandy · ½ lb chopped veal · 2 oz salt pork · salt · thyme · 1 black truffle (optional) · ½ lb chopped pork · 1 egg · pepper · mixed herbs · 3 hard boiled eggs · bay leaves · 1 egg yolk · 2 cups homemade (see p.50) or commercial gelatin*

To garnish: *diced gelatin*

Sift the flour with the salt into a bowl. Using two knives or a pastry blender, cut in the butter or margarine until the mixture is mealy. Add the eggs and water, beating with a fork. Knead the dough quickly for a few moments, form a ball, cover with wax paper and refrigerate for a few hours. Cut the lean veal and ham in 1-inch strips, add half the brandy, cover and marinate for a few hours. In a bowl mix the chopped veal and salt pork with a good pinch each of salt and thyme and remaining brandy. Remove a little of the mixture, add diced truffle if liked and reserve. To the bowl add the chopped pork, 1 egg,

1 2 3

Stuffed Tomato Platter

Tomatoes with Shrimps

Ingredients: 4 *large tomatoes, firm and not too ripe · salt · mayonnaise made with 1 egg (see p.48) or commercial mayonnaise ·* $\frac{3}{4}$ *lb fresh or frozen shrimps · parsley*

Wash and dry the tomatoes, cut tops off each and discard (step 1), vandyke the edges (step 2) and gently scoop out the pulp (step 3), being careful not to break the tomato shells. Salt them and turn upside down to drain. Mix the mayonnaise with most of the shrimps (reserving a few to use as garnish), and pile the mixture into the tomato shells. Place the reserved shrimps around the top of each tomato, as shown in the top picture.

Tomatoes with Russian Salad

Prepare 4 large tomatoes as for Tomatoes with Shrimps. Mix $\frac{3}{4}$ cup Russian salad (see p.26) with $\frac{1}{3}$ cup chicken meat, cooked and cut in thin strips. Fill tomato shells with the mixture and garnish with anchovy fillets.

Tomatoes with Tuna Fish

Prepare 4 large tomatoes as for Tomatoes with Shrimps. Drain the oil from about $\frac{1}{4}$ cup tuna fish, crumble the tuna fish and mix with enough mayonnaise to make a smooth mixture. Add a few capers and fill tomato shells with the mixture. Garnish with extra capers and chill.

Tomatoes with Potatoes

Prepare 4 large tomatoes as for Tomatoes with Shrimps. Combine 2 large potatoes, cooked and diced, with $\frac{1}{4}$ lb Swiss cheese, diced, 1 small onion, finely chopped, and 1 teaspoon minced dill. Season the mixture with oil, vinegar, salt and pepper. Sliced frankfurters may be used if liked as well as potatoes. Fill the tomato shells with the mixture and garnish the tops.

29

Melon with Prosciutto

Ingredients: *1 large or 2 medium ripe cantaloups or other melons · salt · pepper · 8 thin slices of Italian prosciutto · butter*

Chill the melon(s) and cut into eight slices. Remove and discard the skin and seeds (steps 1 and 2). Sprinkle lightly with salt and pepper and wrap each slice with 1 slice of prosciutto (step 3). Place the melon slices wheel-fashion on the serving platter. Garnish with butter curls. The most classic way of serving this dish is to cut the skin from the melon only partially and to serve the melon and prosciutto separately.

Figs with Prosciutto

Place slices of Italian prosciutto on a serving platter. Chill figs, peel them and serve separately.

If desired, the figs can be peeled by each individual diner. This dish is a classic Italian hors d'oeuvre.

Prosciutto Surprise

In a bowl mix boiled chicken meat and Emmenthal cheese, both minced, with sliced celery, a few tablespoons mayonnaise, chopped capers, a little mustard, salt and lemon juice. Divide the mixture between slices of Italian prosciutto and roll up the slices. Pour a thin layer of cool but still liquid gelatin in a deep serving dish, add the prosciutto rolls and cover with a thin layer of gelatin. Refrigerate the dish for a few hours or until the gelatin is set. Garnish with gherkins, cut in fan shapes, or with little artichoke hearts in olive oil.

Prosciutto Roll

In a skillet melt a knob of butter or margarine, add 1 chicken liver, sprinkle with brandy and flame. Add salt and cook for a few minutes. Put $\frac{3}{4}$ cup boiled chicken meat, $\frac{1}{3}$ cup smoked tongue and the cooked chicken liver through the finest blade of a food chopper then work the mixture through a sieve, alternating with $\frac{3}{4}$ cup softened butter. Whip the mixture with a wooden spoon until it is light and fluffy and add a few slices of truffle if liked. Place 6 thick slices of Italian prosciutto, trimmed of their fat, so as to form a rectangle on wax paper, and add the chicken mixture. Roll up the prosciutto, cover the roll with wax paper or aluminum foil and refrigerate for a few hours. Pour a little cool but still liquid gelatin on a serving platter and refrigerate it until it is almost set. Cut the roll in thick slices, place the slices on the gelatin and cover them with more gelatin. Garnish with a border of artichoke hearts in oil and slices of red pepper. Chill before serving. Serves 6.

1   2   3

1   2   3

Liver Mousse

Ingredients: *¾ cup veal or goose liver · 1 slice onion · ¾ cup butter or margarine · ¾ lb veal · 1 bay leaf · salt · 2 tablespoons Marsala · 2 tablespoons grated Parmesan cheese · pepper · mixed herbs · thyme · slices of truffle to taste · 4 cups homemade (see p.50) or commercial gelatin*

In a skillet sauté the onion in a little butter. Discard the onion and add the veal, diced, bay leaf and salt, and cook the mixture without letting it brown on very low heat for 1 hour and 15 minutes. Soak the liver in lukewarm water, slice it finely, add it to the skillet, and

continue cooking for 15 minutes. Put the mixture through the finest blade of a meat chopper twice, add the Marsala, a little more of the butter, Parmesan cheese, salt, pepper, herbs and thyme, and heat the mixture slowly. Work the mixture through a sieve a little at a time, alternating with the remaining butter in pieces. Using a wooden spoon, whip the mixture until it is light and fluffy. Add sliced truffle if liked. Line a long rectangular mold with aluminum foil and pour in the mousse, tightening the foil around it so that there is a 1-inch space between it and all sides of the mold. Refrigerate the mousse until it is set.

Remove the mousse from its mold, put a little cool but still liquid gelatin in the bottom of the mold and refrigerate until almost set. Cut truffle into slices with a knife, or shape with cutters and place on the gelatin (step 1), add the mousse (step 2), and pour the remaining gelatin around it (step 3). Refrigerate until set. To unmold the mousse, dip the mold quickly into boiling water, dry it and immediately turn it over on the serving platter. Garnish with diced gelatin. Serve with olives, if liked. Serves 6–8.

Ham Mousse

Chop and pound in a mortar 1¼ cups ham with ¼ cup butter. Stirring constantly, add 2 tablespoons cold béchamel sauce, made with ½ tablespoon each of butter and flour and 3 tablespoons milk. Put the mixture through the finest blade of a food chopper and add 2 tablespoons diced ham, salt and cayenne pepper. Fold in 1 cup whipped cream. Pour the mixture in a mold lined with a damp cheesecloth and cover with wax paper and a lid so it is airtight. Refrigerate for a few hours.

Unmold the mousse on the serving platter, remove the cheesecloth and garnish with diced gelatin. Serves 4–6.

Tuna Fish Mousse

In a bowl blend ½ cup softened butter or margarine with ½ cup tuna fish in olive oil, 4 desalted anchovy fillets and a few capers, forced through a sieve. Whip the mixture until it is light and fluffy. Add the juice of ½ lemon and pour the mixture into a small fish mold, lined with a damp cheesecloth. Refrigerate for a few hours. Unmold the mousse on the serving platter, remove the cheesecloth and garnish with mayonnaise. Decorate the platter with lemon and green pepper slices, hard-boiled egg and tomato slices, or very simply with diced gelatin.

1

2

3

Tartlets with Ham Mousse

Ingredients: for the flaky pastry, *6 tablespoons sifted flour · 2¼ tablespoons butter or margarine · 1 tablespoon cold water · 1 pinch of salt*

For the filling: *½ cup chopped ham · 1 tablespoon each of mayonnaise and mustard · 1 pinch of paprika · ¼ cup heavy cream · Worcestershire · chopped parsley*

Using two knives or a pastry blender, blend the flour with the butter or margarine, water and salt until it is mealy. Knead the dough for a few minutes, shape it into a ball, wrap in wax paper and let stand in the refrigerator for ½ hour. Roll out the dough on a floured board and cut out 8 rounds to fit tartlet molds. Fill the shells with wax paper and rice or dried beans and bake 'blind' in a hot oven (400°F) for about 15 minutes. Remove the tartlets from their molds, discard the wax paper and rice and allow to cool. Blend the ham with the mayonnaise, mustard and paprika. Fold in the cream, whipped until stiff (step 1), and a few drops of Worcestershire. Fill the tartlets with ham mixture and sprinkle with chopped parsley and paprika (step 2).

Tartlets with Cream Cheese

Mash 6 green olives, pitted and chopped, with ½ chopped celery stalk, 3 small packets cream cheese, 1 or more tablespoons mayonnaise and salt. Using a pastry bag fitted with a large tube, pipe the mixture into 8 tartlets.

Tartlets with Baby Octopus

Make mayonnaise with 1 egg (see p.48) or use commercial mayonnaise, and blend it with Worcestershire and 2 baby octopuses, cooked in boiling salted water and chopped. Fill into 8 tartlets. Garnish each tartlet with 1 baby octopus (step 3).

Tartlets with Liver Mousse

Prepare about ¾ cup liver mousse (see p.31). Using a pastry bag fitted with a star shape, pipe the mousse into 8 tartlets.

Canapés

Ingredients: *sliced white bread · butter · maître d'hôtel butter (see p.49) · smoked salmon · caviar · shrimps · liver mousse (see p.31) · truffles · gherkins · 1 hard-boiled egg · olives · mayonnaise (see p.48) · peeled almonds · homemade (see p.50) or commercial gelatin*

Trim the crusts from the bread slices and cut them into squares and triangles (step 1). Spread the squares with butter and the triangles with maître d'hôtel butter. Spread the canapés with smoked salmon slices, caviar, shrimps and liver mousse, and garnish them with stars of truffles (step 2), gherkins, hard-boiled egg slices, olives, mayonnaise and peeled almonds (step 3). Set the canapés on a serving platter in a decorative way, as seen in the picture, brush them with cool but still liquid gelatin and chill before serving.

Canapé Variations

Trim the crusts from white or rye bread slices and cut them into squares, triangles, circles and flower shapes. Spread them with softened butter mixed with salt or with mustard, anchovy paste or chopped herbs. Spread the canapés with the following mixtures:

Hard-boiled eggs and anchovies: blend 2 hard-boiled eggs with 6 desalted anchovy fillets, mashed, and 2 tablespoons mayonnaise.

Artichokes: in the center of each bread circle spread with butter and anchovy paste, place 1 small artichoke in olive oil, spread it open as a flower and garnish the edges of the canapé with mayonnaise.

Russian salad: spread the bread with butter and with Russian salad (see p.26). In the center put 1 tomato slice, 1 dollop of mayonnaise and 1 cooked shrimp.

Mushroom and egg: spread bread circles with butter. Add hard-boiled egg, mashed with a little mayonnaise and parsley. Garnish with slices of raw mushroom and slices of hard-boiled egg.

1

2

3

1

2

3

Fantasia Torte

Ingredients: *6 eggs · 1 tablespoon flour · a few tablespoons milk · 2 tablespoons grated Parmesan cheese · salt · pepper · ¼ cup fresh or frozen peas · ¼ cup carrots · 1 onion · 2 tablespoons butter or margarine*

Beat the eggs in a bowl with the flour, milk, Parmesan cheese, salt and pepper. Parboil the peas and diced carrots in salted water. Sauté the onion, sliced thinly (step 1), in a little butter until it is golden, add the peas and carrots and cook for a few minutes. Add the vegetable mixture to the beaten eggs (step 2). Melt a knob of butter in a pie dish, add the mixture and cook for about 20 minutes or until the bottom is set (step 3). Bake in a hot oven (400°F) until the torte is golden and com-

pletely cooked. Turn out on to a serving platter and serve cold garnished with a little fried onion, if liked.

Artichoke Frittata

Parboil 4–6 artichoke hearts, dice them and sauté in a little butter. Beat 6 eggs in a bowl with salt, pepper and chopped parsley, and add the artichokes. Melt a little butter or margarine in an omelet or frying pan, add the egg mixture and cook on both sides until set.

Onion Frittata

Melt 2 tablespoons butter or margarine in a cast-iron frying pan, add 1½ cups thinly sliced

onions and cook over low heat for about 20 minutes. Beat 6 eggs in a bowl with salt and pepper and add the onions. Melt a little butter in the frying pan, add the egg mixture and cook on both sides until set. Turn out on a serving platter and serve immediately.

Spinach Frittata

Beat 8 eggs in a bowl with ¾ cup fresh cooked spinach, chopped, 3 tablespoons grated Parmesan, chopped parsley and salt. Sauté ½ onion in butter in a frying pan until golden, discard onion. Pour the egg mixture in the frying pan and cook over low heat for 8–10 minutes. Turn out onto a serving platter and serve immediately.

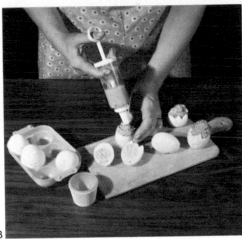

1   2   3

Egg Flowers

Ingredients: *4 eggs · 1 tablespoon softened butter · 1½ tablespoons anchovy paste · 1 tablespoon mayonnaise · salt · pepper · capers*

Cook the eggs in boiling salted water for 9 minutes, pass them under cold running water and shell them (step 1). Using a small sharp knife, cut off the top of each egg, without touching the yolk (step 2). Whip the butter with the anchovy paste, mayonnaise, salt and pepper to taste until the mixture is fluffy. Using a pastry bag fitted with a star tube, pipe the mixture on each egg (step 3) and garnish with 1 caper. Chill before serving.

Eggs with Shrimps

Halve hard-boiled eggs lengthwise. Blend the yolks with enough mayonnaise, ketchup and Worcestershire to make a smooth mixture.

Fill the whites with the mixture and garnish each half with 1 big shrimp (cooked in boiling salted water for a few minutes, shelled and deveined), a few slices of black olive and sprigs of parsley. Chill before serving.

Spring Eggs

Halve hard-boiled eggs lengthwise, work the yolks through a sieve and blend them with enough mayonnaise to make a smooth mixture. Add salt and pile the mixture in the whites. Garnish as shown in the picture by using pieces of red pepper or tomato and parsley.

Eggs with Radishes

Halve hard-boiled eggs lengthwise, work the yolks through a sieve and blend with a little cottage or cream cheese, 1 or 2 tablespoons

mayonnaise, a few drops of Worcestershire, salt and pepper. Pile the mixture in the whites and garnish with slices of radishes, as shown in the picture. Chill before serving.

Eggs with Tuna Fish

Halve hard-boiled eggs lengthwise and work the yolks through a sieve with 2 tablespoons tuna fish in olive oil and 1 teaspoon capers. Add 2 tablespoons softened butter and whip the mixture until it is fluffy. Using a pastry bag fitted with a small tube, pipe the mixture in the whites and garnish with petals of green peppers or carrots and 1 caper in the center.

Vegetables à la Grecque

Ingredients: *4 small artichokes · 2 celery hearts · ½ cauliflower · 2 carrots · 2 zucchini · 1 eggplant · 8 asparagus · 4 mushroom caps · 4–8 small white onions · 4 tablespoons olive oil · 2 tablespoons white wine vinegar or the juice of 1 lemon · 1 clove of garlic · 6 peppercorns · salt · bouquet garni made of parsley, 1 bay leaf, and thyme*

Wash and clean thoroughly all vegetables. Discard the hard outer leaves of the artichokes, halve them and discard the chokes; halve the celery hearts, separate the cauliflower in flowerets, scrape and slice the carrots (step 1), and dice the zucchini and eggplant. Put the vegetables in a saucepan with the oil, vinegar or lemon juice, garlic, pepper, salt and the bouquet garni, and add enough boiling water to just cover. Bring to a boil and cook over moderate heat until the vegetables are *al dente* (step 2). Strain the cooking liquid into a pan (keeping the vegetables on one side) and cook over low heat until reduced by half. Put the vegetables in an earthenware casserole, add the cooking liquid (step 3) and let stand until cool. Chill for a few hours before you serve the vegetables.

Marinated Mushrooms

Clean and wash 8 large mushroom caps and slice them finely. Very small mushroom caps may also be used but kept whole (the tails can be kept for use in soups, stews or casseroles). Put the mushrooms in a deep serving platter with the juice of 1–2 lemons, 2 tablespoons olive oil, salt and freshly ground pepper. Let the mushrooms marinate for 2½ hours before serving.

Olives with Garlic

Pound ¾ cup green olives lightly so as to be able to pit them without breaking them too much. Put the olives in a sterilized jar with 2 cloves of crushed garlic, 1 piece of pimiento and olive oil to cover. Seal immediately and let stand for 2–3 days.

Hot Hors d'Oeuvres

Rice Croquettes

Ingredients: for the risotto, $1\frac{1}{2}$ cups rice · $\frac{1}{2}$ chopped onion · 2 tablespoons butter or margarine · 4 cups stock · 1 egg · 2 tablespoons grated Parmesan cheese

For the filling: $\frac{1}{2}$ chopped onion · 2 tablespoons butter or margarine · 2 tablespoons diced ham · 1 tablespoon dried mushrooms, softened in water and sliced · 4 tablespoons chopped veal · 2 tablespoons chopped chicken giblets · $\frac{1}{2}$ glass dry white wine · flour · salt · pepper · 4 tablespoons diced mozzarella or Bel Paese cheese (optional) · 1 egg · breadcrumbs · oil

To prepare the risotto sauté the onion in the butter or margarine until golden, add the rice and pour in the stock slowly (reserving a little for the filling). Cook the rice until it is *al dente* and has absorbed the stock, remove it from the heat, add the beaten egg and grated cheese, transfer the mixture to a working surface, spreading it out, and let cool (step 1).

To prepare the filling sauté the onion in butter until it is golden, add the ham, mushrooms, veal and giblets and cook the mixture for a few minutes. Add the wine and continue cooking until it has evaporated. Sprinkle with flour, salt and pepper, add some stock and cook over low heat until the sauce has thickened. Remove from the heat. Put a generous tablespoon of rice in the palm of the left hand, make a depression in the center (step 2), and fill it with some filling and a few pieces of mozzarella cheese if liked (step 3). Close the croquette with more rice and pat it into a ball. Dip the croquettes in flour, in egg beaten with salt and in breadcrumbs. Fry a few at a time. Drain and serve immediately garnished with parsley.

Chicken Croquettes

Chop about $1\frac{1}{2}$ cups cooked and boned chicken and add diced ham or salami. Prepare a béchamel sauce (see p.47) and add it to the meat mixture with 2 tablespoons grated Parmesan cheese, chopped parsley and 1 egg yolk. Prepare and cook as above.

1

2

3

Barquettes of Mussels

Ingredients: for the flaky pastry, *6 tablespoons sifted flour · 2¼ tablespoons butter or margarine · 1 tablespoon cold water · 1 dash of salt (or use frozen puff pastry)*

For the filling: *1 lb mussels · ½ glass dry white wine · 1 slice of onion · 1 tablespoon butter mixed with ½ tablespoon flour (beurre manié) · 1 teaspoon chopped parsley · 1 tablespoon dried mushrooms, softened in water and sliced · pepper · breadcrumbs · butter*

Using two knives or a pastry blender, blend the flour with the butter or margarine, water and salt until it is mealy. Knead the dough for a few moments, shape it into a ball, wrap it in wax paper and let it stand in the refrigerator for ½ hour. Roll out the dough on a floured board and cut out 8 boat-shaped pieces to fit barquette molds. Fill the shells with wax paper and rice or dried beans and bake 'blind' in a hot oven (400°F) for 15 minutes. Meanwhile, wash and scrub the mussels, put them in a deep pan with the wine and chopped onion and cook them on high heat until all the shells have opened. Strain the cooking liquid through a cheesecloth into a pan (step 1), cook over high heat until reduced by ⅔; remove from heat, add beurre manié (step 2) and return to high heat until mixture boils and is thick. Remove from heat, add the parsley, mushrooms, mussels, with shells removed, and pepper. Remove the barquettes from their molds, discard the wax paper and rice and fill them with the mussel mixture (step 3). Sprinkle them with breadcrumbs and melted butter and brown them in a hot oven (400°F) for a few minutes. Serve immediately garnished with sprigs of parsley.

Barquettes of Shrimps

Prepare 8 barquettes as in the basic recipe above. Cook about 24 shrimps in boiling salted water, drain, shell and devein them. Put 3 shrimps in each barquette, cover them with Mornay sauce (see p.47), sprinkle with grated Parmesan cheese and cook in a very hot oven (425°F) for a few minutes or until golden. Serve immediately, garnished with sprigs of parsley.

38

Piedmontese Fondue

Ingredients: *10 oz Italian fontina or Gruyère cheese · 1 cup milk · 3 egg yolks · 1 tablespoon butter · salt · truffle (optional)*

Slice the cheese into a bowl, add ¾ of the milk (step 1) and let it stand for 2–3 hours. Pour the mixture in a fondue dish (step 2) or in the top of a double boiler and cook, stirring constantly and always in the same direction, until the cheese is completely melted. Add the egg yolks mixed with remaining milk, warmed, and the butter a little at a time and continue cooking, stirring constantly, until the fondue is smooth and creamy (step 3). Add salt to taste and a few slices of truffle, if liked.

Swiss Fondue

Cut ½ lb each of Swiss Emmenthal and Gruyère cheese into cubes and put the cheese in a fondue dish or in the top of a double boiler, previously rubbed with a cut clove of garlic, with ½ cup Neuchâtel or other dry white wine. Melt the cheese over low heat, stirring constantly and adding another ½ cup white wine a little at a time. As soon as the mixture starts to boil, add 3–4 teaspoons potato flour mixed with 3 tablespoons kirsch (cherry brandy) or brandy. Continue cooking, stirring constantly, until the mixture is smooth, and add salt, pepper and grated nutmeg to taste. Remove the fondue from the heat and put it on a fondue burner or heater in the middle of the dining-room table, adjusting the heat so that it is kept simmering very gently. A little more kirsch can be added if the fondue thickens too much.

Fondue is served with bread cubes or with bread croûtons fried in butter. Each diner impales a bread cube with a long-handled fork, dips it in the fondue, coating the bread completely, lifts it and twists it until it stops dripping, and quickly brings it to his plate. Black tea and a small glass of kirsch or dry white wine are the traditional drinks to serve with the fondue.

1

2

3

Vegetable Molds and Soufflés

Spinach and Carrot Mold

Ingredients: for the spinach mold, *1 lb spinach · 1 egg · 1 tablespoon butter · 1 tablespoon flour · ⅓ cup milk · salt · grated nutmeg · ½ teaspoon potato starch · 1 tablespoon grated Parmesan cheese*

For the carrot mold: *½ lb carrots · 1 tablespoon butter · 1 tablespoon flour · ⅓ cup milk · 1 tablespoon grated Parmesan cheese · salt · grated nutmeg · 2 eggs*

Cook the spinach in boiling salted water for a few minutes, work through a sieve (step 1), leave to cool, then mix in the egg yolk, reserving the white. Make a béchamel sauce with the butter, flour, milk and salt and grated nutmeg to taste, and blend into the spinach, together with the potato starch and Parmesan cheese.

Cook the carrots in boiling salted water until tender, work through a sieve (step 2), then sauté in butter for a few minutes. Add the flour, stirring constantly, then the milk a little at a time off the heat. Cook over low heat for 10 minutes. Remove from heat, stir in the Parmesan cheese, and salt and grated nutmeg to taste, and leave to cool. Add 2 egg yolks, reserving the whites, and beat the mixture for 10 minutes.

Add 2 egg whites, beaten until stiff, to carrot mixture and 1 egg white, also beaten until stiff, to spinach mixture. Butter a high-sided ovenproof mold and carefully pour in the spinach mixture and the carrot mixture, without mixing the two (step 3). Bake in a bain-marie in a moderate oven (350°F) for about 1 hour. Unmold and serve immediately.

Other vegetables, such as cauliflower, may also be used in this manner to make vegetable molds.

Cheese Soufflé

Ingredients: *4 tablespoons butter ·*
6 tablespoons flour · 2 cups boiling milk ·
2 tablespoons grated Parmesan cheese ·
6 tablespoons grated Gruyère cheese · salt ·
4 eggs

Heat the butter in a pan, add the flour and
cook for a few minutes. Add the milk and cook,
stirring constantly, for 5 minutes. Remove
from heat, add cheeses and salt (step 1). Beat
the egg yolks until foamy and add gradually.
Whip the egg whites until stiff, then fold in
gently (step 2). Pour into a soufflé dish, buttered
and lightly sprinkled with flour (step 3) and
bake in a hot oven (400°F) for 20 minutes or
until risen and golden. Serve immediately.

Asparagus Soufflé

Cook the tender parts of 1 lb asparagus in
boiling salted water for a few minutes, drain
and place in a buttered soufflé dish. Heat 1 cup
milk with 3 slices onion and ½ bay leaf; strain.
In a pan heat 3 tablespoons butter, add 3 tablespoons flour and cook for a few minutes. Add
the milk all at once and cook, stirring constantly, for about 5 minutes. Remove from
heat and stir in 3 egg yolks, beaten with salt,
pepper and paprika to taste, and 3 tablespoons
grated Parmesan cheese. Leave to cool and
fold in 3 egg whites, whipped until stiff. Pour
mixture on the asparagus and bake in a hot
oven (400°F) for about 20 minutes or until
risen and golden on top. Serve immediately.

Fish Soufflé

Melt 2 tablespoons butter in a pan, add 3 tablespoons flour and cook for a few minutes. Add
1 cup boiling milk all at once and cook,
stirring constantly, for about 5 minutes.
Remove from heat and stir in salt and pepper
to taste, 5 tablespoons grated Gruyère cheese,
3 egg yolks, one at a time, and 6 tablespoons
cold white fish, freshly cooked and shredded.
Fold in 3 egg whites, beaten until stiff, and
pour mixture into a buttered soufflé dish. Bake
in a hot oven (400°F) for 20 minutes, or until
risen and golden on top. Serve immediately.

Brussels Sprouts Soufflé

Cook 1 lb Brussels sprouts and ½ lb potatoes,
peeled, in boiling salted water for 20 minutes,
or until tender, then work through a sieve or
food chopper. Add 3 egg yolks, 4 tablespoons
butter and salt and pepper to taste, and beat
the mixture until smooth. Fold in 3 egg whites,
beaten until stiff, and pour mixture into a
soufflé dish. Sprinkle with grated Gruyère
cheese and bake in a hot oven (350°F) for 20
minutes or until risen and golden on top.
Serve the soufflé immediately. Serves 6.

1

2

3

1

2

3

Pasta

Ravioli

Ingredients: for the pasta, *2¼ cups sifted flour · 4 eggs · 6 tablespoons water*

For the filling: *10 oz beef · 1 tablespoon bacon · 2½ oz pork fillet ·*
2 tablespoons butter or margarine ·
onion, celery, carrot, all chopped together ·
salt · pepper · ½ glass dry white wine ·
¼ lb Savoy cabbage · 2½ oz mortadella ·
1 handful white bread soaked in milk and
squeezed dry · milk · 1 egg
grated Parmesan cheese · grated nutmeg

For the sauce: *meat sauce or gravy from a roast or braised meat ·*
grated Parmesan cheese for sprinkling

For the filling: 1 day before serving, put the beef, barded with the bacon, in a pan with the pork, butter or margarine, onion, celery and carrot, and sauté over moderate heat, turning the meat occasionally, until all the ingredients are golden. Add salt and pepper to taste and the white wine, and cook the mixture, covered, over very low heat for 2 hours. Remove the meat from the pan and reserve. Add the cabbage, cooked in boiling salted water for 10 minutes, to the pan and sauté for a few minutes. Work the cabbage, meats and mortadella through the medium blade of a food chopper. Add the white bread, egg, grated Parmesan cheese, salt, pepper and grated nutmeg to taste, and blend well.

Make a dough of the flour, eggs and water (see p.45), and roll out thinly. Shape the filling into small balls and set them about 2 inches apart on the dough (step 1). Fold the dough over (step 2) and cut with a ravioli or cookie cutter (step 3) or with a small glass. Seal the edges. Cook the ravioli in boiling salted water until it is *al dente*, drain, and put on a warm serving platter. Cover with meat sauce or gravy and sprinkle with grated Parmesan cheese. Serves 5–6.

Genoese Ravioli

Boil ½ cup each of endives and spinach in salted water for 5 minutes and drain. Dice 6 oz veal, 2½ oz pork, 3 oz sweetbreads, scalded and peeled, and sauté in 2 tablespoons butter for a few minutes. Add a piece of brain, scalded and peeled, and 1 oz beef marrow and cook for a few minutes. Chop with marjoram and pound in a mortar. Add 1¼ oz sausage meat, a little bread, soaked in milk and squeezed dry, grated Parmesan cheese and salt, and mix well. Prepare the dough and proceed as above.

1

2

3

Gratinéed Cannelloni

Ingredients: for the dough, *2 cups sifted flour ·
4 eggs · 3 tablespoons water*

For the filling: *2 tablespoons butter ·
1 slice onion, chopped ·
3 tablespoons ham, chopped · ¾ lb beef, diced ·
½ bay leaf · 1 tablespoon flour · stock · salt ·
pepper · grated nutmeg · 1 egg ·
1 handful white bread, soaked in milk and
squeezed dry · Parmesan cheese ·
tomato or béchamel sauce · butter ·
grated Parmesan cheese*

Prepare the dough (see p.45) and let stand.
Roll out thinly and cut into 4 or more 5-inch
by 4-inch rectangles. Cook these, a few at a
time, in boiling salted water until tender, drain
(step 1), and place on a damp cloth. In a pan
heat the butter, add the onion and ham and
cook for a few minutes. Add the beef and the
bay leaf and cook for a further few minutes.
Stir in the flour, add a little stock, salt, pepper
and grated nutmeg to taste. Cook the mixture
over low heat for 45 minutes, discard the
bay leaf. Work mixture through the medium
blade of a food chopper, add the egg, the bread
and grated Parmesan cheese and work mixture
until well blended. Put a little filling on each
rectangle and roll up (step 2). Place the
cannelloni side by side in a buttered ovenproof
dish. Cover with tomato sauce (step 3) or with
a rather thin béchamel sauce, dot with butter
and sprinkle with grated Parmesan cheese.
Gratiné the cannelloni in a hot oven (400°F)
until golden. Serve immediately.

Cannelloni Maison

Prepare 12 little crêpes: in a bowl mix 2 eggs
with 10 tablespoons sifted flour and 1 pinch
salt, add 1 cup milk or water and 1 tablespoon
melted butter gradually. Beat the batter with a
wire whip until smooth. Heat a 7-inch frying
pan and add a little oil. Pour in 2 tablespoons
batter and quickly tilt and rotate the pan so that
the batter coats the bottom thinly and evenly.
Cook the crêpe on both sides until golden.
Continue until all the batter is used. Prepare a
béchamel sauce with 2 tablespoons butter or
margarine, ¼ cup sifted flour, 2 cups milk,
salt, pepper and grated nutmeg to taste.
Remove from heat and stir in 2½ tablespoons
grated Gruyère cheese. Pour a little béchamel
sauce onto each crêpe, add ½ slice ham to each
and roll up crêpes. Place side by side in a
buttered ovenproof dish, add 1 cup heavy
cream and sprinkle with grated Parmesan
cheese. Bake in a hot oven (400°F) for 15
minutes and serve immediately. Cannelloni
may also be filled with meat or vegetables.

Baked Lasagne

Ingredients: for the pasta, *2½ cups sifted flour · 4 eggs · 1 lb spinach*

For the sauce: *¼ cup butter or margarine · 1 carrot, 1 celery stalk, 1 onion, all chopped together · 6 oz ground beef · salt · pepper · grated nutmeg · 1 cup milk · tomato sauce*

For the béchamel sauce:
2 tablespoons butter or margarine · 2 tablespoons flour · 2 cups milk · salt · grated nutmeg · grated Parmesan cheese

Heat half the butter or margarine, add the onion, celery and carrot, and cook until golden. Add the beef, salt, pepper and nutmeg to taste and cook the mixture for 20 minutes. Add the tomato sauce, thinned with a little hot water, cover the pan and simmer until the tomato sauce is well blended. Add the milk and cook,

covered, over low heat for 1 hour.

Meanwhile prepare the dough (see p.45) with the flour, eggs and spinach, cooked in boiling salted water, drained well and worked through a sieve. Roll out the dough in a very thin sheet and cut into 3½-inch squares (step 1). Make the béchamel sauce with the butter or margarine, flour, milk, salt and grated nutmeg to taste, remove from the heat and stir in 2–3 tablespoons grated Parmesan cheese. Cook the lasagne, a few at a time, in boiling salted water with 1 tablespoon butter or margarine so that the squares do not stick, for a few minutes (step 2), wash under cold running water, drain and dry on a clean cloth. Grease a baking dish with butter or margarine, add a layer of lasagne, cover with a little béchamel sauce, a little meat sauce (step 3), grated Parmesan cheese and curls of butter or margarine. Continue until all the ingredients

are used. Bake in a hot oven (400°F) for 30–40 minutes until top is golden. Serves 5–6.

Lasagne 16th Century Style

Prepare and cook the dough as above using 1½ cups sifted flour and 3 eggs.

Wash and pat dry ¾ lb perch or sole fillets, dip them in egg beaten with salt, then in breadcrumbs and sauté them lightly. Prepare a béchamel sauce with 2 tablespoons butter, 2 tablespoons flour, 2 cups milk, salt and grated nutmeg, remove from heat and stir in 2 tablespoons grated Gruyère cheese. Grease a baking dish, add a layer of lasagne, cover with béchamel sauce and add a few fish fillets. Continue in this manner until all the ingredients are used. Add curls of butter and bake the lasagne in a moderate oven (350°F) for about 30 minutes or until the top is golden.

1

2

3

4

Noodles Bolognese

Ingredients: for the pasta, *2 cups presifted flour · 4 eggs · $\frac{2}{3}$ cup spinach, cooked and chopped (optional)*

For the sauce: *2 tablespoons bacon, chopped · 2 tablespoons butter · 1 celery stalk, 1 carrot and $\frac{1}{2}$ onion, all chopped together · 6 oz ground beef · a few dried mushrooms, soaked in lukewarm water, squeezed dry and sliced (optional) · $\frac{1}{2}$ glass white or red wine · salt · pepper · grated nutmeg · 2 tablespoons tomato paste · $1\frac{1}{2}$ cups stock or water · 1 glass milk (optional)*

Prepare the pasta: sift the flour on a lightly floured board, make a well in the center and break in the eggs (step 1). Add the spinach if green noodles are required. Work flour and eggs together with a round-bladed knife (step 2) until a smooth dough is formed. Roll out, not too finely (step 3). Let dough dry for a few minutes then fold over to form a 4-inch wide strip and cut into $\frac{1}{4}$-inch strips. Pick up 5–6 strips at one time, shake out gently and let dry on the board (step 4).

Prepare the sauce: in a pan sauté the bacon in the butter for a few minutes, add the chopped vegetables and cook until they start to brown. Add the beef and mushrooms (if using), and cook for a few minutes. Stir in the wine, add salt, pepper and nutmeg to taste, and cook the sauce until wine has evaporated. Add the tomato paste, thinned with $\frac{1}{4}$ cup stock or water, and cook, covered, over very low heat for about 2 hours, adding a little more stock or water occasionally. Add the milk (if using) gradually and continue cooking for 1 hour. Pour the sauce on the noodles, cooked in boiling salted water until they are *al dente* and drained. Mix well and serve immediately.

Curried Noodles

Sauté 1 medium onion, finely chopped, in $3\frac{1}{2}$ tablespoons butter without browning. Add 2 teaspoons curry powder, salt, and 4 tablespoons ham, chopped, and cook the mixture for a few minutes. Pour the seasonings on $\frac{3}{4}$ lb noodles, cooked in boiling salted water until *al dente* and drained. Mix well and serve immediately. Serve grated Parmesan cheese separately.

45

Rice

Paella

Ingredients: *1 quart mussels · 3½ tablespoons oil · a 2-lb chicken · ½ cup veal · ½ cup beef · 2 onions, chopped · 3 cups shrimps · 2 green peppers, deseeded and quartered · salt · pepper · 1–2 zucchini, peeled and diced · ¾ cup tomatoes, peeled and diced · 4 tablespoons sausage, peeled and sliced · 2 cloves of garlic, peeled and crushed · 1 cup rice · 2 teaspoons saffron · 1 cup peas · 4 artichoke hearts, sliced · a few olives, pitted*

Wash and scrub the mussels thoroughly and cook in a little oil over high heat until the shells have opened. Drain and shell, reserving a few in their shells for garnish. Strain the cooking liquid through a fine cloth and reserve. Cut the chicken into 8 pieces and cube the meats. Sauté the meat in a frying pan, preferably an iron one, in remaining hot oil (step 1). Add the onions, raw shrimps, green peppers, salt and pepper (step 2). Mix well and cook the mixture, covered, for 10 minutes. Add the zucchini, tomatoes, sausage, garlic and the reserved cooking liquid from the mussels. Cover pan and cook over low heat for 1 hour and 10 minutes. Add the rice and saffron (step 3) and boiling water to cover. Cook covered, over low heat for 10 minutes. Add the peas, artichoke hearts, shelled mussels and a few olives, and continue cooking for 10 minutes. Add reserved mussels, heat through and serve immediately. Serves 6–8.

Rice à la Grècque

Heat 2 tablespoons butter in a flameproof earthenware casserole with a cover. Add 1 onion, chopped finely, and cook without browning. Add 1 clove of garlic, peeled and crushed, 4 lettuce leaves, shredded, 2 tablespoons dried mushrooms, softened in lukewarm water, squeezed dry and sliced, 2–3 tomatoes, peeled and chopped, 4 oz sausage, peeled and chopped, or sausage meat, 1½ cups rice, 4 cups hot stock, salt and pepper. Cover the casserole and bake in a hot oven (400°F) for 20–25 minutes. When cooked, add 1 tablespoon melted butter, ¾ cup cooked peas, 1 diced red pepper and 3 tablespoons raisins, cooked in a little butter. Mix gently and serve.

1

2

3

1 2 3

Béchamel Sauce

Ingredients: *2¼ tablespoons butter · ¼ cup flour · 2 cups milk · salt · pepper · nutmeg*

Melt the butter over low heat (step 1), blend in the flour (step 2) and cook the mixture for 1 minute. Add the lukewarm milk all at once (step 3), salt, pepper and grated nutmeg, and cook the mixture, stirring constantly, with a wooden spoon or a wire whisk, over low heat for 10 minutes or until the béchamel has thickened. Yield: 2 cups sauce.

Aurore Sauce

For eggs, vegetables and poultry: add 2 tablespoons tomato sauce and 1 tablespoon butter to 2 cups hot béchamel sauce.

Maître d'Hôtel Sauce

For eggs and boiled, fried or grilled fish: blend 4 tablespoons hot water with 1 cup hot béchamel sauce. Add 3–4 tablespoons butter, one at a time, the juice of ½ lemon and 1 tablespoon chopped parsley.

Caper Sauce

For boiled fish: add 3–4 tablespoons capers, coarsely chopped, 1 teaspoon lemon juice and 2 tablespoons fresh butter to 2 cups hot béchamel sauce.

Curry Sauce

For meat, hard-boiled eggs and asparagus: melt 1 teaspoon butter over low heat, add 1 garlic clove, pressed, and 1 teaspoon each of minced shallots, chives or onion and curry powder.

Cook the mixture for 3 minutes, add 1 cup béchamel sauce and bring to a boil.

Mornay Sauce

For pasta, egg, vegetable, fish and poultry gratins: add 1 or 2 egg yolks, beaten with 1 cup cream, to 1 cup béchamel sauce. Bring the mixture to a boil and remove from the heat. Add 2 tablespoons butter and 3 tablespoons grated Gruyère cheese.

Cream Sauce

For eggs, vegetables, fish and poultry: add 1 cup cream and 2 tablespoons fresh butter, a little at a time, to 1 cup hot béchamel sauce.

Soubise Sauce

For eggs, fish, meat, poultry and vegetables: cook ¾ cup chopped onion in boiling water for 2–3 minutes, drain and sauté in 1 tablespoon butter until soft but not browned. Add the onion to 2 cups hot béchamel sauce and continue cooking the mixture for 10–12 minutes. Pass the sauce through a sieve, return to the heat and add ⅞ cup cream, a little at a time, and salt to taste.

White Wine Sauce

For eggs and boiled, fried and grilled fish: add 2–3 egg yolks, one at a time, and 1 tablespoon grated Parmesan cheese alternately with 5 tablespoons dry white wine to 1 cup hot béchamel sauce. Cook over low heat.

Mayonnaise

Ingredients: *2 egg yolks at room temperature · ¼ teaspoon salt · dash of pepper · the juice of 1 lemon, or 2–3 tablespoons vinegar · 1½ cups oil*

Put the egg yolks, salt, pepper and a few drops of lemon juice or vinegar in a bowl (step 1). Stirring slowly with a wooden spoon and then faster, add the oil drop by drop and then in a thin stream as the mayonnaise thickens, alternating with the remaining lemon juice (steps 2 and 3). If the mayonnaise turns or curdles, put 1 egg yolk in a clean bowl and add, stirring constantly, the turned mayonnaise drop by drop at first and then in small amounts. Yield: 1 cup.

Mayonnaise can also be made in an electric blender or bought commercially.

To make a successful mayonnaise all ingredients must be at room temperature, the oil must be added very slowly at first and stirring must be done in the same direction.

Aspic Mayonnaise

For salads and to cover a variety of dishes: prepare a mayonnaise following the basic recipe above. Soften about ¼ oz gelatin in a little warm water or in meat or fish stock and let it cool. Blend the cool but still liquid gelatin into the mayonnaise, a little at a time. Use the aspic mayonnaise immediately (before it sets) to cover hard- or soft-boiled eggs, fish, boiled chicken, etc. If a firmer mayonnaise is desired, add more gelatin.

Chantilly Mayonnaise

For asparagus and other cold boiled vegetables: fold 3–4 tablespoons whipped cream into 1 cup mayonnaise. If a lighter sauce is preferred, add the white of 1 egg, beaten until stiff.

Cocktail Sauce

For shellfish cocktail: add 3 tablespoons tomato ketchup, 1 teaspoon Worcestershire, 1 teaspoon brandy or gin, 2–3 tablespoons heavy or whipped cream, salt and paprika to 1 cup mayonnaise.

Aïoli Mayonnaise

For snails, cod, and vegetables: pound 4 garlic cloves in a mortar. Put the garlic, 1 egg yolk, a little salt and a small boiled potato in a bowl. Stirring constantly with a wooden spoon, add ¾ cup oil drop by drop and then in a thin stream until the mayonnaise has thickened.

Tuna Mayonnaise

For boiled meat, poultry, and eggs: work ¾ cup tuna fish in olive oil, 2 anchovy fillets, desalted, and a few capers through a sieve. Blend the mixture into 1 cup mayonnaise. If the sauce is too thick, thin it with a few tablespoons cold stock and add a few drops of lemon juice to taste.

Rémoulade Sauce

For boiled and grilled meat and fish: add 2–3 gherkins and 2 tablespoons capers, both chopped and dried with a clean cloth, 1 tablespoon mustard and 1 tablespoon chervil, tarragon and parsley, all chopped together, to 1 cup mayonnaise. If the sauce is too thick, thin with lemon juice.

Tartare Mayonnaise

For eggs, fish and meat: add 1 tablespoon each of chopped green olives, gherkins, parsley, shallots or chives and tarragon, 1 teaspoon mustard, a dash each of salt and freshly ground pepper to 1 cup mayonnaise and mix well.

1   2   3

Hot and Cold Savory Butters

Very fresh butter, kept at room temperature, must be used to make these various butters, particularly the cold ones. Margarine also gives very good results.

Shrimp Butter

For various dishes: work 4 tablespoons salted butter in a bowl until it is creamy. Pound 15 shrimps, cooked in boiling salted water for a few minutes, drained, shelled and deveined, in a mortar and add them to the butter. Work the mixture through a very fine sieve (steps 1, 2 and 3).

Anchovy Butter

In a bowl beat 4 tablespoons butter with 2 tablespoons anchovy paste or 3–4 anchovy fillets, drained, desalted and mashed to a paste, until it is light and foamy. Work the mixture through a fine sieve.

Garlic Butter

For steak and other dishes: peel 5 cloves of garlic, scald them in boiling water for a few minutes, dry them and pound them in a mortar. Add them to 4 tablespoons butter, beat until light and foamy and sieve.

Clarified Butter

For sauces and fine pastry: melt the necessary quantity of butter in a bowl in a bain-marie. Carefully pour the clear fat through a cheesecloth placed in a fine sieve, (leaving the milky sediment caught in the cloth).

Maître d'Hôtel Butter

For grilled fish, poultry, and meat: beat 4 tablespoons butter in a bowl with ½ tablespoon chopped parsley, 1 tablespoon lemon juice, and salt and pepper until light and foamy.

Beurre Manié

To bind sauces: make a paste of equal amounts of butter and flour and add it a little at a time to bind the sauce.

Beurre Meunière

For fish: melt 4 tablespoons butter and add a little lemon juice, chopped parsley, salt and pepper.

Paprika Butter

For cold hors d'oeuvres, canapés, grilled fish and poultry: blend 4 tablespoons butter with 2 teaspoons paprika. Or cook 1 tablespoon butter with 2 teaspoons paprika and 2 teaspoons finely chopped onion over low heat for a few minutes. Strain the butter through a fine sieve, let it cool and blend it well with 2½ tablespoons salted butter.

Horseradish Butter

For various dishes: pound 5 teaspoons fresh grated horseradish in a mortar and blend it with 4 tablespoons butter. Sieve.

Green Butter

For garnish and for fish: in a small saucepan put 12 spinach leaves, chopped, 2 tablespoons chopped parsley and 2 teaspoons chopped tarragon, add water just to cover and cook the mixture over high heat for 5 minutes. Drain, dry, sieve. Blend with 4 tablespoons butter and sieve again.

1

2

3

4

Savory Jellies

Jellied Stock, Gelatin or Aspic

Ingredients: *2 calf's feet, cracked (about 4 lb) ·
1 lb veal knuckle, cracked · ¼ lb fresh or salt
pork rind · ¼ cup onion · ¼ cup carrot ·
1 tablespoon celery · bouquet garni made of
parsley, bay leaves and thyme · salt · pepper ·
12 cups cold water · ¼ cup chopped beef ·
2 egg whites*

Put the feet, knuckles, salt pork, onion, carrot,
celery, bouquet garni, salt, pepper and water
in a large pan (step 1). Bring the mixture
slowly to a boil, skim for about 5 minutes
or until there is no scum left and cook for
about 3½ hours or until the stock has reduced
to 6 cups. Strain the stock into a bowl, let
it cool and remove the fat completely (step 2).
A perfect jellied stock must be transparent,

brilliant and light amber in colour. To achieve
this the stock must be clarified in the following
manner: transfer the stock into a pan, add
the chopped beef and the egg whites and
whip the mixture gently with a wire whisk
(step 3). Bring the mixture to a boil and cook
it over moderate heat, stirring with a wooden
spoon, for 15 minutes. As the egg whites cook,
they will come up to the surface taking with
them all the particles in the stock. Strain the
stock through a fine sieve covered with a thin
cloth dipped in lukewarm water and wrung
out (step 4). The stock is now ready for use.
Yield: 4 cups.

Use the same method of clarification for
consommés and fish stocks. Add wine (port,
Marsala or Madeira) only after clarification.

Jellied Game Stock

Put 2 cracked veal knuckles, 1 lb bones and
bits of the game to be cooked, ¼ lb fresh or
salt pork rind, ¼ cup each of onion and carrot,
1 tablespoon celery, 3 crushed juniper berries,
a bouquet garni made of parsley, thyme and 1
bay leaf, salt, peppercorns and 12 cups cold
water in a large pan and follow the basic
recipe above. To clarify the stock, add ¼ cup
each of chopped lean beef and chopped game
meat and 2 egg whites, and proceed as for
above recipe.

Jellied Fish Stock

Put 1 lb fish, cut into cubes (including the
heads, mashed bones, etc.), ¼ cup sliced onion,
1 sprig of parsley and 1 bay leaf, salt and a
few peppercorns in a large pan. Add 8 cups
water, bring to a boil and cook for about 40
minutes. Proceed as for the basic recipe. To
clarify the stock, add ½ cup cod or other white
fish, chopped, and 1 egg white. In this case, add
¼ oz powdered gelatin, softened in cold water.
Yield: 4 cups.

Fish & Egg Dishes

Sea Fish

Fresh Herring au Vert

Ingredients: *1½ lb fresh small herring or mackerel · 2½ tablespoons butter · garlic and parsley, chopped · 2 anchovy fillets, desalted and mashed · ½ cup dry white wine · salt*

To garnish: *lemon*

Remove the head and main bone from the fish (step 1) without opening them, wash and dry with absorbent paper. Melt the butter in a pan, add the chopped garlic and parsley to taste, cook for 1–2 minutes then remove from heat and add the mashed anchovy fillets (step 2). Continue cooking on low heat, then add the white wine and a small pinch of salt. After a few minutes arrange the fish in the pan (step 3) and cook for about 10 minutes. Serve hot with the sauce. Garnish with lemon slices.

Neapolitan Herring

Prepare 1½ lb small herring or mackerel as above. Sauté chopped garlic and parsley to taste in ¼ cup oil. Add 1¼ cups canned tomatoes, chopped, cover with stock and simmer for a few minutes. Arrange 2 cups potatoes, thinly sliced, in a buttered dish, cover with the prepared fish and spread over the tomato sauce. Cover and cook slowly for about 30 minutes or until potatoes are tender. If there is too much sauce, reduce on high heat for a few minutes.

Herring with Tomato Sauce

Sauté 1 clove of garlic, soaked in a little milk and mashed, in 1 tablespoon butter, add 1 cup canned tomatoes, chopped, and cook for about 20 minutes. Meanwhile prepare 1½ lb small herring or mackerel as above and sauté them in ¼ cup oil for about 10 minutes. Sprinkle with a little salt. Pour the sauce into a warm serving platter, put in the cooked fish, sprinkle with chopped basil and parsley to taste, and serve immediately.

Herring in Batter

Prepare a batter by blending 1¼ cups flour, 1 egg, salt and ¾ cup beer. Add a little water and let stand for 1–2 hours. Clean, wash and dry 1½ lb small herring or mackerel, and sprinkle with salt. Whip 2 egg whites, and fold into the batter. Roll fish in batter and fry in hot deep fat. Remove, and cut off heads and tails. Serve with tartare sauce or tomato sauce.

Rolled Herring with Capers

Remove heads and bones from 1½ lb small herring or mackerel, and cut each into 2 fillets. Place a few capers on each and roll up. Sauté chopped garlic to taste in ¼ cup oil, arrange the fillets in the pan and cook slowly for 10 minutes. Season, add ¼ cup parsley, chopped, and ½ cup dry white wine. Increase heat and cook until the sauce has reduced.

1

2

3

Neapolitan Salt Cod

Ingredients: *1½ lb salt cod fillets, soaked overnight in 2 changes of cold water · flour · oil · 2–3 large onions, sliced · 2 cups canned tomatoes, chopped · salt · pepper*

Wash the cod under cold running water and dry. Cut into large pieces (step 1), roll in flour, and fry in plenty of hot oil until cooked (step 2), and keep warm. Brown the onions lightly in a few tablespoons oil. Add the tomatoes, season with salt and pepper to taste, and cook slowly until a rich sauce has formed. Ten minutes before removing the pan from the heat, add the fried pieces of cod (step 3) and heat through. Transfer to a warm serving platter and coat the fish with the sauce. Serve immediately.

Salt Cod Provençal

Prepare and cut into pieces 1½ lb salt cod fillets as above. Roll in flour and fry in ¼ cup oil until cooked, drain and keep warm. In the same pan, add a little more oil and brown 2 cloves of garlic, crushed. Remove the garlic, add 2 cups canned tomatoes worked through a sieve, 1 tablespoon capers, ¾ cup pitted black olives and 1 pinch oregano. Cook for 10 minutes. Add the pieces of cod to the sauce and heat through. Serve immediately.

Salt Cod Croquettes

Bake 1½ cups potatoes in their jackets in the oven, halve, and remove the insides. Poach 1½ lb salt cod fillets (prepared as above) in water to cover for a few minutes – do not allow to boil. Drain and mash with ½ cup onion, finely chopped, 2 eggs, salt and pepper to taste, and the potato. Shape the croquettes on a floured board, roll in an egg beaten with a little oil and salt, and fry until golden in medium-hot oil. Serve with a tomato sauce, if liked.

Salt Cod in Brandade

Soak 1½ lb salt cod fillets overnight in 2 changes of water. Wash under cold running water, dry, and poach until tender. Mash in a mortar with 1¼ cups potatoes, boiled and drained, and a few

drops oil and milk, until creamy. Add pepper and check the seasoning before adding salt.

Salt Cod with Aïoli Mayonnaise

Soak, wash and dry 1½ lb salt cod fillets as above. Cut into 4 pieces and poach in water to cover for 15–20 minutes. Do not allow to boil. In a separate pan, cook 1 small cauliflower,

cut into flowerets, 1½ cups carrots, peeled, and 2 cups potatoes, unpeeled, in boiling salted water until just tender. Meanwhile, make the aïoli (garlic) mayonnaise: in a mortar, crush 6 cloves of garlic, peeled, add 1 pinch salt, white pepper to taste and a dash of vinegar. Mix in 1 egg yolk and pour in very slowly 1 cup olive oil, stirring constantly, until thick. Drain the cod and vegetables and serve with the aïoli.

1

2

3

Fillets of Sole Meunière

Ingredients: *2 soles (1–1¼ lb each) or 1½ lb sole fillets, fresh or frozen · flour · salt · pepper · ¼ cup butter · juice of 2 lemons · parsley, chopped*

To garnish: *lemon slices*

Remove and discard the heads from the soles, and skin them (step 1). Wash and drain. Make an incision along the center bone of each sole (step 2) and detach the 4 fillets carefully with a knife (step 3). Roll the fillets lightly in flour seasoned with salt and pepper, and cook slowly in a pan in 4 tablespoons of the butter until they are golden on all sides. Arrange them on a warm serving platter, sprinkle with the lemon juice, and the chopped parsley to taste. Melt the remaining butter in the pan, cook until lightly golden, then pour evenly over the sole. Serve immediately, garnished with lemon slices.

Sole Bonne Femme

Arrange 8 sole fillets, prepared as above, in a buttered ovenproof dish. Sprinkle over ½ cup shallots and ½ cup mushrooms, finely chopped, season with salt and pepper to taste, and add 1 cup dry white wine and a little fish stock. Cover with buttered wax paper or foil and bake in a moderate oven (350°F) for 15–20 minutes. Strain the cooking juices, thicken over heat with a little beurre manié (equal quantities of butter and flour kneaded together), remove from the heat, and blend in 2 egg yolks. Pour the sauce back over the sole, and return to the oven for a few minutes to gratiné.

Fillets of Sole Florentine

Clean and wash 2½ cups spinach, and cook until tender in a little boiling salted water, drain, and keep warm. Melt 2½ tablespoons butter in a pan, stir in 2 tablespoons flour, and cook for 1–2 minutes. Remove from heat and stir in 1 cup boiling milk, and salt, pepper and grated nutmeg to taste. Simmer for 10 minutes, stirring with a wire whisk or wooden spoon. Remove from heat and stir in ½ cup light cream and 2½ tablespoons Gruyère cheese, grated. Roll 8 sole fillets, prepared as above, in flour seasoned with salt and pepper, and cook them slowly in 4 tablespoons butter until golden on all sides. Put the spinach in a buttered ovenproof dish, and arrange the sole fillets over the spinach. Blend 2 egg yolks into the sauce, and pour it over the fillets. Sprinkle with grated Gruyère cheese, and put in a hot oven (425°F) for a few minutes to gratiné.

1

2

3

Fritto Misto Mare

Ingredients: *8 small sole fillets · 1 cup shrimps · ¾ lb small frying fish (sprats, whitebait, sardines) · ½ lb cuttlefish · oil · flour · salt*

To garnish: *lemon quarters · parsley (optional)*

Clean and wash the fish and prepare for cooking (step 1). Cut the cuttlefish into small pieces (step 2) and fry gently in oil until tender (this may take 20 minutes to 1 hour). Dry all the fish well and roll in flour. Fry the fish in very hot deep oil (step 3) until golden. Drain on absorbent paper, sprinkle with salt, and serve piping hot with lemon quarters, and fried parsley, if liked.

Salt Cod Beignets

Soak, wash and dry 1½ lb salt cod fillets (see p.54) and cut into small pieces. To prepare the batter: beat in a bowl 1 egg yolk with 1 tablespoon melted butter, add 1 cup flour, sifted, 1 pinch salt, and 1 cup beer. Mix without beating. Let the mixture stand for 1 hour, then fold in 1 egg white, whipped until stiff. Dip the fish pieces into the batter and fry in very hot deep oil until golden and crusty. Drain, and serve immediately, garnished with lemon quarters.

Sole Dugléré

Prepare 8 sole fillets (see p.43) and place in a buttered ovenproof dish. Surround with ½ cup onions, finely chopped, 2 cups tomatoes, peeled, seeded and chopped, and chopped parsley to taste. Add ½ cup dry white wine, and season with salt and pepper to taste. Cover with wax paper or foil, and poach in a moderate oven (350°F) for 15–20 minutes. Remove the sole, and keep warm on a serving platter. Reduce the cooking juices over high heat on top of the stove, then remove from heat and add ½ cup light cream and the juice of ½ lemon. Pour over the sole and serve immediately.

1

2

3

1

2

3

Hake Provençal

Ingredients: *4 slices hake (about 6 oz each) ·
1 cup mushrooms · 2½ tablespoons butter ·
salt · pepper · ½ onion, finely chopped · ½ clove
of garlic, crushed · 1 tablespoon chopped
parsley · 1¼ cups canned peeled tomatoes,
chopped · ½ cup dry white wine*

Clean the mushrooms, slice them (step 1) and
sauté in 1 tablespoon butter; reserve. Arrange
the hake slices, sprinkled with salt and pepper,
in a generously buttered ovenproof dish (step 2).
Sprinkle with the onion, garlic and parsley
(step 3), add the tomatoes, the cooked mushrooms and the wine. Cover, bring to a boil,
then lower the heat and cook for about 15

minutes or until the fish is tender. If the sauce
is too liquid, reduce it on high heat. Transfer
to a warm serving platter and serve immediately.

Hake au Gratin

Clean, wash and dry thoroughly 2 lb hake.
Place in each fish 1 clove of garlic, peeled, and
a few leaves of rosemary. Leave to stand for
½ hour in 6 tablespoons oil, seasoned with salt
and pepper to taste and a few sprigs rosemary.
Drain, reserving the oil, and roll in breadcrumbs,
then arrange in a buttered ovenproof dish.
Pour the reserved oil over and cook in a hot
oven (425°F) for about 20 minutes or until the

fish is tender and golden. Baste occasionally
with the cooking juices. Serve immediately.

Breaded Hake a l'Anglaise

Make an incision along the back of 4 hake,
about 5 oz each, then, taking hold of the tail
remove it, together with the main bone, and
cut off the head. Flatten the fish with a knife,
and dip into 2 eggs beaten with salt and pepper
to taste, and ½ cup oil. Roll the fish in 2½ tablespoons breadcrumbs mixed with 1 tablespoon
flour. Fry in a pan in a mixture of half oil, half
butter until tender and golden. Arrange fish
on a warm platter with parsley and serve.

1   2   3

Grilled Sea Bass

Ingredients: *1 sea bass, or salmon trout, about 2 lb · salt · pepper · olive oil · 2½ tablespoons butter, melted · juice of ½ lemon · 2 tablespoons chopped rosemary and parsley*

To garnish: *lettuce leaves · lemon slices · parsley · canned red pimiento (optional)*

Clean the sea bass or salmon trout and remove the central bone (step 1). Wash and dry, sprinkle with salt and pepper (step 2) and dip in oil. Place in a double grill or under the broiler, and cook slowly, turning frequently, and basting with the butter mixed with the lemon juice and the chopped herbs (step 3). Transfer to a warm serving platter and garnish with lettuce leaves, lemon slices and parsley. Stuff the eye with a little parsley and a small slice of canned red pimiento, if liked. Serve immediately.

Sea Bass Forestière

Prepare a 2-lb sea bass or salmon trout as above, flatten it and remove the head. Place 1 cup fresh mushrooms mixed with 1 table-spoon chopped parsley at the bottom of an ovenproof dish. Put in the fish and sprinkle with salt. Add ½ cup dry white wine and ½ cup fish stock, prepared with the head and bones of the fish and thickened with ½ teaspoon flour. Bring to a boil on top of the stove, then cover the dish with wax paper or foil and bake in a moderate oven (350°F) for 20–25 minutes or until the fish is tender. Remove the foil and continue cooking for another 5 minutes. Lift out the fish and keep warm on a serving platter. Mix 2 tablespoons butter gradually into the cooking juices, and heat through. Pour the sauce and mushrooms over the fish, and serve immediately.

Sea Bass with Tomato Sauce

Clean, wash and dry a 2-lb sea bass or salmon trout as above. Heat 2 tablespoons oil in a pan, put in the fish and brown lightly for a moment. Add ¼ cup dry white wine, ¼ cup water, 1 twig thyme, 1 bay leaf, and salt and pepper to taste. Cook for 35–40 minutes, basting the fish occasionally with the cooking juices. Meanwhile, in a separate pan sauté 1 small onion, finely chopped, in 1 tablespoon oil until golden. Add 2 cups canned peeled tomatoes worked through a sieve, and salt and pepper to taste, and cook slowly for ½ hour. Remove the fish from the pan, drain, and place on a warm serving platter. Reduce the cooking juices on high heat after removing the thyme and bay leaf, add the tomato sauce and 1 tablespoon chopped parsley, mix well and pour over the fish. Serve immediately.

Gratin of Sardines

Ingredients: *2 lb fresh sardines, or small herring or mackerel · 2½ tablespoons breadcrumbs · 2 cloves of garlic, chopped · chopped parsley · salt · pepper · juice of 1 lemon · 2½ tablespoons butter · 2 eggs · ½ cup milk*

To garnish: *parsley*

Open fish, remove heads and bones (step 1), wash and dry. Arrange half the fish side by side in a buttered ovenproof dish (step 2). Mix together the breadcrumbs, garlic and parsley, and salt and pepper to taste, and spread half over the fish (step 3). Sprinkle with lemon juice and dot with half the butter. Arrange another layer of fish over this, and cover with the remaining breadcrumb mixture. Pour over the eggs beaten with the milk, melt the remaining butter and pour over the top. Bake in a moderate oven (350°F) for 30 minutes or until golden. Serve in cooking dish, garnished with parsley.

Sardine Croquettes

Clean, wash and dry 1 lb sardines, small herring or mackerel, and cut into small pieces after removing the heads and bones. Mix 1 egg in a bowl with 1 tablespoon pine nuts, 1 tablespoon raisins, 2 tablespoons breadcrumbs, 2 tablespoons grated Parmesan or Swiss cheese, 1 tablespoon chopped parsley, and salt and pepper to taste. Add the fish and mix well. Shape into croquettes about 2½ inches long on a floured board. Roll in flour, then sauté. Serve with tomato sauce (see p.58).

Portuguese Sardines

Clean, wash and dry 1 lb sardines, small herring or mackerel, and remove the heads and bones. Mash ½ lb cod with 2 egg yolks, and salt, pepper and basil to taste. Add 1 tablespoons fine breadcrumbs. Stuff the fish with this mixture. Cook ½ cup onion, chopped, in butter until transparent. Add 2 cups tomatoes, peeled, seeded and chopped, 1 pinch basil, 1 tablespoon chopped parsley, 2 cloves of garlic, crushed, and salt and pepper to taste, and cook slowly until a thick sauce has formed. Roll fish in flour and cook in ½ cup oil and ½ cup butter until golden. Pour the sauce into a warm dish, arrange fish over and serve.

1 2 3

Grilled Swordfish

Ingredients: *4 slices swordfish (6–8 oz each, about 1 inch thick) · salt · pepper · 2½ tablespoons butter kneaded with anchovy paste or chopped mixed herbs to taste*

To serve: *melted butter · chervil · rosemary · basil · juice of 1 lemon*

To garnish: *green beans · canned peeled tomatoes*

Season the fish slices with salt and pepper, cover with the butter (step 1), and cook on a buttered grill (step 2) for 5–6 minutes on each side (step 3). Serve with melted butter mixed with chopped chervil, rosemary, basil and lemon juice in a separate dish. Garnish the serving platter with sliced green beans and tomatoes.

Spanish Swordfish

Put ½ cup oil in an earthenware dish with ½ cup onion, finely chopped, 2 cloves of garlic, crushed, ½ cup green and red peppers, seeded and sliced, and 2 cups tomatoes, peeled, seeded and chopped. Cook slowly for 20 minutes, then add 1½ lb swordfish in 1 piece. Season with salt and pepper to taste, and add 1 twig thyme and 1 bay leaf. Cook the fish for 5 minutes on each side. Serve in the cooking dish.

Salmon Trout au Gratin

Clean, wash and dry a 2-lb salmon trout (see p.58). Season it inside with salt, pepper and lemon juice to taste. Place the fish in a buttered ovenproof dish and spread over it

½ cup onion, chopped, ½ cup shallots, chopped, 1 tablespoon chopped parsley, ½ cup mushrooms, sliced, then add 1 cup dry white wine, 2½ tablespoons butter in small pieces, and 1 tablespoon breadcrumbs. Cover the dish and bake in a moderate oven (350°F) for 35–40 minutes. Serve immediately.

Swordfish with Capers

Take 4 slices swordfish (about 1½ lb). Cook in ¼ cup oil until golden on both sides. Sprinkle with salt. Add 2 tablespoons tomato sauce, thinned in a little hot water, and 2 tablespoons capers. Cook slowly for about 30 minutes, and serve with the reduced cooking juices.

1   2   3

Cod Provençal

Ingredients: *2 lb cod fillets · salt · pepper · flour · 2 tablespoons grated Parmesan cheese · grated nutmeg · 1 small onion, chopped · 1 clove of garlic, chopped · ½ cup oil · 6 anchovy fillets, soaked in a little milk and mashed · 1 teaspoon chopped parsley · ½ cup dry white wine · 3 cups hot milk · 1 tablespoon butter*

To serve: *polenta or mashed potatoes*

Clean and skin cod and cut in large pieces. Sprinkle with salt and pepper and roll in flour (step 1). Arrange in 1 layer in an ovenproof dish and sprinkle with the Parmesan cheese mixed with a pinch of nutmeg. In a pan, sauté the onion and garlic lightly in oil, then add the anchovy fillets, parsley and white wine. Reduce on low heat, then pour in the hot milk (step 2), stirring thoroughly, and add the butter in small pieces. Pour over the fish (step 3), bring to a boil, cover, and cook in a slow oven (250°F) for 2 hours. After cooking, the cooking juices should be almost completely absorbed. Serve with piping hot polenta or mashed potato.

Ligurian Cod

Sauté 1 clove of garlic, crushed, and 1 teaspoon chopped parsley lightly in ½ cup oil. Add 4 anchovy fillets, desalted and mashed, ½ cup pitted green olives, 2½ tablespoons pine nuts, lightly sautéed in butter, and a few capers. After a few minutes, add 2 lb cod fillets, cleaned, skinned and cut into pieces. Season to taste, cover, and cook gently for 1½ hours, adding 1 cup dry white wine gradually during cooking.

Cod Casserole

Clean and skin 2 lb cod fillet, and cut into pieces. Place in a casserole with 3 onions, sliced, 2 cups canned peeled tomatoes, chopped, ½ cup oil and a little water. Cover and cook gently for 2 hours. Serve with polenta or mashed potato.

Cod Niçoise

Prepare 1½ lb cod fillet as above, and sauté in a casserole with ½ cup onion, chopped, 2 cloves of garlic, chopped, and 1 cup olive oil. Add 1½ cups tomatoes, peeled, seeded and crushed, chopped parsley, 1 bay leaf, and salt and pepper. Cook briefly, then add 3 cups potatoes, quartered. Cover with boiling water and cook for about 1 hour. Add ½ cup pitted black olives.

1   2   3

Spiced Cod

Ingredients: *1½ lb fresh cod, cut into 4 slices ·
1 small onion, chopped · 1 teaspoon chopped
parsley · ½ cup oil · salt · 1 tablespoon flour ·
1 bay leaf · ground cinnamon · ¼ cup dry white
wine*

To garnish: *parsley sprigs*

Sauté the chopped onion and parsley lightly in
the oil. Add the slices of cod and cook on both
sides until golden (step 1). Sprinkle with salt.
After about 15 minutes, add the flour blended
with a little water, the bay leaf (step 2), and a
pinch of cinnamon, and continue cooking a
further 15 minutes. Before removing from the
heat, add the white wine (step 3), and reduce.
Transfer to a warm serving platter and garnish
with parsley sprigs.

Cod with Olives

Soak 1½ lb fresh cod in cold water for ½ hour.
Dry it, and place in an ovenproof dish with
2½ tablespoons melted butter. Sprinkle the fish
with breadcrumbs, place over it 2 tomatoes,
sliced, 4 tablespoons pitted green olives, finely
chopped, 1 tablespoon capers, and salt and
pepper to taste. Add ¼ cup oil, and bake in a
moderate oven (350°F) for about 30 minutes.
This dish can also be cooked on top of oven.

Cod with Tomatoes

Roll 4 slices fresh cod, seasoned with salt and
pepper, and cook until golden in ¼ cup oil. In a
separate pan, sauté ½ onion, chopped, in ¼ cup
oil. Add 1 teaspoon chopped parsley, then ½ cup

dry white wine, and reduce. Add 3 anchovy
fillets, desalted, and 1½ cups canned peeled
tomatoes. Cook for 15 minutes, then add the
fish slices. Cook for about a further 15 minutes
and serve immediately.

Broiled Cod with Tartare Sauce

Season 4 slices fresh cod (about 1½ lb) with
salt and pepper. Roll in flour, brush with oil,
and place under a hot broiler. Turn them over
when they are well broiled on one side. Prepare a tartare sauce with mayonnaise, chopped
onion, parsley, tarragon, chervil, chives,
gherkins and capers (see p.48). Serve the fish
on a warm serving platter, with the tartare
sauce in a separate dish.

Stuffed Salmon Slices

Ingredients: *2 slices fresh salmon, or other similar fish such as halibut, ¾ inch thick and about 10 oz each · 1 slice chopped onion · 1 tablespoon chopped parsley · butter or margarine · 1 generous handful of bread, soaked in milk and squeezed dry · 1 cup finely sliced mushrooms · salt · pepper · 1 cup light cream*

To serve: *chopped parsley · boiled potatoes*

Fry the onion and parsley lightly in 2½ tablespoons butter or margarine on low heat. Mix in a bowl with the bread, mushrooms, and salt and pepper to taste (step 1). Butter generously an ovenproof dish, put in one salmon slice, and spread the mushroom mixture over it (step 2). Cover with the second salmon slice, pour over the cream, previously heated (step 3), dot with butter, and sprinkle with salt and pepper. Cook in a moderate (350°F) oven for about ½ hour, basting occasionally with the cooking juices. Transfer to a warm serving platter, sprinkle with chopped parsley and serve with boiled potatoes.

Fish Scabecia Style

Clean, wash and dry 1½ lb sole fillets, or sardines, or other fish according to taste, roll in flour and fry in oil a few at a time. Arrange in a bowl. In the remaining oil (add more if necessary) cook until golden 1 onion, sliced, and 2–3 cloves of garlic, crushed. Remove from the heat, add 4 bay leaves, 1 twig of thyme, vinegar and salt and pepper to taste. Pour immediately over the fried fish, and let stand in the refrigerator for at least 2 days.

Salmon Brochettes

Arrange on oiled skewers 1½ lb fresh salmon, or swordfish, or halibut cut into pieces, alternating with mushroom caps, halved tomatoes, slices of onion and green pepper. Sprinkle with salt and pepper, and pour over 1 cup olive oil and ½ cup dry white wine. Let stand for 3½ hours. Broil, turning occasionally and basting with the marinade. (This is a perfect dish to prepare over charcoal.)

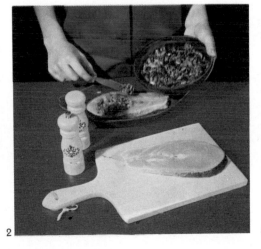
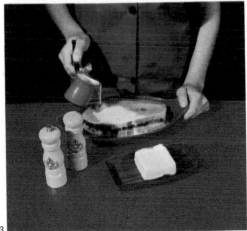

1   2   3

1

2

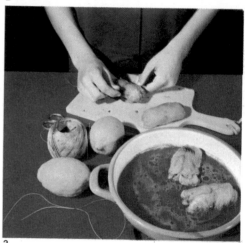

3

Sicilian Stuffed Swordfish

Ingredients: *4 large, flattened slices swordfish · 4 tablespoons breadcrumbs · 4 tablespoons grated Parmesan cheese · 1 tablespoon chopped capers · a few pieces tomato · salt · pepper · butter · 2 cups tomato sauce*

To garnish: *capers · parsley sprigs*

Mix together the breadcrumbs, Parmesan, chopped capers and tomato, add salt and pepper to taste, and enough melted butter to obtain a smooth paste (step 1). Spread over the 4 fish slices. Roll them (step 2), tie them with string (step 3), and cook for about ½ hour in the tomato sauce, turning them over carefully half way through the cooking. Transfer to a warm serving platter and garnish with capers and parsley sprigs.

Salmon Bellevue

Put 1 quart dry white wine in a fish poacher or kettle with 2 quarts water, 2 carrots, sliced, 2 onions, sliced, a few cloves, 1 bouquet garni, made with 2–3 sprigs of parsley, 1 sprig of thyme, 1 bay leaf, 1–2 cloves of garlic, a handful of rock salt and 6 whole peppercorns. Bring to a boil, skim the scum, and cook for 45 minutes. Scale, clean and wash a whole salmon (6–8 lb). Trim off gills and fins, and trim the tail. Place it in the court bouillon and simmer slowly for 25–30 minutes. Turn off the heat and cool in the court bouillon. Remove the salmon from the liquid when cool, discard the skin and place the fish on a folded white napkin on a large platter. Cover the fish with cool, liquid aspic (see p.50) and allow to set.

Prepare 16 hard-boiled eggs. Halve them lengthwise, remove the yolks and mash them together with mayonnaise to make a stiff cream. Fill the egg whites with this mixture, using a pastry bag fitted with a star nozzle. Cut off the tops of 10 tomatoes, remove seeds and pulp and fill with a macédoine mixed with mayonnaise (see p.48). To prepare the macédoine: cook until tender 1 lb carrots, diced, with 2 cups green peas, shelled, and 2½ tablespoons turnips, diced, in boiling salted water; drain. Cook until tender 10 artichoke hearts in boiling salted water with a little vinegar; drain. Place small shrimps dipped in mayonnaise on top of artichoke hearts. Arrange everything around the salmon on the platter with lettuce leaves and lemon slices. Serve with a tartare sauce (see p.48) in a separate dish.

Red Mullet en Papillote

Ingredients: *4 red mullet or red snapper ($\frac{1}{2}$–$\frac{3}{4}$ lb each) · 1 cup mushrooms, sliced · butter · 2 tablespoons tomato paste · $\frac{1}{2}$ cup stock or dry white wine · chopped parsley · salt · pepper · oil · $\frac{1}{4}$ lb cooked ham, cut into strips*

To serve: *tomatoes · parsley*

Scale and clean the fish and remove the gills. Make a few deep slits in the sides with a knife (step 1), and dry. Cook the mushrooms in butter, add the tomato paste and the stock or white wine, and parsley, salt and pepper to taste, and continue cooking slowly. Cut out 4 ovals of wax paper or aluminum foil, each one large enough to enclose a fish (step 2), and oil generously on one side. Place on each sheet some of the mushroom sauce and 1 fish, and over the fish a few strips of cooked ham. Fold the papillotes, twisting the ends so that they are sealed and juices will not escape (step 3). Arrange them in a buttered ovenproof dish and bake in a moderate oven (350°F) for about 15 minutes. To serve, unwrap the fish carefully and arrange on warm serving plates garnished with whole baked tomatoes and parsley.

Red Mullet Provençal

Scale and dry 4 red mullet (about $\frac{1}{2}$ lb–$\frac{3}{4}$ lb each). Remove the gills. Sprinkle with salt and pepper and roll them lightly in flour. Cook in a little oil on moderate heat until golden brown on all sides. Remove carefully from pan with a spatula and keep warm on a serving platter. Heat $\frac{1}{4}$ cup oil in a pan, add 1 slice of onion, chopped, and 1 clove of garlic, peeled, and cook until golden. Remove the garlic, add a pinch of crumbled thyme and 1 bay leaf, $1\frac{1}{4}$ cups peeled tomatoes, and salt and pepper to taste. Cook for a further 10 minutes, then pour the sauce over the fish. Sprinkle with chopped parsley and serve.

Stuffed Red Mullet

Prepare 4 red mullet as above and remove the center bone. Prepare a stuffing with 4 tablespoons breadcrumbs, chopped rosemary, 1 clove of garlic, chopped, salt, pepper and chopped rosemary to taste, and a few tablespoons oil. Mix well together. Put a portion of this mixture inside each fish. Heat plenty of oil in a frying pan with 1 clove of garlic, peeled. Remove the garlic, add the red mullet to the pan and cook on high heat until golden brown on all sides (about 15 minutes each side). Serve piping hot with lemon quarters.

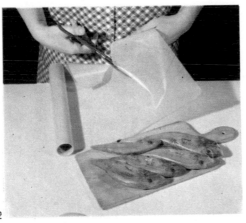

1   2   3

Fish Stew with Red Wine

Ingredients: *3 lb mixed fish (halibut, cod, flounder, mackerel, bass, red snapper, shrimps mussels, scallops, squid cut into rings) · 1 celery stalk, chopped · 1 carrot, sliced · 1 onion, sliced · 2 cloves of garlic, crushed · ½ cup oil · 1 slice red pepper · parsley, chopped · 1 cup red wine · 2 cups canned peeled tomatoes · salt · pepper*

To serve: *French bread · garlic*

Clean, wash and dry the fish, cutting the larger fish into pieces and leaving the smaller ones whole (step 1). Boil in salted water the heads, bones, tails and skins of the fish, together with the celery, carrot and onion. Cook the garlic lightly in the oil, then add the red pepper and parsley to taste (step 2). Add the wine, let it reduce, then add the tomatoes. Strain the stock and add it gradually to the sauce. Cook for 10 minutes, add the squid and continue cooking for 15 minutes. Transfer to a large flameproof pan – preferably earthenware – taste for seasoning and add the remaining fish, scallops, shrimps and mussels last (step 3). Cover and cook for 20–30 minutes, adding more stock if necessary. (Many connoisseurs believe the dish is best if left to stand for a few hours and re-heated on low heat before serving.) Just before serving, toast slices of French bread, rub them with garlic, arrange them in each individual plate, and spread the fish, seafood, and sauce over them.

Mediterranean Bouillabaisse

Prepare for cooking 5 lb mixed fish (whiting, red mullet, halibut, perch, cod, hake, conger eel, mackerel, bass, lobster, crab). Cut the larger fish into pieces and leave the smaller ones whole. Put the fish (except for the tender varieties like red mullet) into a large pan, together with ¾ cup onion, sliced, 2–3 cloves of garlic, crushed, 2 tomatoes, peeled and cut into pieces, 1 bay leaf, and parsley, saffron, salt and fennel to taste. Cover with water, bring to a boil and cook for 15 minutes. Add the remaining fish and cook very slowly for a further 7–8 minutes. Serve piping hot with slices of dry bread. Serve in a separate dish a mayonnaise (see p.48).

1

2

3

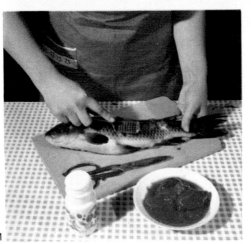
1

2

3

Fresh-water Fish

Baked Carp

Ingredients: *1 carp (about 2½ lb) · 1 slice onion finely chopped · ½ cup oil · a few leaves sage · salt · pepper · ground cinnamon · 1¼ cups tomatoes, peeled (fresh or canned)*

Scale the carp (step 1), clean, wash, salt, and let stand between 2 plates for about 2 hours. Cook the onion until golden in the oil in a fish poacher or kettle. Put in the carp (step 2), and brown on both sides. Add the sage leaves, salt and pepper to taste, and a pinch of cinnamon and continue cooking for about 15 minutes, adding a few spoonfuls of hot water from time to time. Add the tomatoes (step 3), and continue cooking for another 20 minutes. The sauce must be thick. Transfer the carp to a warm serving platter and surround with the sauce.

Perch Fillets with Olives

Float ¼ cup oil in a pan, then add chopped parsley to taste. Add to the pan 1¼ lb perch, sliced, or rainbow trout, sliced, and sauté lightly on moderate heat. Sprinkle with salt and pepper to taste and add ¼ cup dry white wine. Let it reduce by half, then add ½ cup pitted green olives. Continue cooking for a few minutes, adding a few spoonfuls hot water or stock if necessary.

Golden Perch Fillets

Cover 8 perch fillets or rainbow trout in a marinade of oil, lemon juice, salt, pepper and chopped onion. Let stand for about 1 hour, turning them over occasionally. Remove them from the marinade, dry carefully, roll in flour, beaten egg and breadcrumbs. Brown them in ½ cup very hot oil, and arrange on a warm serving platter. Add ¼ cup oil and a few sage leaves to the pan, and cook on high heat. Pour over the fillets and serve with lemon quarters.

Trout with Almonds

Clean 4 trout (8–10 oz each), sprinkle with salt and pepper, and roll in flour. Brown them on both sides in a mixture of half butter, half oil. Add 1 small glass brandy, bring to a boil and flame. Reduce the heat to low and add salt and pepper to taste, and ½ cup light cream. Heat through gently, without letting the cream boil. Serve the trout with the cooking juices and sprinkle with ½ cup almonds, sliced and toasted.

Stuffed Pike

Ingredients: *1 large pike (about 3 lb) · 1 egg ·*
1 handful breadcrumbs · ½ cup grated Parmesan
or Gruyère cheese · chopped parsley · garlic,
crushed · salt · pepper · ½ cup oil · a few sage
leaves · 1 bay leaf

To serve: *macédoine of vegetables or polenta*

Clean the pike and remove the center bone
(step 1), wash and dry. Mix in a bowl the egg,
breadcrumbs, Parmesan or Gruyère cheese,
parsley, garlic, and salt and pepper to taste.
Stuff the pike (step 2) with mixture, sew with
string (step 3), and put it in an ovenproof
dish, with the oil, sage and bay leaves. Cover,
and cook in a moderately hot oven (350°F) for
40–50 minutes, basting occasionally with the
cooking juices. Transfer to a warm serving
platter, and surround with a buttered macédoine of vegetables or with polenta.

Baked Pike with White Wine Sauce

Prepare 1 large pike (about 3 lb) as above. Cut
slits under the skin of the fish, and insert small
strips of bacon. Put in a buttered ovenproof
dish, cover and cook in a moderately hot oven
(375°F) for 25 minutes. Remove the fish and
keep warm on a serving platter. Pour 1½ cups
dry white wine into the baking dish, and mix
with the cooking juices. Add 2½ tablespoons
butter, simmer for 5 minutes, then pour over
the fish.

Pike Fricassee

Prepare 1 large pike (about 3 lb) as above, and
cut into pieces. Put in a pan with ¼ cup oil,
¾ cup mushrooms, chopped, and a bouquet
garni of parsley, thyme and 1 bay leaf.

Sprinkle the fish with 1 teaspoon flour, and salt
and pepper, then add 3 tablespoons stock and
½ cup dry white wine. Cook on fairly high heat
until fish is tender, stirring carefully from time
to time. Take out the fish and keep warm on a
serving platter. Remove the bouquet garni,
and blend into the sauce 1 egg yolk, beaten
with a little lemon juice. Let thicken without
boiling, then pour over the fish.

Pike Médaillons

Prepare 1 large pike (about 3 lb) as above, and
cut into slices 1½ inches thick, removing the
bones. Dip the slices in egg beaten with a little
salt, then roll in breadcrumbs. Heat plenty of
oil in a pan and brown the fish on all sides.
Transfer to a warm serving platter, garnish
with parsley, and serve with tomato sauce (see
p.6) in a separate dish.

1

2

3

1

2

3

Trout in Aspic

Ingredients: *1 trout (about 3 lb)*

For the court bouillon: *4 quarts water · ½ cup white (distilled) vinegar · 1 medium-sized onion, sliced · 1 carrot, sliced · 1 slice of lemon · 2–3 sprigs parsley · ½ bay leaf · a few crushed peppercorns · 1 handful of rock salt*

For the aspic: *5 oz whiting or flounder, chopped · 2 egg whites · 1 leek, finely chopped · a few parsley sprigs · 6 sheets isinglass, soaked in tepid water and squeezed*

To garnish: *radishes · gherkins · black olives*

To prepare the court bouillon: put the water in a large pan with the vinegar, onion, carrot, lemon, parsley, ½ bay leaf, peppercorns and salt. Bring to a boil, then simmer gently for

¾ hour. Strain the liquid and let cool. Scale, clean and wash trout. Place it on grid of a fish kettle, cover it with 3 quarts cold court bouillon, and poach it for 10 minutes at a temperature just below boiling. Turn off heat and let cool in court bouillon; drain and reserve. Strain liquid through a wet cloth.

To prepare the aspic: add the whiting or flounder to 1 quart of the strained cooking liquid, blend in the egg whites, leek and parsley sprigs. Bring to a boil, and add the isinglass. Skim the scum, and cook on very low heat for about ½ hour, stirring occasionally. Do not allow to boil. Strain through a fine wet cloth, and pour a thin layer into a long, narrow serving platter. Put in the refrigerator to set. Meanwhile, let the remaining aspic cool, without getting too hard. Carefully remove the center skin of the trout, leaving the tail and head

whole (step 1). When the aspic in the serving platter is set, place the trout on top (step 2), and garnish the skinned part with slices of radish, gherkin, and olive (step 3). Pour over a few spoonfuls of aspic. Garnish the platter with more gherkin and radish slices.

Salmon Cutlets Pojarski

Mash 1¼ lb cooked salmon (leftovers from a poached salmon are ideal) and mix it with ¾ cup breadcrumbs. Add ½ cup milk, and salt and pepper to taste. Stirring continuously, blend in 4 egg yolks one by one. Let stand for 15 minutes, then shape into cutlets. Dip them in 2 eggs beaten with a few drops oil, 1 pinch each of salt and pepper, and roll in fine white breadcrumbs. Brown in butter; serve with tartare sauce (see p.6) in a separate dish.

Shellfish

Lobster Bellevue

Ingredients: *1 live lobster (about 2½ lb)*

*For the court bouillon: 1 tablespoon butter ·
1 carrot, sliced · 2 onions, sliced · 1 quart dry
white wine · 1 quart water · 1 bouquet garni of
parsley, thyme and bay leaf · salt · peppercorns*

*To garnish: 6 artichoke hearts, fresh, frozen or
canned · 2 cups Russian salad, commercially
prepared or homemade (see p.26) · 4 hard-
boiled eggs · mayonnaise, commercially prepared
or homemade · 1¼ cups rice · lettuce leaves ·
aspic (optional) · truffles (optional) · radish roses*

To prepare the court bouillon: heat the butter
in a large pan, add the carrot and onions and
cook until golden. Add the wine, water,
bouquet garni, and salt and peppercorns to
taste. Bring to a boil, then put in the live
lobster. Cook for 20–25 minutes, then leave to
cool in the cooking liquid. Meanwhile, cook
fresh artichoke hearts in boiling salted water,
drain, allow to cool, then fill with the Russian
salad. Halve the hard-boiled eggs, remove the
yolks carefully with a spoon, work them
through a sieve, and mix with mayonnaise to
make a stiff cream. Fill the eggs with this
mixture, using a pastry bag fitted with a star
nozzle. Cook the rice in boiling salted water
until it is *al dente*, drain, and place at one end
of an oval serving platter, making a hollow in
the center. Cover with lettuce leaves. Remove
the lobster, put it on its back on a towel, and
cut it lengthwise with scissors from head to
tail (step 1). Take the flesh out carefully in one
piece, then cut into regular slices (step 2).
Arrange lobster shell on the platter, the head
resting on the rice and lettuce. Cover with
lobster slices, garnished with little liquid aspic
(step 3) and truffles cut into star shapes, if
liked. Place artichoke hearts and eggs round
lobster and garnish with lettuce and radish
roses.

Lobster American Style

Cut 1 lobster (about 3 lb) into pieces. Leave
both tail and claw meat in the shell, and remove
and reserve the soft flesh, tomalley and liver.
Heat 2 tablespoons oil in a shallow pan and put
in the lobster pieces. Turn, and add salt, saffron,
and red and cayenne peppers. Pour in ½ cup
brandy, bring to a boil and flame. Lower heat,
add ½ cup shallots, chopped, 1 clove of garlic,
crushed, and 1 cup tomatoes, peeled, seeded
and chopped. Add 1 cup dry white wine, and
fish stock to cover lobster pieces. Put in 1 twig
thyme and 1 bay leaf, and cook slowly for 20
minutes. Take out the lobster and keep warm
on a serving platter. Let the pan juices simmer
until reduced by half. Blend in reserved meat,
finely chopped, and add 2½ tablespoons butter
and ½ cup light cream gradually; heat through.
Pour over lobster and serve with a rice pilaff
in a separate dish.

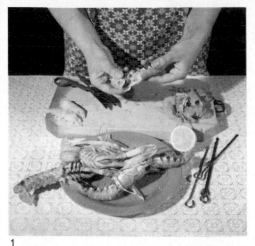

1

2

3

Brochettes of Scampi

Ingredients: *24 scampi tails (langoustines) ·*
3 zucchini · 16 mushroom caps · butter or oil

For the marinade: *a few spoonfuls olive oil ·*
1 clove of garlic, crushed · 1 bay leaf, crumbled ·
salt · pepper · lemon juice

To garnish: *lemon slices or wedges · green*
salad leaves

Shell the raw scampi tails (step 1), slice the
zucchini (step 2), clean the mushroom caps,
and put everything into a bowl. Mix all the
marinade ingredients together, pour into the
bowl, and let stand for 1 hour. Drain the
scampi, zucchini and mushrooms (reserving
the marinade), and arrange them on oiled
metal skewers (step 3). Spread a shallow baking

dish with butter or oil and put in the brochettes.
Cook in a hot oven (425°F) for about 15
minutes, basting occasionally with the reserved
marinade. Transfer the brochettes to a warm
serving platter and garnish the edges of the
platter with lemon slices or wedges and
green salad leaves.

Serve with mixed salad, dressed according
to taste, in a separate dish.

Algerian Shrimps

Blend together 3 cloves of garlic and $\frac{1}{4}$ cup
parsley, chopped. Heat 1 cup oil. When very
hot, put in 32 large shrimps and sauté, adding
salt and cayenne pepper. Add the garlic and
parsley, cook for a further 2 minutes and serve
immediately.

Shrimps with Mayonnaise

Put 2 quarts water in a large pan with 1 celery
stalk, chopped, 1 onion, sliced, 2 bay leaves,
1 twig of thyme, and parsley and salt to taste.
Boil for a few minutes, put in the tails of about
$2\frac{1}{2}$ lb shrimps, and poach for 5 minutes. Drain,
and leave to cool. Shell them, brush with oil
and lemon juice, and let stand for a few hours.
Serve with mayonnaise (see p.48), and garnish
with salad and hard-boiled eggs.

Mussels au Gratin

Ingredients: *3 lb mussels · ¼ cup dry white wine · 1 slice of onion, finely chopped · freshly ground pepper · vinegar · chopped parsley · 2 cloves of garlic, chopped · breadcrumbs · salt · pepper · 3 tablespoons oil mixed with 1 tablespoon vinegar or lemon juice*

Scrape the mussels (step 1), wash in running water, discarding any that are open, and put in a large pan together with the white wine, onion, pepper, and a few drops vinegar. Cover and cook on high heat, shaking the pan from time to time, until the mussels are all opened (discard any that do not open). Drain them and discard the empty halves of the shells, keeping those where the mussel is attached. Arrange the mussels in an ovenproof dish (step 2), and cover each with a mixture of parsley, garlic, breadcrumbs, and salt and pepper to taste (step 3). Pour the oil and vinegar over, and put the dish in a hot oven (425°F) for a few minutes to gratiné. Serve immediately.

Stuffed Mussels

Prepare 3 lb mussels as above, heat them in a frying pan until they are all opened (discard any that do not open). Meanwhile, prepare the stuffing: mix 3 oz mortadella, chopped finely, with 3 oz sausage meat, and a handful of the white part of bread, soaked and squeezed dry, 1 tablespoon chopped parsley, 1 clove of garlic, chopped, and salt and pepper to taste. When the mixture is smooth, stuff mussels, close them and tie them with string. Cook in a large pan 2 cups tomatoes, peeled, seeded, and crushed, a few basil leaves, a little chopped onion, a few spoonfuls oil and a pinch of salt. Then put in the mussels and cook for another 30 minutes. Remove mussels from sauce, discard string, then return mussels to sauce to reheat. Serve piping hot.

Mussel Soup

Prepare 5 lb mussels as above. Heat them in a frying pan until they are all open (discard any that do not open). Add a few spoonfuls hot water, and cook for about 15 minutes. Meanwhile, cook 1–2 cloves of garlic, peeled, in ½ cup oil until golden; remove the garlic and add a generous measure of chopped parsley

and basil. Pour over the mussels, adding more hot water if necessary, and boil for a few minutes. Arrange in individual dishes slices of bread fried in butter, pour over the mussels and their sauce, and serve immediately.

Mussels Marinière

Put 1 cup dry white wine in a pan with 1 twig thyme and 1 small bay leaf. Add 3 lb mussels (prepared as above). Cover and cook on high heat until mussels are all opened (discard any that do not open). Take out the mussels and keep warm on a serving platter. Make a roux with 2½ tablespoons of butter, 2 tablespoons flour, and the cooking juices from the mussels. Pour over the mussels, and sprinkle them with a mixture of finely chopped parsley to taste and ¼ cup shallots, finely chopped, or finely chopped garlic to taste.

1

2

3

Snails Bourguignon

Ingredients: *48 large snails · rock salt ·*
vinegar · flour · dry white wine · 1 carrot and 1
onion sliced together · 1 shallot, chopped ·
garlic to taste, peeled · 1 bouquet garni ·
peppercorns

For the stuffing: *2 cups butter, softened ·*
1 tablespoon shallot or onion, finely chopped ·
4 cloves of garlic, crushed · 2 tablespoons
chopped parsley · 1 teaspoon salt · 1 pinch each
pepper and spices

To garnish: *parsley sprigs*

You can now buy canned snails, already
cleaned and prepared, accompanied by clean
empty shells, and ready to cook. If, however,
you choose to use fresh snails, there must be
lengthy preparations. First, the snails must be
left to disgorge for 2–3 days in a container
where they can get enough air, but from which
they cannot escape. If the snails are bought
live in a shop, this has usually been done. Dip
the snails in plenty of cold water and stir well
to rid the shells of the diaphragm and particles
of earth. Put the washed snails in a pan containing rock salt, vinegar, and a little flour.
Let them disgorge for 2–3 hours, shaking the
pan occasionally. Wash once more in running
water. Put the snails in a large pan, cover with
cold water, and bring to a boil on low heat.
Skim the scum, and boil on high heat for 8
minutes. Lift the snails out, drain and put in
cold water for a moment. Put them back in a
pan, and cover with equal parts of water and
white wine. Add rock salt ($\frac{1}{2}$ tablespoon for 1
quart of liquid), the carrots and onions, shallot,
bouquet garni, and garlic cloves, and peppercorns to taste. Bring to a boil on a moderate
heat, and continue cooking for 2–3$\frac{1}{2}$ hours,
according to the size of the snails. When cooked
put them in a sieve to drain. Remove snails
from shells (step 1), and remove the black part
at the end of the helix. Wash the shells thoroughly in warm water, and dry in the oven.

To make the stuffing, blend together the
butter, chopped shallots or onion, crushed
garlic, parsley, salt, pepper and spices (step 2).
Put some of this mixture at the bottom of each
empty shell (step 3), put in the snail, and seal
the shell with more of the mixture, pressing it
down firmly. Arrange the shells, open side up,
on special snail dishes (*escargotières*), or on
ovenproof dishes filled with a layer of rock
salt, and bake in a hot oven (425°F) for 5
minutes. Garnish with parsley sprigs before
serving.

1

2

3

1

2

3

Eel with Peas

Ingredients: *2 lb eel · ½ onion, chopped · 1 clove of garlic, crushed · 3 tablespoons oil · salt · pepper · 1 cup white wine · 1 tablespoon tomato sauce · 1 tablespoon hot water · 6 cups fresh green peas, shelled, or 4 cups canned peas · chopped parsley*

To serve: *polenta or mashed potatoes*

To skin the eel, make an incision around the body just under the head. Holding head with a cloth, pull skin off from top to tail at one stroke (step 1). Clean the eel and cut into 2-inch sections, discarding the head. Brown the onion and garlic in the oil in a pan, then add the eel slices, and salt and pepper to taste (step 2). When the eel slices are golden brown, and the liquid has evaporated, add the white wine, tomato sauce, water and peas (step 3). Continue cooking for 20–30 minutes or until eel is

tender; add more water if fish becomes dry. (If using canned peas, add near end of cooking time.) Transfer to a warm serving platter, sprinkle with chopped parsley and serve with piping hot polenta or mashed potato.

Stewed Eel en Matelote

Prepare and slice 2 lb eel as above. Put the slices in a pan with ½ cup onions, sliced, and ½ cup mushrooms, sliced, 1 bouquet garni, 3 cloves of garlic, crushed, salt and pepper to taste, and 1½ cups dry white wine. Bring to a boil and, after a few seconds, add ½ cup brandy. Cook slowly for 20–30 minutes or until the eel is tender. Remove the eel slices and keep warm on a serving platter. Continue cooking the sauce on high heat until reduced by half. Remove from the heat, stir in 1 tablespoon butter, pour sauce over the eel, and serve.

Eel with Herbs

Prepare and slice 2 lb eel as above. Cook on high heat for 5 minutes in 2½ tablespoons butter with 1 tablespoon chopped celery and 1 tablespoon chopped onion, stirring occasionally. Add 2 cups dry white wine. 1 pinch thyme, 1 bay leaf, crumbled, salt and pepper to taste, a handful each of sorrel leaves, spinach leaves and watercress, all washed and finely chopped, 1 pinch tarragon, and 1 tablespoon each of chopped parsley and chervil. Add a few leaves of sage and mint, wrapped in a piece of muslin. Cook on high heat, stirring with a spatula, for 10–15 minutes or until the eel is tender. Remove from the heat. Take out the sage and mint bag, and stir into the sauce 3 egg yolks, beaten. Add 1 teaspoon lemon juice. Arrange the eel slices in a platter, and pour the sauce over. This dish is equally delicious hot or cold.

1

2

3

Eggs

Poached Eggs in Mornay Sauce

Ingredients: *4 eggs · 4 round croûtons, toasted and buttered · 1 cup fresh mushrooms, sliced and cooked in butter and brandy · ½ cup mornay sauce (see p.47) · grated Parmesan cheese · a few asparagus tips*

To finish: *4 whole button mushrooms · grated Parmesan cheese · tomatoes*

Poach the eggs, place each on a croûton (step 1) and put in an ovenproof dish. Add the mushrooms to the mornay sauce and cover each egg with the mixture (step 2). Sprinkle with grated Parmesan cheese (step 3) and gratiné in a hot oven (400°F) until golden. Put the asparagus tips in a hot serving dish, arrange the eggs on top, place a mushroom cap on each and sprinkle with grated Parmesan cheese. Garnish the dish with whole skinned tomatoes and serve with a hot tomato sauce.

Poached Eggs in Fish Stock

Prepare 2 cups stock with fish leftovers or fish pieces, celery, carrot, ½ bay leaf, onion and 1 stock cube. Strain through a fine wet cloth. In the same pan melt ¾ tablespoon butter or margarine, stir in about 1 tablespoon flour, then pour in stock. Add salt and pepper, bring to a boil, stirring with a whisk, and simmer for 10 minutes. Cut 4 slices of bread into 8 triangles and brown lightly in oil. Place 2 bread triangles on each plate, add 1 poached egg, and pour over the boiling fish stock.

Eggs Letizia

Brown 1 small onion, chopped, in butter. Add ¾ cup rice, 1 teaspoon curry powder, and let stand 2 minutes. Pour in gradually 3 cups boiling stock (preferably chicken stock), and cook for about 20 minutes, stirring occasionally. Meanwhile, poach 4 eggs. Melt ½ tablespoon butter in a pan, stir in 1 tablespoon flour and 1 teaspoon curry powder and cook for 1 minute. Remove from the heat, gradually stir in 1 cup chicken stock, return to heat and cook for about 10 minutes. On a warm serving platter or individual plates, arrange the cooked rice in 4 heaps, making a hollow in each one. Place 1 egg in each hollow and pour over hot sauce. Garnish with parsley.

Eggs with Brussels Sprouts

Clean 2 cups Brussels sprouts and cook for 5 minutes in boiling salted water; drain. Put sprouts into fresh boiling salted water and cook for another 15–20 minutes, or until tender. Drain thoroughly and mix with 1 tablespoon butter. (This way of cooking sprouts makes them more digestible. Frozen sprouts can be used if liked.) Arrange sprouts in a crown in a buttered ovenproof dish, break 4–6 eggs in center of dish, add salt and pepper to taste, sprinkle with grated Parmesan cheese and dot with melted butter. Place the dish in a moderate oven (350°F) and cook for a few minutes until eggs are set.

Poached Eggs with Mushroom Sauce

Ingredients: *4 eggs · 2½ tablespoons butter or margarine · 1–2 cloves of garlic, peeled · 2 tablespoons dried mushrooms soaked in lukewarm water, squeezed dry and sliced, or 1¼ cups fresh mushrooms, sliced · 2 cups canned peeled tomatoes, roughly chopped · ½ bay leaf · salt, or 1 stock cube · pepper · 4 slices bread · chopped parsley*

Heat the butter or margarine, add 1 clove of garlic, and cook until golden-brown. Remove garlic, put in the mushrooms and sauté for 2–3 minutes. Add the tomatoes, the bay leaf, the salt, or stock cube to taste, and the pepper. Let the sauce simmer for 45 minutes, adding a few spoonfuls water if it becomes too thick. Poach the eggs (step 1), drain and trim them

(step 2) and place on slices of bread toasted in the oven (step 3). If liked, the bread may be rubbed with a clove of garlic. Pour the sauce around the bread slices, sprinkle with chopped parsley, and serve immediately.

Poached Eggs Allegria

Melt 1 tablespoon butter with 2 tablespoons flour, pour in 1 cup water, add salt, pepper or paprika to taste, and simmer for 5 minutes. Remove the sauce from the heat, mix in 2 egg yolks and the juice of ½ lemon, and keep warm in a double boiler, stirring occasionally. In a lightly oiled frying pan brown on both sides. Toast in oven 4 slices of bread and place on a platter or on individual plates. Put on

each bread slice 1 slice ham, 1 slice tomato and 1 poached egg. Season with salt and pepper to taste, and pour the hot sauce over the top.

Poached Eggs Burgundy Style

In a covered pan boil for 30 minutes, or until the wine is reduced by half, 2 cups red wine (preferably Burgundy type), onion, chopped, 1 clove of garlic, peeled and crushed, parsley to taste, 1 sprig of thyme and 1 bay leaf. Poach 4 eggs and place each egg on 1 fried croûton. Strain the sauce through a sieve. Add 2 egg yolks, 2 tablespoons butter, salt and pepper to taste, and blend thoroughly. Reheat the sauce gently, pour over the eggs and serve.

Oeufs à la Coque

Bring salted water to a boil (salting the water will usually prevent the cracking of the egg shell), slide in 4 eggs carefully with a spoon (step 1), and count 3 minutes from the moment the water starts boiling again. Remove the eggs, put them in egg cups (step 2), and cut off the tops (step 3).

Eggs in a Cup

Soft boil 2 eggs per person, as above. Break them on the edge of a heated cup, take the eggs out of the shells with a spoon, and drop them into the cup. Add salt and pepper to taste, and eat with buttered toast.

Oyster Eggs

Use only the freshest eggs. Break 1 raw egg and separate the yolk from the white. Put the yolk in a tablespoon, season with a pinch of salt, a generous measure of pepper, and a few drops of lemon juice. Eat it immediately – swallowing it whole if possible. This is the simplest way of eating an egg, and also the most digestible. It is recommended for convalescent or anaemic people. The taste is most pleasant, faintly recalling that of an oyster.

Soft-boiled Eggs on Toast

Toast slices of bread (2 per person), butter them and break 1 soft-boiled egg (see above) on each slice of bread. Season generously with salt and pepper.

Eggs with Russian Salad

Place on a serving platter a layer of Russian salad (a mixture of carrots, turnips, potatoes, French beans, peas and mayonnaise). Make 4 hollows and put in each hollow 1 egg, cooked for 6 minutes as above. Cover with mayonnaise (see p.48). Garnish with capers and keep cool.

Eggs Mimosa

Ingredients: *4 hard-boiled eggs, shelled · 2½ tablespoons butter, at room temperature · 1 cup tomato sauce · salt · pepper · 1 cup béchamel sauce (p.47)*

To garnish: *2 hard-boiled egg yolks · chopped parsley*

Halve the hard-boiled eggs lengthwise. Remove the yolks carefully with a teaspoon, mash with a fork and mix with the butter, 3 tablespoons of the tomato sauce and salt and pepper to taste (step 1). Fill the egg whites with the mixture, and place in a buttered ovenproof dish. Cover with a lid or foil and heat through in a moderate oven (350°F) for 10–15 minutes. Meanwhile, blend together the béchamel sauce and the remaining tomato sauce, both piping hot (step 2). Pour the sauce over the eggs (step 3), sprinkle with the hard-boiled egg yolks worked through a sieve and the chopped parsley, and serve immediately.

Egg Rolls with Eggplant

Prepare a flaky pastry with 1 cup flour, ½ cup butter or margarine, 2 tablespoons cold water and 1 pinch salt, wrap in wax paper and let stand in the refrigerator for ½ hour. Or use frozen flaky pastry. Roll out very thinly and use it to line the bottom and sides of an 8-inch pie pan. Prick the dough with a fork and bake in a hot oven (425°F) for 20–25 minutes. Meanwhile prepare 4 hard-boiled eggs, shell and cut each into 4 pieces. Work through a sieve 1½ cups canned peeled tomatoes until a purée is formed. Heat until golden brown 1 tablespoon butter with 1 slice onion. Remove the onion. Add the tomato purée and cook for a few minutes on high heat with a few basil leaves and 1 pinch salt. Peel and slice lengthwise 3 eggplants, to make 16 slices. Fry a few at a time in a little hot oil until golden, taking care they do not become dry, then drain on absorbent paper. Cover each slice with 1 teaspoon of the tomato sauce, and put on it 1 slice hard-boiled egg. Fold each eggplant slice to form a roll, and arrange them in a ring inside the pastry crust. Sprinkle generously with grated Parmesan cheese or cover with 3 slices Emmenthal cheese. Pour the remaining tomato sauce over and put in a hot oven (450°F) for 10–15 minutes, or until the cheese is melted.

Hard-boiled Eggs with Curry

Halve 4 shelled hard-boiled eggs lengthwise. Remove yolks carefully with a teaspoon and mash them with a fork together with 3 tablespoons mayonnaise, ½ tablespoon curry powder, ½ tablespoon chopped onion, ½ tablespoon chopped parsley, and salt and pepper to taste. Fill the egg whites with the mixture and keep in the refrigerator for a few hours. Place the eggs in a buttered ovenproof dish and cover with 2 cups béchamel sauce (see p.8). Put the dish in a moderate oven (350°F) to gratiné for about ½ hour.

Scotch Eggs

Ingredients: *4 hard-boiled eggs, shelled · ¾ lb sausages or sausage meat · chopped basil and parsley · 1 egg · 1 tablespoon water · breadcrumbs · oil for frying*

To garnish: *sprigs of parsley*

Roll the hard-boiled eggs in flour (step 1). Peel the sausages, if using sausages, or crumble the sausage meat, and blend in the chopped basil and parsley to taste. Divide the meat into 4 and completely cover each egg (step 2). Roll them again in flour, then in the egg beaten with the water, and finally in breadcrumbs. Let stand 15 minutes, then fry them in hot deep fat (step 3), preferably using a deep fat bath. Drain and serve them hot, whole or halved, garnished with parsley sprigs and with tomato sauce served in a separate dish, or green salad.

Egg Croquettes

Keep 6 hard-boiled eggs in their shells in cold water. Melt in a pan 2½ tablespoons butter or margarine, add 4 tablespoons flour, and, stirring constantly, 1 cup milk all at once. Add salt, pepper and grated nutmeg to taste. Let simmer for 8–10 minutes, then cool thoroughly. Shell the hard-boiled eggs, dice them and add to the sauce with 4 oz salami, diced, and 1 tablespoon grated Parmesan cheese. Mix well and shape with the hands into croquettes. Roll them in beaten egg then in breadcrumbs, let stand ½ hour, then fry them, a few at a time, in hot deep oil until golden brown and crisp. Drain the croquettes and serve hot. Serves 6.

Golden Stuffed Eggs

Halve 4 shelled hard-boiled eggs lengthwise, remove the yolks carefully with a teaspoon and mash them with a fork. Mix in a pan 2 tablespoons melted butter and 1 teaspoon anchovy paste. Add 1 cup fresh mushrooms, chopped, or 1 tablespoon dried mushrooms, soaked in lukewarm water, squeezed dry and chopped, a little onion to taste, and cook, stirring, for 2 minutes. Add 2–3 tablespoons light cream, 1 teaspoon chopped parsley and 1 pinch pepper. Mix with the mashed egg yolks, fill the egg whites with the mixture, and put egg halves back together. Dip them in a beaten egg, then roll in breadcrumbs. Put in the refrigerator for 1 hour (they can be prepared the day before), then fry, a few at a time, in hot deep oil until golden. Drain and serve with tomato sauce, if liked.

Stuffed Eggs Lidia

Ingredients: *6 hard-boiled eggs, shelled · 1 tablespoon anchovy paste · mayonnaise, commercially prepared or homemade (see p.48) · Worcestershire · chopped parsley · 2–3 tomatoes · paprika*

To garnish: *parsley sprigs · 1 hard-boiled egg (optional)*

Halve the hard-boiled eggs lengthwise. Remove the yolks carefully with a teaspoon (step 1) and work them through a sieve (step 2). Mix them with the anchovy paste, a little mayonnaise, and a few drops Worcestershire, to form a rather stiff paste. Shape into small nut-size balls, and roll in the chopped parsley. Put a layer of mayonnaise in each egg white, and put in the prepared balls. Place the eggs on raw tomato slices, and sprinkle with paprika before serving. Garnish the platter with parsley sprigs and put a whole hard-boiled egg in the center for decoration, if liked.

Mushroom Eggs

Put on the bottom of a serving platter a layer of mayonnaise mixed with chopped parsley, or thin strips of chicory tossed in oil, vinegar, salt and pepper to taste. Cut off the bottoms of 4 hard-boiled eggs, shelled, and set them upright on the platter. Top them with halves of tomatoes, slightly hollowed, and dot with mayonnaise. Garnish the edge of the platter with slices of hard-boiled egg, alternating with halves of stuffed olive.

Marinated Eggs

Cook slowly for a few minutes 1 tablespoon sugar, 1 teaspoon salt, 1 celery stalk, chopped, 1 cup vinegar and 8 tablespoons water. Strain and cool the liquid. Put 6 hard-boiled eggs, shelled, in a tureen and pour the marinade over them, adding $\frac{1}{2}$ clove of garlic, crushed. Cover and let stand in the refrigerator for 3 days before serving. Drain the eggs, and serve sliced.

1

2

3

Eggs Stuffed with Prosciutto

Ingredients: *4 hard-boiled eggs · 4 oz prosciutto or cooked ham, chopped · 1 tablespoon chopped capers · 1 teaspoon mustard · 1 tablespoon butter or margarine · 1 tablespoon mayonnaise · salt*

To garnish: *capers · shrimps · anchovy fillets, desalted · mayonnaise*

Shell the hard-boiled eggs (step 1), remove the yolks carefully with a teaspoon, and work them through a sieve (step 2). Blend in the chopped prosciutto (or cooked ham) and capers, the mustard, butter or margarine, mayonnaise, and salt to taste. Fill the egg whites with the mixture, using a pastry bag (step 3). Garnish some eggs with capers, some with whole shrimps, and some with anchovy fillets rolled around dots of mayonnaise, on top of the eggs. Keep cool until serving.

Eggs Stuffed with Anchovy

Halve 4 shelled hard-boiled eggs lengthwise. Remove the yolk carefully with a teaspoon and work them through a sieve together with 2 tablespoons butter or margarine at room temperature and 2–3 desalted anchovy fillets, or 1 teaspoon anchovy paste. Mix well, adding enough mayonnaise to obtain a soft smooth mixture. Fill the egg whites with the mixture, using a pastry bag. Garnish each egg with 1 anchovy fillet, desalted and rolled around a dot of mayonnaise, if liked.

Eggs Stuffed with Shrimps

Halve 4 shelled hard-boiled eggs lengthwise. Remove the yolks carefully with a teaspoon, mash them with a fork, and mix with a few shrimps, finely chopped, and tomato ketchup. Fill the egg whites with the mixture, garnish with mayonnaise and 1 whole shrimp. Refrigerate, and serve on lettuce leaves.

Eggs Stuffed with Olives

Halve 4 shelled hard-boiled eggs lengthwise. Remove yolks, mash and mix with 4 oz chopped ham, a few green olives, chopped, and mayonnaise to bind mixture. Fill the egg whites with the mixture.

1   2   3

Spanish Fried Eggs

Ingredients: *4 eggs · ¼ cup oil · 2 onions · butter · 2 peppers · garlic · 2 tomatoes · salt · sugar*

Fry the eggs in the oil (step 1) and arrange them in a circle on a round platter. Slice 1 onion into rings, fry in butter (step 2) and place it in the center. Place around the eggs a piperade (step 3) prepared in advance in the following manner: cook 1 chopped onion in oil until golden brown, add the seeded peppers, chopped garlic, and tomatoes, peeled, seeded and crushed. Season with salt and sugar and cook slowly. Serve immediately.

Fried Eggs with Emmenthal Cheese

Melt some butter or margarine in a pan, or in individual ovenproof dishes. Break eggs into the pan, sprinkle with grated Emmenthal cheese and salt and pepper to taste. Cover and cook on moderate heat until eggs are cooked. Gratiné in a hot oven before serving.

Italian Fried Eggs

Fry eggs in oil, and arrange them in a circle on a warm round serving dish, alternating with slices of prosciutto fried in butter. Pour tomato sauce in the center of the dish, and serve piping hot.

Fried Eggs with Eggplants

Fry thick eggplant slices in oil, and arrange them in a circle on a warm serving platter. Place a fried egg on each eggplant slice and pour tomato sauce in the center. Sprinkle with chopped garlic, parsley and basil to taste.

Fried Eggs Boulangère

In a large frying pan cook 1 clove of garlic, peeled, in butter until golden. Remove garlic, add 4 slices of bread, diced, without crusts. Cook slowly, stirring, until golden. Break 4 eggs into the pan, lower the heat and cook very slowly until the eggs are set. Season with salt and pepper to taste, remove the eggs carefully, making sure there is some bread with each egg.

1

2

3

1   2   3

Eggs and Bacon

Ingredients for each serving: *2 eggs · ½ tablespoon butter or margarine · 1–2 rashers bacon · salt · pepper*

Melt the butter or margarine in a pan or an ovenproof dish, brown the bacon slices on a high heat (step 1), drain and reserve. Break the eggs into the pan, lower the heat and cook for a few minutes until set (step 2). Add salt to taste, depending on the saltiness of the bacon, pepper, and the fried bacon (step 3). Serve immediately.

Fried Eggs Bercy

Fry 4 eggs, season with salt and pepper to taste. Serve immediately with small sausages or small frankfurters, broiled separately for a few minutes, and tomato sauce served in a separate dish.

Swiss Eggs

Melt 1 tablespoon butter or margarine in a pan. Break in 4 eggs, season with salt and pepper to

taste, and cook briefly on low heat. Place on each egg ½ slice Emmenthal cheese, and pour 4–5 tablespoons light cream over. Cover and keep on very moderate heat until the cheese begins to melt. Serves 2.

Egg Cutlets

Put a layer of breadcrumbs on a large shallow dish, and break 6–8 whole eggs carefully on them, taking care to keep the eggs separate. Cover with more breadcrumbs and let stand for 1 hour. With a slotted spoon transfer 1 egg at a time to a frying pan, letting the excess breadcrumbs fall, and cook until golden on both sides in butter or margarine. Drain on absorbent paper, and serve immediately with tomato sauce.

Eggs Harlequin

Dice 2 potatoes, 2 carrots and 2 zucchini, chop ½ onion, quarter 2 tomatoes, peeled and seeded and shell 1 cup peas, or use frozen vegetables.

Melt 2 tablespoons butter or margarine in a pan, add the vegetables and cook slowly, adding a little stock occasionally if necessary. When the vegetables are cooked, mix in chopped parsley and basil to taste, and, using a wooden spoon, make 4 hollows in the mixture, or 1 large hollow in the center. Break in 4 eggs, season with salt and pepper to taste, and cook on moderate heat until the eggs are set.

Eggs Daisy

Melt a little butter in a pan, add 1 slice onion and sauté for a few minutes. Remove the onion, add 4 chicken livers, and cook them for a few minutes. Sprinkle with Marsala and salt to taste. In a separate pan sauté 4 tablespoons cooked or canned green peas in butter. On each plate place 2 eggs fried in butter or oil according to taste and garnish with 1 chicken liver and 1 tablespoon peas. Serve piping hot.

1   2   3

Scrambled Eggs with Shrimps

Ingredients: *6 eggs · 1 cup cooked shelled shrimps · 2 tablespoons butter · 1 cup milk · salt · pepper · chopped parsley · round slices of bread, toasted and buttered*

To garnish: *sprig of parsley (optional)*

Chop the shrimps, reserving 6 whole ones for the garnish. Melt the butter, add the milk, salt and pepper to taste, and chopped shrimps, and heat through. Beat the eggs, without making them too foamy, pour them into the milk (step 1) and cook on low heat, stirring constantly with a wooden spoon (step 2). When soft and smooth, add the chopped parsley to taste, and pour the mixture on the buttered toast (step 3). Garnish with the reserved whole shrimps, and a sprig of parsley, if liked. Transfer to a warm serving platter and serve immediately.

Eggs Marta

Melt 1 tablespoon butter or margarine in a frying pan, add 4 eggs beaten with salt and pepper to taste, and 2 oz grated Swiss cheese. As soon as the eggs are set, place them on a warm serving dish, spread a few tablespoons tomato sauce over them, and sprinkle with chopped basil and parsley to taste. Serve immediately. The eggs could also be served in puff pastry *vol-au-vent* cases.

Scrambled Eggs with Cheese

Separate 4 eggs, reserve the yolks and beat the whites until they are stiff. Put in a flameproof pan $\frac{1}{2}$ lb grated Swiss cheese, and dot it with 2 tablespoons butter. Pour in 1 cup dry white wine, add $\frac{1}{2}$ teaspoon chopped parsley, and salt, pepper and grated nutmeg to taste. Put the pan on low heat and stir constantly until the cheese is melted. Turn the heat down to very low and add the egg yolks one at a time, beating the mixture constantly. Add the egg whites and continue cooking, stirring constantly, until the eggs are set. Serve on buttered toast, or toast spread with a mixture of butter and anchovy paste. Serve immediately.

Scrambled Eggs with Ham

Melt 2 tablespoons butter, and add 6 oz cooked ham, diced. After a few minutes, pour in 6 eggs beaten with salt and pepper to taste, and cook on low heat, stirring constantly with a wooden spoon, until the eggs are about set. Add 1 teaspoon finely chopped parsley, and serve piping hot.

Frittata with Mozzarella Cheese

Ingredients: for the frittata, *6 eggs · 2 tablespoons flour · 2 tablespoons milk · salt · 2½ tablespoons butter*

To garnish: *1 mozzarella cheese, sliced · 1 cup thick tomato sauce · black olives · oregano (optional) · anchovy fillets, desalted (optional)*

Beat the eggs, add the flour and milk (step 1), and the salt to taste. Cook the mixture on both sides in the butter (step 2) until set. Arrange mozzarella cheese slices over the frittata, pour tomato sauce between the slices (step 3), and decorate with a few black olives. Sprinkle with oregano, if liked. Anchovy fillets can also be added at this stage. Cover, and cook on low heat until the cheese has melted. Serve hot.

Omelet Poulard

Separate 8–10 eggs. Beat the yolks and add salt and pepper to taste. Beat the whites separately until stiff. Heat 4 tablespoons butter in a pan, pour in the yolks and stir when they begin to set. Mix in about ½ cup light cream, and fold in the whites. Shake the pan quickly over high heat. Fold the omelet and flip it into a long platter. Serve immediately.

Spanish Frittata

Broil 2 peppers, remove skins and seeds. Dip 2 tomatoes in boiling water, peel, halve, and squeeze them to remove the seeds. Crush the peppers and tomatoes together. Beat 8 eggs. Heat 2½ tablespoons butter or olive oil in a pan. Put in the peppers and tomatoes, and salt, pepper and chopped garlic to taste. Add the eggs and stir until they are set. Serve immediately.

Portuguese Omelet

Dip 3 tomatoes in boiling water, peel, halve, squeeze to remove the seeds, and crush them. Beat 8 eggs. Heat 2½ tablespoons butter in a pan, add the tomatoes and 1 clove of garlic, chopped. Add salt and pepper to taste. Cook for a few minutes, then pour in the eggs. Stir until the eggs are set, fold the omelet, and serve immediately on a long warm platter.

Zucchini Frittata

Ingredients: *5 eggs · 2 tablespoons butter · 1 tablespoon oil · 1 small onion, finely chopped · ¾ lb zucchini, washed, dried and sliced · salt · pepper · 3 ripe tomatoes, peeled, seeded and crushed*

Heat the butter and oil in a pan, add the onion and cook until golden brown. Add the zucchini (step 1), the salt and pepper to taste, and the tomatoes. Cook until the zucchini are almost tender. Beat the eggs with a pinch of salt. Pour them over the zucchini (step 2), and mix together. When the frittata is golden-brown on 1 side, turn it over and cook on the other side on moderate heat (step 3).

Asparagus Frittata

Beat 6 eggs with 1 tablespoon flour, 2 tablespoons grated Parmesan cheese, 2 tablespoons milk and salt and pepper to taste. Melt 2½ tablespoons butter in a pan, add the egg mixture and cook on both sides until set. Cover with asparagus tips cooked in boiling salted water, and 1 cup ricotta, or cottage cheese. Cook on low heat for a moment to melt the cheese, then serve immediately.

Omelet Argenteuil

Cook 1 lb asparagus in boiling salted water. Cut off the tips — 1½ inches long. Beat 8 eggs, add salt and pepper to taste, and 3½ fl oz light cream. Heat 2 tablespoons butter in a frying pan, pour in the eggs when the butter is very hot. Stir, and add the asparagus tips. Roll the omelet, and serve immediately on a long warm platter.

Old-Fashioned Omelet

Dice ½ lb lean bacon. Cook it for 5 minutes in boiling water, drain. Fry in butter until lightly golden 20 small croûtons (½-inch bread squares). Beat 8 eggs, and season with salt and pepper to taste. Sauté the bacon and croûtons in 2 tablespoons butter in a frying pan. Add the eggs. Serve the omelet immediately, without folding.

Tomato frittata

Cook on high heat with a little salt 10 oz tomatoes, peeled, seeded, and chopped. Beat 6–8 eggs, add grated Parmesan cheese, basil, parsley, salt and pepper to taste. Add tomatoes when their liquid has boiled away. Heat 2 tablespoons butter, pour in egg and tomato mixture, and cook frittata on both sides until golden.

Potato Frittata

Cook 1 lb potatoes, diced, in 2 tablespoons butter until golden. Season and cook until tender, drain. Beat 6 eggs, add the potatoes and grated Parmesan cheese, pour mixture back into pan. Cook for 5 minutes, turn it over, and cook on other side for another 5 minutes; add more butter if necessary. Serve immediately, piping hot.

1   2   3

1   2   3

Tyrolean Eggs

Ingredients: *2 hard-boiled eggs, quartered ·*
· butter · 1 large can tomatoes, drained · anchovy
paste · parsley · breadcrumbs · salt · pepper ·
3 eggs · 1 cup light cream

Butter generously an ovenproof dish, and place
a layer of tomatoes on the bottom (step 1).
Beat a few tablespoons butter until foamy, with
anchovy paste to taste, spread over the
tomatoes and sprinkle with chopped parsley
to taste. Arrange the hard-boiled egg quarters
on top, then sprinkle with breadcrumbs
seasoned with salt and pepper to taste (step 2).
Beat the eggs together with the cream and a
little salt and pepper, pour the mixture over
the eggs (step 3) and bake in a hot oven
(425°F) for about ½ hour, until the eggs are
well set in the cream. Serve piping hot in the
baking dish.

Eggs Gratiné

Boil 4 eggs for 10 minutes, dip them in cold
water, shell, and slice. Prepare a béchamel
sauce with 2½ tablespoons butter, 4 tablespoons flour, 2 cups milk, and salt, pepper and
grated nutmeg to taste (see p.47). When
cooked, blend in 1 tablespoon grated Parmesan
cheese. In a buttered ovenproof dish, arrange a
layer of white bread (without crusts) crumbled
and mixed with grated Parmesan cheese to
taste. Top with a layer of hard-boiled egg
slices, then a layer of cooked ham, chopped
(about ½ lb), and finally a layer of béchamel
sauce. Repeat, finishing with crumbled bread.
Sprinkle with grated Parmesan cheese, and dot
with butter. Bake in a hot oven (425°F) for
about 10–15 minutes, or until a golden crust
has formed on top.

Eggs Françoise

Boil 4 eggs for 10 minutes, shell, and halve.
In a pan, melt 1 tablespoon butter, add 2 oz
salt pork, soaked in cold water for 1 hour,
drained and cut into strips, 1 slice onion, and
1 clove of garlic, finely chopped, and cook until
golden. Add 1 cup water, ½ cup dry white wine,
3 tablespoons tomato sauce, 1 bay leaf, and salt
and pepper to taste. Cook for 10 minutes, then
add 1 tablespoon butter blended with 1 tablespoon flour, and let the sauce reduce slowly.
Cook 1 cup tagliatelle in boiling salted water
until *al dente*. Drain, and put into a buttered
ovenproof dish. Arrange the hard-boiled eggs
in the center of the dish. Pour the sauce over
and sprinkle with 3 tablespoons grated
Parmesan cheese. Dot with butter and put in a
hot oven (425°F) for a few minutes to gratiné.

87

Tartlets Primavera

Ingredients: *6 eggs · 1 lb asparagus tips · 4 tablespoons butter · 12 tartlets, bought or homemade with 8 oz rich shortcrust or flaky pastry · salt · pepper*

Cut off the asparagus tips (step 1), cook them in salted boiling water until tender, then sauté them in ½ the butter. Cook the tartlets in a hot oven (400°F) for 15–20 minutes until golden; if using bought tartlets heat them through. Melt the remaining butter in a pan, add the eggs, beaten with salt and pepper to taste, and cook, stirring constantly, until they begin to set (step 2). Fill each tartlet with the egg mixture (step 3), garnish with asparagus tips and serve piping hot.

Eggs with Peas

Cook 1 cup green peas in boiling salted water for a few minutes and drain, or use canned peas.

Finish cooking peas in 1 tablespoon butter with 2 oz cooked ham cut into strips. Ten minutes before serving, melt 1 tablespoon butter in a pan, then stir in 1 tablespoon flour and 2–3 tablespoons milk. Cook for 2–3 minutes, stirring constantly, and add 3–4 eggs, beaten with salt and grated nutmeg to taste. Do not allow mixture to boil. When creamy, remove from heat. Arrange the peas on a warm serving platter, cover with the egg mixture, and serve immediately with bread croûtons fried in butter.

Scrambled Eggs with Cod

Shred ½ lb fresh cod and sauté in 2½ tablespoons butter. Add 1 cup milk, a little chopped onion, chopped parsley to taste, and ½ bay leaf. Cook for 8–10 minutes, stirring occasionally, then add 4–5 eggs, lightly beaten with pepper (but no salt). Continue cooking until the eggs are creamy, and serve immediately.

Scrambled Eggs with Tomato Sauce

Beat 6 eggs lightly, add a few drops cold water, and season. Melt 2½ tablespoons butter in a pan, pour in eggs, and cook gently until creamy, stirring constantly. Remove from heat; add 1 tablespoon soft butter. Serve with tomato sauce, parsley and basil.

Scrambled Eggs with Cream

Fry 4 slices of bread in 4 tablespoons butter or margarine and keep warm. In another pan, melt 1 tablespoon butter and pour in 6 eggs beaten with ¼ cup milk or light cream, 4 tablespoons grated Parmesan cheese, and salt, pepper and grated nutmeg to taste. Cook on very low heat, stirring constantly, until set. Spread on the fried bread, and serve.

1

2

3

Stuffed Crêpes Bolognese

Ingredients: for the crêpes, *3 eggs · ¾ cup flour · salt · 1 cup milk · 4 tablespoons butter*

For the stuffing: *Bolognese sauce (see p.45) · 12 thin slices Emmenthal cheese*

To garnish: *¼ tomato (optional)*

Mix the eggs with the flour and 1 pinch salt in a bowl. Add the milk, gradually, and 1 tablespoon butter, melted. Whip the mixture thoroughly. Heat a 6-inch frying pan on high heat, and, using a small amount of batter at a time (2 tblspns), make 12 small crêpes (step 1). Place 1 at the bottom of a buttered round ovenproof dish, slightly larger in size than the crêpes. Cover with Bolognese sauce, and put 1 slice Emmenthal cheese over the sauce (step 2). Repeat these layers (step 3) until all ingredients are used up, ending with a crêpe. Dot with remaining butter and bake in a hot oven (425°F) for 10 minutes or until crêpes are heated through and cheese has melted. If liked, garnish with ½ tomato, grilled or fried.

Stuffed Crêpes with Spinach

Prepare 12 small crêpes as above. Cook 1¼ lb spinach in a little boiling salted water, wash, drain and chop, then mix with ½ cup grated Parmesan cheese. Place a layer of spinach and 1 desalted anchovy fillet on each crêpe. Roll the crêpes and arrange them in a buttered ovenproof dish. Sprinkle with grated Parmesan cheese and put in a hot oven (425°F) for a few minutes to gratiné.

Crêpe Mold

Discard the outer leaves of 3 artichokes, and cut artichokes in small pieces with 1 carrot, 1 celery stalk and 1 tablespoon dried mushrooms, soaked in lukewarm water and squeezed dry.

Melt 4 tablespoons butter in a pan, add a little onion, chopped, and cook until golden. Add the vegetables, together with 2 cups green peas, shelled. Cook for 2 minutes, sprinkle with ½ tablespoon flour, cook for a further 2–3 minutes, stirring, then add 2 tablespoons tomato sauce, diluted with stock. (The liquid should cover the vegetables.) Season with salt and pepper to taste, cover and let simmer for 1½ hours until the sauce has reduced. Prepare 12 small crêpes (see p.38) and let cool. Butter an ovenproof dish, about 8 inches wide and 2 inches high, and line the bottom and sides with crêpes. Fill the dish with layers of crêpes and vegetable mixture, ending with a crêpe. Cook in a bain-marie in a moderately hot oven (375°F), or in the top of a double boiler, for 1¼ hours. Remove from the heat, leave to stand for 10 minutes, then unmold onto a warm serving platter.

Eggs en Cocotte with Spinach

Ingredients: *4 eggs · 2 tablespoons butter · 4 tablespoons spinach, cooked and roughly chopped · 4 tablespoons light cream · salt · pepper*

Butter 4 individual soufflé or ramekin dishes (step 1) and put 1 tablespoon spinach in each (step 2). Break 1 egg into each dish and pour in 1 tablespoon cream (step 3). Dot with butter and sprinkle with salt and pepper to taste. Place the dishes in a baking dish half full of hot water, and bake in a very hot oven (450°F) for 8–10 minutes, or until the whites of the eggs are set.

Farmhouse Eggs en Cocotte

Melt in a pan 2½ tablespoons butter, stir in 2 tablespoons flour, cook for 1–2 minutes, remove from heat, then stir in 2 cups boiling milk. Cook for 2 minutes, stirring constantly, add salt to taste and ½ cup grated Parmesan or Swiss cheese. Cook until the cheese is melted. Pour the mixture into 8 buttered individual soufflé or ramekin dishes. Break 1 egg into each, sprinkle with salt and pepper to taste, place the dishes in a baking dish half full of hot water, and bake in a hot oven (450°F) for 8–10 minutes, or until the whites of the eggs are set.

Eggs en Cocotte with Cheese

Butter 8 individual soufflé or ramekin dishes. Break 1 egg into each, season with salt and pepper to taste, and cover with a little light cream. Place a thin slice of Emmenthal cheese over each egg, and add another tablespoon cream. Cook as above.

Eggs en Cocotte with Mushrooms

In each buttered dish put 1 tablespoon chopped cooked mushrooms, add 1 egg, 1 tablespoon light cream, dot with butter, and sprinkle with salt and pepper to taste. Cook as above.

Eggs and Spinach Gratiné

Boil 4 eggs for 10 minutes, dip them in cold water, shell and slice. Clean and wash 3 cups fresh spinach. Sauté in butter 1 slice onion until golden, remove onion, add 1¼ cups canned tomatoes, chopped, the spinach, and 1 pinch salt. Simmer, stirring occasionally, until the liquid has reduced. Arrange the spinach, hard-boiled egg slices, and grated Parmesan cheese to taste, in layers in a buttered ovenproof dish. Top with grated Parmesan cheese and dot with butter. Put in a hot oven (425°F) for a few minutes to gratiné.

Eggs en Cocotte with Bacon

In the bottom of each buttered dish place 1 slice smoked bacon. Add 1 egg, season with salt and pepper to taste, and cook as above.

Meat Dishes

Beef

Steak Tartare

Ingredients: 1¼ lb raw fillet steak or rump, minced · salt · freshly ground pepper · parsley · 4 egg yolks · 4 tablespoons chopped onion · 4 tablespoons capers · 4 teaspoons mustard · oil · lemon · Worcestershire

Divide the raw beef into 4 portions (step 1), season with salt and pepper to taste. Chop the parsley (step 2) and sprinkle it over the meat. Make a hollow in each meat portion, and put 1 raw egg yolk in each (step 3). Arrange on the edge of each plate 1 tablespoon chopped onion, 1 tablespoon capers and 1 teaspoon mustard. Serve oil, lemon and Worcestershire separately.

Hamburgers

Mix in a bowl 1¼ lb ground beef, 1 finely chopped onion, and salt and pepper to taste. Shape the mixture into a ball, and beat it repeatedly against the bottom of the bowl. Divide into 4, shape into patties, roll in flour and cook in a frying pan on high heat in 2 tablespoons butter or oil. Cook on both sides, lower the heat, and continue cooking more slowly until done according to taste. Serve the hamburgers, covered with fried onion rings and spread with tomato ketchup, in buns.

Hamburgers with Barbecue Sauce

Mix in a bowl 1 lb 2 oz ground beef, 4 tablespoons crushed cornflakes (optional), 2 tablespoons grated onion, and salt and pepper to taste. Work the mixture as above and divide into 4 patties. Brown on both sides in ¼ cup butter or oil, and remove them from the pan. Add to the cooking juices 1 onion and 1 celery stalk, both sliced, 1 green pepper, deseeded and cut into strips, 4 teaspoons mustard, ¼ cup stock and salt and pepper to taste. Cook for 10 minutes, then add the hamburgers and continue cooking on low heat for ½ hour. Serve with the reduced sauce.

Steak alla Pizzaiola

Ingredients: *4 tender beef steaks ·
¼ cup butter or 4 tablespoons oil · salt ·
pepper · 2 cloves of garlic, peeled ·
1¼ cups canned peeled tomatoes, roughly
chopped · 1 generous pinch oregano*

To garnish: *parsley*

Brown the steaks on both sides in the butter
or oil on high heat (step 1) and continue
cooking according to taste. Remove them,
place on a warm serving platter, and season
with salt and pepper to taste. Cook the cloves
of garlic in the juices remaining in the pan
until golden, remove them, add the tomatoes
(step 2), salt and pepper to taste, and oregano.
Continue cooking for 8–10 minutes, put the
steaks back into the pan (step 3), re-heat
quickly, and serve, coated with some of the
sauce, on the hot serving platter. Garnish with
parsley and serve with remaining sauce.

Steak à la Bismark

Brown on both sides, on high heat, 4 slices
fillet steak (each about 6 oz) in ¼ cup butter
or oil. Continue cooking according to taste.
Season with salt and pepper to taste, arrange
them on a hot serving platter, and keep warm.
Place on each steak 1 egg, fried in ¼ cup
butter. Add a few spoonfuls stock to the
cooking juices of the meat, mix well, boil
rapidly for a few seconds, then pour over the
steaks. Serve immediately.

Steak Chasseur

Brown 4 tender steaks on both sides in ¼ cup
butter or oil on high heat, and continue
cooking according to taste. Remove the steaks
and put them on a warm platter. In the cooking
juices remaining in the pan, cook 1 slice
onion, chopped, and 1 cup mushrooms,

cleaned, trimmed and sliced, until golden.
Stir in 1 glass dry white wine, ¼ cup stock and
1 tablespoon tomato paste. Continue cooking
on low heat for 10–15 minutes, then return
steaks to the pan to reheat, and add chopped
parsley.

Steak Lyonnaise

In 1 tablespoon butter cook until transparent,
but not browned, 2 large onions very thinly
sliced. Remove and reserve. Brown 4 steaks
(4–6 oz each) on both sides in 2 tablespoons
butter or oil on high heat. Continue cooking
according to taste. Season with salt and
pepper to taste halfway through the cooking.
Remove the steaks from the pan and place
on a warm serving platter. Add ½ glass dry
white wine to the cooking juices, boil for 2
minutes, add the onions, and, as soon as they
are hot, pour over the steaks.

Fillet of Beef Stuffed with Mushrooms

Ingredients: *1 whole piece of fillet of beef, preferably the middle part (about 2 lb) · 1 cup dry white wine · ¼ cup butter or oil · 1 small glass brandy · 1 bay leaf · 1 pinch thyme (optional) · salt · 1 medium-sized onion, thinly sliced · 10 oz fresh mushrooms, or 1½ tablespoons dried mushrooms, soaked in water, squeezed dry and sliced*

To garnish: *mushrooms · parsley*

Put the beef in a bowl, add the white wine, and leave to marinate overnight. Melt in a pan half the butter, add the brandy, bay leaf, thyme, and salt to taste. Add the onion and cook slowly until golden. Add the mushrooms and continue cooking. Meanwhile, drain the beef, reserving the marinade, and make an incision along the narrow side with a sharp knife (step 1). Stuff with the mushrooms (step 2), seal the two ends with 2 pieces of meat from the inside of the fillet, and tie the meat with string to keep the stuffing inside (step 3). Brown the fillet on all sides over high heat in the remaining butter or oil, baste it with some wine from the marinade, cover the pan, lower the heat, and continue cooking for about 40 minutes — or less, according to taste. Alternatively the fillet may be cooked in the oven. Baste with the cooking juices from time to time. Serve the steak sliced, with the cooking juices, and garnish with whole mushrooms sautéed in butter, and parsley.

Fillet of Beef with Olives

Put one 2-lb piece of fillet of beef in a baking pan with ¼ cup butter or oil. Place in a moderate oven (350°F), and cook for 25–30 minutes, basting occasionally with dry white wine and stock. Brown in a separate pan ¼ cup butter mixed with 2 tablespoons flour, add the cooking juices of the meat, and continue cooking for 8–10 minutes, adding more wine and stock if necessary, until the sauce is smooth and creamy. Add about 1 cup pitted green olives, pepper, a little salt, and, when the mixture is hot, some chopped parsley. When the fillet is cooked, slice it and arrange on a warm serving platter with the sauce.

Fillet of Beef with Parsley

Mix a few tablespoons olive oil with chopped parsley and freshly ground pepper. Put into the mixture 1 whole piece of fillet of beef (1½–2 lb) and let stand for 24 hours, turning occasionally. Then put everything in a flame-proof casserole, and cook on high heat for 20–25 minutes, or more according to taste. Halfway through the cooking time season with salt and pepper to taste, and add more chopped parsley. Add a few spoonfuls stock if the meat becomes too dry.

Slice the meat and serve immediately on a warm serving platter, covered with the cooking juices.

1

2

3

Fondue Bourguignonne

Cut 1 lb fillet of beef into 1-inch cubes (step 1), removing any fat and gristle. Put in a small pan — the classic pans for this dish are usually made of copper — a generous measure of oil, 1 pinch of thyme or 1 bay leaf (optional) and bring slowly to a boil. Place the pan over a portable burner in the center of the table so that it continues to boil.

Each guest spears a cube of meat with a long fork, dips it into the hot oil until cooked to taste, transfers it to his own plate and dips it into one of several sauces which accompany the dish. The sauces (see the following suggestions) should be prepared beforehand (steps 2 and 3).

Garlic Sauce

Crush in a mortar 1 head of garlic (about 1 oz). Mix with 1 raw egg yolk and 1 pinch salt in a bowl. Stirring constantly with a wooden spoon, pour in gradually 1 cup oil and the juice of 1 lemon, as for mayonnaise. If the sauce is too thick, dilute with a few drops hot water. If, on the contrary, the sauce does not stiffen, or curdles, beat a fresh egg yolk in a separate bowl and add the sauce to it gradually — again as for mayonnaise.

Andalusian Sauce

Roast 1 pepper in the oven or over a flame, peel and sauté it in a skillet in a little oil with a pinch of salt, let cool, deseed it, and cut into thin strips. In a bowl, mix the strips with 1 cup mayonnaise, diluted with $\frac{1}{4}$ cup homemade tomato sauce, sieved, reduced and cooled.

Caper Sauce

Mix into 1 cup mayonnaise a handful of capers, and some gherkins, finely chopped.

Rémoulade Sauce

In a bowl, mix 1 cup mayonnaise with 4 gherkins and 1 tablespoon capers, finely chopped, $\frac{1}{4}$ teaspoon anchovy paste or $\frac{1}{2}$ teaspoon mustard, 1 teaspoon chervil, 1 teaspoon chopped parsley, 1 teaspoon chopped shallot, and 1 pinch cayenne pepper. Add salt if necessary.

Mustard Sauce

In a bowl mix 6 tablespoons mayonnaise with 2 tablespoons French mustard, and 2 chopped scallions or 1 tablespoon chives.

Kishaili Sauce

In a bowl, mix $\frac{2}{3}$ cup fresh ricotta or cottage cheese with celery salt and pepper to taste, and enough oil and vinegar to obtain a smooth paste. Add 1 bunch radishes, washed, trimmed and sliced thinly, and let stand 48 hours.

Aurore Sauce

In a bowl mix 1 cup mayonnaise with 1 teaspoon paprika, 2 tablespoons tomato ketchup, 1 tablespoon ground pine nuts, 1 tablespoon capers chopped with 1 slice onion and some parsley, 1 tablespoon brandy, and salt.

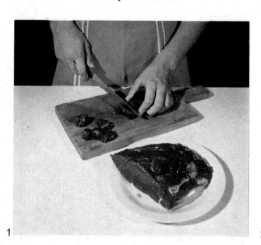

1   2   3

1   2   3

Grandmother's Meat Loaf

Ingredients: 1¼ lb top rump of beef ·
1 slice mortadella (6 oz) · ¾ lb frozen chopped
spinach, thawed according to package
instructions (or fresh spinach, cooked and
worked through a sieve) · 4 tablespoons butter
or oil · 1 cup ricotta or cottage cheese ·
1 egg yolk · 2 tablespoons grated Parmesan
cheese · salt · pepper · nutmeg ·
1 small glass Marsala or ½ glass dry white
wine · stock

To garnish: carrots

Dry the spinach over moderate heat with 1
tablespoon butter. When it has cooled, add the
ricotta or cottage cheese, the egg yolk,
Parmesan cheese, and salt, pepper and nutmeg to taste (step 1). Pound the meat well,
put the mortadella slice on top, cover with the
spinach mixture (step 2), roll up, and sew it

(step 3). Brown the loaf on all sides over high
heat in ¼ cup butter or oil, add the Marsala or
wine and let it reduce. Sprinkle the meat with
salt, and add ¼ cup stock. Cover, lower the
heat and cook slowly for about 2 hours,
adding more stock if the meat becomes dry.
Remove the loaf from the pan, let stand for
5–10 minutes, then slice, and arrange on a
warm serving platter with the reduced cooking
juices. Garnish with diced carrots. This dish is
also very good when served cold – perhaps
with aspic.

Meat Loaf with Frittata

Pound 1½ lb top rump of beef in the slice.
Prepare a frittata (a flat, Italian-style omelet)
in the following way: beat 2 eggs with 1
tablespoon chopped parsley, 2 tablespoons
grated Parmesan cheese, 2 tablespoons milk,

and salt and pepper to taste, and cook the
mixture on both sides in 1½ tablespoons
butter or margarine, then let it cool. Place on
the beef 1 or 2 slices cooked ham (each ¼ inch
thick), the frittata, and a few slices Emmenthal
cheese. Roll up the meat, tie with string, and
brown on all sides over high heat in ¼ cup
butter. Add 1 small glass brandy or grappa,
and flame it, or add ½ glass dry white wine and
allow to reduce. Season with salt and pepper
to taste, add ¼ cup stock, cover, lower the heat
and cook slowly for about 2 hours, adding
more stock if the meat becomes dry. Remove
the loaf from the pan, let stand for 5–10
minutes, then slice it and arrange on a warm
serving platter with the reduced cooking
juices. Veal may equally well be used for this
recipe as beef.

Ground Meat Loaf

Ingredients : *1¼ lb ground beef ·*
4 oz mortadella · 2 eggs · 1 handful white
bread, soaked in milk and squeezed dry ·
¼ lb boiled potatoes (optional) ·
2 tablespoons grated Parmesan cheese ·
parsley · salt · pepper · nutmeg · flour ·
4 tablespoons butter or margarine ·
2 tablespoons Marsala or dry white wine ·
¼ cup hot stock · 3 hard-boiled eggs, shelled ·
3 carrots, blanched

To garnish: *petits pois*

Mix in a bowl the ground beef, chopped
mortadella, eggs, bread, and the potatoes (if
using) worked through a sieve, Parmesan
cheese, chopped parsley, and salt, pepper and
nutmeg to taste (step 1). Make a ball of the
mixture and pound it repeatedly against the
bottom of the bowl. Flatten the mixture on a

board, place the hard-boiled eggs and carrots
in the center (step 2), and roll up, shaping it
into a loaf. Roll it in flour (step 3), and brown
on all sides on high heat in butter or margarine.
Season with salt, sprinkle with Marsala or
wine and when it has reduced, add the hot
stock. Cover, lower the heat, and cook slowly
for about 1 hour, adding more stock if the loaf
becomes dry. Remove the loaf from the pan, let
stand for 5–10 minutes, then slice it and
arrange on a warm serving platter with some
of the reduced cooking juices. Garnish with
petits pois and serve cooking juices separately.

Meat Loaf Clementina

Mix in a bowl 1¼ lb ground beef, ¼ cup chopped
mortadella, ¼ cup grated Parmesan cheese,
1 egg, and salt, pepper and nutmeg to taste.
Shape the mixture into a ball, and beat it

repeatedly against the bottom of the bowl, then
spread it about ½ inch thick on a piece of cloth.
Put over the meat one ½-inch thick slice
cooked ham, cut into strips, and 2 hard-boiled
eggs. Roll the meat, wrap it in the cloth and tie
at both ends. Boil in a generous amount
salted water for about 2 hours, topping up
with more hot water as it evaporates. Prepare
a sauce in the following way : cook in a few
spoonfuls hot oil in a pan ¼ cup mashed
anchovy fillets until well blended, without
allowing them to brown. Add 1 tablespoon
chopped capers and some chopped parsley,
and continue cooking slowly for a few minutes.
Remove the sauce from heat and add the
juice of 1 lemon. Remove the loaf from the
pan, let stand for 5–10 minutes, then slice it
and arrange on a warm serving platter, with
the sauce poured over. Serve with mashed
potato or green vegetables.

Roast Beef

Ingredients: *2 lb roast of beef (sirloin, rump, fillet or rib) · ¼ cup melted butter · 1 carrot and 1 onion, peeled and cut in quarters · salt · pepper*

To garnish: *tiny whole potatoes, boiled*

Tie the meat with string (step 1), brush it with half the butter (step 2) and place on a rack in a roasting pan with the carrot and onion. Put it in a very hot oven (450°F) and cook for 25–30 minutes, turning it and basting occasionally with the remaining butter (step 3). (Do not puncture the meat during cooking; use 2 spoons to turn it over.) Sprinkle it with salt and pepper halfway through the cooking. To check whether the meat is done, prick it with a fork: a drop of pink juice should escape. When cooked, remove beef from the pan, untie, and let stand. Pour off excess fat from the pan, discard carrot and onion, then add a few tablespoons stock to the pan to detach the glazed cooking juices, and bring to a boil. Slice the beef, arrange on a warm serving platter, and pour the gravy over, or, if preferred, serve it separately in a sauce boat. Garnish the platter with tiny whole boiled potatoes if liked.

Roast beef can also be cooked in a pan on top of the stove: tie the meat with a sprig of rosemary, and put it in the pan with 3–4 tablespoons oil. Brown on high heat on all sides, cover the pan, lower the heat, and continue cooking slowly for 15–20 minutes, sprinkling the meat with salt and pepper halfway through the cooking. When cooked, remove the meat, let stand, then slice it, and serve as above.

Roast Beef in Salt

Put at the bottom of a high and narrow pan 2 lb rock salt. Place in the center a 2-lb roast of beef and put another 4 lb rock salt around and over the meat, covering it completely. Cover the pan and put in a hot oven (375–400°F) for about ¾ hour. Overturn the pan on a sheet of thick paper and crack the salt crust with a hammer. Remove all the salt from the meat with a brush, and serve the meat hot or cold. The salt can be used again. Serves 6–8.

Roast Beef Croquettes

Chop 1 lb rare roast beef and 7 oz Italian prosciutto. Mix with chopped parsley and salt and pepper to taste. Form croquettes with the mixture, roll them in flour, brown them on all sides over high heat and cook them for a few minutes in 1½ tablespoons butter or margarine.

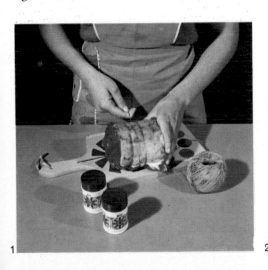

1   2   3

1

2

3

Beef Braised in Wine

Ingredients: *1 rump roast (2 lb) · 4 oz salt pork · ¼ cup butter · 1 slice onion · flour · salt*

For the marinade: *1 pint Barolo or other Burgundy-type wine · 1 stalk celery · 1 medium sized onion and 1 carrot, both sliced · 1 clove of garlic, peeled and crushed · rosemary · 1 bay leaf · 3 peppercorns*

To garnish: *tiny whole potatoes, boiled · butter · parsley*

Lard the beef with half the salt pork (step 1), tie it with string, pour the prepared marinade over (step 2) and leave overnight. Chop the remaining salt pork, brown it in butter together with the onion. Drain the meat (reserving the marinade), dry it, roll in flour,

add to the pan and brown on all sides over high heat (step 3). Add the reserved marinade, salt, cover, lower the heat and cook very slowly for about 3 hours. When cooked, remove the meat from the pan and let stand. Strain the sauce, boiling to reduce if too thin. Slice the meat and arrange on a warm serving platter with some of the sauce poured over. Serve the remaining sauce separately, and garnish the platter with tiny whole potatoes, tossed in butter and sprinkled with parsley.

Braised Beef

Lard a 2-lb rump roast with strips of salt pork, chopped garlic (optional), and chopped parsley mixed with pepper and mixed herbs. Tie the meat with string, brown it on all sides over

high heat in 1 tablespoon butter and 2 tablespoons oil. Sprinkle with salt and pepper. Add chopped celery, carrot and onion, 1 bouquet garni made of parsley, thyme and 1 bay leaf, and 1 small onion stuck with 1 clove. Pour in 1 cup good red wine, and 2 tablespoons brandy (optional). Cover the pan with wax paper or aluminum foil, lower heat, and cook very slowly for about 3 hours (or 1¼ hours in a pressure cooker), turning the meat over with 2 spoons occasionally. After 2 hours, strain the cooking juices, put them back into the pan, and thicken them with a little beurre manié (equal parts of butter and flour, blended together). When the cooking is done, remove the meat from the sauce and let stand 5–10 minutes, slice, and arrange on a warm serving platter with the sauce poured over it. Serves 6.

Tournedos Renata

Ingredients: *4 slices fillet of beef, 1½ inches thick · 1 cup butter · 2 lb mushrooms · 1 clove of garlic, peeled · salt · pepper · 1 small glass brandy · 1 cup light cream · thyme · marjoram · 4 slices lemon · 1 tablespoon chopped parsley*

Cut out 4 pats of butter – ¼ inch thick – with a small round cutter (step 1), and keep them in the freezer or ice box. Trim the stems of the mushrooms, wash and dry, and slice them. Brown the garlic in the butter then remove it. add the mushrooms and sauté them quickly. Add salt and pepper to taste, pour in the brandy, and flame it. Add half the cream, cover, lower the heat and cook slowly for about ½ hour. In the last few minutes add the rest of the cream, and prepare the tournedos. In a separate pan, cook them quickly in 2 table-spoons browned butter, adding pepper, thyme, marjoram and salt to taste. Put the mush-rooms in a warm oval serving platter, arrange the tournedos in the center (step 2), and place over each 1 lemon slice and 1 pat of butter sprinkled with chopped parsley (step 3). Serve immediately.

Tournedos Rossini

Brown in 1 tablespoon butter 1 carrot and 1 small onion, both roughly chopped. Mix in 1 teaspoon flour, add ½ cup stock, ½ glass dry white wine, 1 bouquet garni made of parsley, thyme and bay leaf, and salt and pepper to taste. Cook very slowly for 25 minutes, then strain through a sieve. Fry 4 large bread croûtons in 2 tablespoons butter and keep warm on a serving platter. Cook in 2 table-spoons browned butter, on high heat, 4 tournedos for 2–3 minutes on each side. Season with salt and pepper to taste. Arrange them on the croûtons, and place on each 1 slice liver pâté and 1 slice truffle. (Where truffles are not easy to obtain, a flat mush-room may be substituted.) Dissolve the cooking juices in the pan with 1 small glass Madeira, and mix with the sauce. Pour some of the sauce over the tournedos, and serve immed-iately with the rest of the sauce separately.

 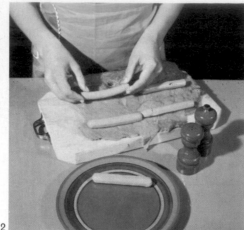 

Veal

Rolled Veal with Frankfurters

Ingredients: $1\frac{1}{2}$ lb veal in the slice ·
4 frankfurters · $\frac{1}{4}$ cup butter or oil ·
$\frac{1}{2}$ glass dry white wine · salt · $\frac{1}{2}$ cup hot stock

Pound the meat slice (step 1), place the frankfurters over it lengthwise (step 2), roll and tie it with string (step 3). Brown on all sides over high heat in the butter or oil, add the white wine, and, when the wine has reduced, sprinkle the meat with salt, add the hot stock, cover, lower the heat, and cook slowly for $1\frac{1}{2}$ hours. If there is too much juice, reduce it on high heat during the last minutes of cooking. Remove the roll from the pan and let stand 5–10 minutes. Slice it, arrange on a warm serving platter and pour the cooking juices over. The dish can also be served cold, in aspic, if desired. Beef can be used instead of veal.

Veal Loaf Cesira

Chop $\frac{1}{2}$ lb veal, mix it with 1 egg, 2 tablespoons grated Parmesan cheese, and salt and grated nutmeg to taste. Quarter 2 hard-boiled eggs and cut 3 oz cooked ham and 3 oz mortadella into strips. Pound $1\frac{1}{2}$ lb veal in the slice, spread over it a layer of the chopped meat mixture, then a layer of hard-boiled eggs, ham and mortadella strips, and continue until all the ingredients have been used. Roll the meat, tie with string, and brown on all sides over high heat in $\frac{1}{4}$ cup butter. Cover, lower the heat and cook for $1\frac{1}{2}$ hours, adding stock occasionally. When cooked, lift out the loaf, add to the pan 2 tablespoons beurre manié (1 tablespoon butter blended with 1 tablespoon flour), the juice of 1 lemon and more stock if necessary. Cook for a few minutes, then return loaf to the pan and reheat. Transfer to a warm serving platter, slice, and serve with the juices poured over. Serves 4–6.

1 2 3

Stuffed Breast of Veal Home Style

Ingredients: *2 lb breast of veal, boned ·
1 celery stalk · 1 onion, peeled and quartered ·
1 carrot, peeled and quartered · ½ bay leaf ·
salt*

*For the stuffing: 1 slice onion · ¼ cup butter ·
4 oz lean veal · 4 oz veal brains ·
4 oz sweetbreads · 1¾ oz marrow, scalded,
skinned and cut into pieces · 1 small carrot,
sliced · ¾ cup shelled green peas or canned peas ·
3 tablespoons grated Parmesan cheese ·
1 pinch marjoram (with a little garlic if
desired) · 1 tablespoon pistachio nuts · salt ·
pepper · grated nutmeg · 6 eggs*

To garnish: *lettuce · tomatoes*

Have the butcher make a pocket in the breast
of veal. Prepare the stuffing: sauté the onion
in the butter (it can then be removed, according to taste), the veal, cut into thin slices, the
brains, the sweetbreads, chopped, and the
marrow. Add the carrot and cook slowly for
20–30 minutes. Add ⅓ of the green peas,
cooked in boiling salted water, and divide the
mixture into 2 parts. Work 1 part through a
sieve, and chop the other part. Put both in a
bowl, add the remaining green peas (step 1),
the Parmesan cheese, marjoram, the pistachio
nuts, scalded and peeled, and salt, pepper and
nutmeg to taste. Beat the eggs, blend them
into the mixture, and pour it – it will be fairly
liquid – into the pocket cut in the breast of
veal (step 2), taking care that it does not fill
more than ⅔ of it. Sew it up with string (step 3)
and wrap it in a wet piece of cloth. Tie well.
Put in a pan, cover with cold water, add the
celery, onion, carrot, bay leaf, and salt to
taste, and bring slowly to a boil, pricking it
occasionally with a trussing needle so that it

does not burst as it swells. Continue cooking
for about 2 hours, remove it from the stock,
and put it on a plate with a weighted plate on
top of it. Serve sliced, hot or cold, garnished
with lettuce leaves and tomato slices. Serves 8.
Any leftovers can be rolled in beaten egg and
breadcrumbs, sautéed in butter and served
with lemon quarters. Or they may be rolled
in beaten egg and breadcrumbs, heated for a
few minutes and served with green peas and
homemade tomato sauce.

1 2 3

Roast Veal Sirloin

Ingredients: *2 lb veal sirloin ·*
2 oz diced salt pork · chopped rosemary mixed
with salt and pepper · 1 tablespoon oil ·
¼ cup butter or margarine · salt · pepper ·
dry white wine (optional)

To garnish: *green beans, sliced*

Make lengthwise incisions in the meat (step 1), roll the salt pork in the rosemary mixture (step 2), and insert in the meat (step 3). Tie the meat with string, brush it with the oil, and place it on a rack in a roasting pan, with the butter or margarine, in small pieces. Put the pan into a moderate oven (350°F) and roast the meat for 1½–1¾ hours. When the meat is brown, sprinkle with salt and pepper, and dry white wine according to taste. Turn it over occasionally during the cooking, basting it with its own juices. When the meat is cooked, remove from pan, let stand for 5–10 minutes, then slice it and arrange on a warm serving platter.

Roast Veal in Piquant Sauce

Lard 2 lb veal sirloin with 2 cloves of garlic, peeled and sliced, and 4 anchovy fillets, desalted. (Shoulder of veal, boned, rolled and tied, may also be used for this recipe.) Put the meat in a bowl with 1 cup dry white wine and let stand for 24 hours, turning it over occasionally. Drain the meat, reserving the wine, brush with oil, place it on a rack in a roasting pan, and cook it for 1½ hours in a moderate oven (350°F). Baste frequently with the reserved wine. When the cooking is done, remove the meat, cover, and keep warm. Add to the pan 1 tablespoon flour mixed with a little cold water, stir with a wooden spoon to incorporate all the cooking juices, and continue cooking for a few minutes. Add ½ cup light cream, 1 tablespoon washed and dried capers (whole if small, chopped if large), and heat the cream without boiling. Slice the meat and arrange on a warm serving platter. Serve the sauce separately. Serves 4–6.

Veal Pot Roast with Kidneys

Have the butcher bone 2 lb shoulder of veal. Halve 1 veal kidney lengthwise, let it stand in water and lemon juice for 1 hour, drain, and remove the membrane and skin. Put the 2 kidney pieces inside the roast, in place of the bone. Tie the meat with string, brush with oil, and put in a pan with ¼ cup butter or margarine in small pieces, and a sprig of rosemary. Brown it on all sides over high heat, pour over 1 small glass of brandy, and flame it. Cover, lower the heat, and cook on moderate heat for about 2 hours, adding a little stock occasionally if the meat becomes dry. Sprinkle with salt and pepper halfway through the cooking. When the cooking is completed, remove the meat from the pan, let stand for 5–10 minutes, then slice it and arrange on a warm serving platter with the reduced cooking juices poured over.

Mexican Paupiettes

Ingredients: *1¼ lb veal cut into 8 small scallops · 3 oz pork loin · 3 oz prosciutto · ¼ clove of garlic (optional) · ¼ cup white bread, soaked in milk and squeezed dry · 1 egg yolk · grated lemon peel · 1½ tablespoons grated Parmesan cheese · salt · pepper · grated nutmeg · sage leaves · 4 tablespoons butter or margarine · flour · stock*

To serve: *mashed potato*

Trim and pound the veal scallops (they should be about 3 by 5 inches). Mince until very fine the pork loin, the prosciutto, the garlic (if using), and the bread. Mix in the egg yolk, grated lemon peel, Parmesan cheese, and salt, pepper and nutmeg to taste. Blend the mixture thoroughly, then spread over the meat slices with a knife (step 1). Roll them up tightly, and stick them 2 by 2 on toothpicks, with 1 sage leaf between (step 2). Melt the butter or margarine in a pan, put in the paupiettes lightly coated with flour, and brown them on all sides over high heat. Add some stock (step 3), cover, lower the heat, and cook slowly for about ¾ hour, or until the paupiettes are cooked and the juice is reduced. Serve on a bed of mashed potato.

Italian Paupiettes

Trim 8 small veal scallops (about 1¼ lb), and pound well. Chop 4 oz lean prosciutto, and mix it with 4 mashed and desalted anchovy fillets. Add 1 egg yolk, 3 tablespoons grated Parmesan cheese, and some grated white truffle (optional). Shape the mixture into 8 balls and put one in the center of each meat slice. Roll the slices, tie with string, and brown them on all sides over high heat in ¼ cup butter or margarine. Cover, lower the heat, and cook slowly for about 45 minutes. If you want to have a sauce add some stock during the cooking and let it reduce.

Florentine Paupiettes

Pound 8 small veal scallops (about 1¼ lb). Trim the edges and chop the trimmings together with 4 oz pork loin, a handful of spinach, celery, carrot and parsley. Cook the mixture in 2 tablespoons butter. Allow to cool, and mix with 1 egg, grated Parmesan cheese, and salt and grated nutmeg to taste. Spread the mixture over the meat slices, roll them, tie with string, and brown on all sides over high heat in ¼ cup butter or margarine with a little chopped onion. Sprinkle with salt, add 1 tablespoon tomato sauce diluted with a little water or stock, cover, lower the heat and cook slowly for about ¾ hour.

You could use beef instead of pork for the stuffing, in which case cook a little longer.

1

2

3

1

2

3

Ossobuco

Ingredients: *four 2-inch thick slices (about 2 lb) of veal shank (ossobuco) · 4 tablespoons butter or margarine · flour · ½ glass dry white wine · 1 celery stalk, 1 small carrot, ½ onion, 2 desalted anchovy fillets, all chopped · salt · pepper · 1¼ cups canned peeled tomatoes, chopped · stock · garlic, parsley and the zest of ½ lemon, all chopped*

To serve: *mashed potato or risotto*

Melt the butter or margarine in a pan, and immediately put in the floured veal slices (step 1). Brown them on all sides over high heat, add the dry white wine and let it reduce. Add the chopped celery, carrot, onion and anchovy fillets, and salt and pepper to taste. Cook until golden and add the tomatoes

(step 2). Cover, lower the heat, and cook slowly for about 1¼ hours, adding stock occasionally to obtain a fairly thick juice. A few minutes before completing the cooking, add the chopped garlic, parsley and lemon zest to taste (step 3). Transfer to a warm serving platter and serve with mashed potatoes, or with a risotto.

Ossobuco with Mushrooms

Roll 4 slices of veal shank (about 2 lb) in flour mixed with salt and pepper. Brown them on all sides over high heat in ¼ cup butter or margarine. Add ½ glass dry white wine, let it reduce, then add chopped onion, carrot, garlic, parsley and grated lemon zest to taste, and 1 tablespoon dried mushrooms, soaked in

lukewarm water and squeezed dry. Add 2 tablespoons tomato sauce and ½ cup stock. Cover, lower the heat, and cook slowly for about 1 hour.

Ossobuco with Green Peas

Brown 4 floured slices of veal shank (about 2 lb) on all sides over high heat, in 4 tablespoons butter or margarine with 1 chopped onion. Sprinkle with salt. Add ½ glass dry white wine, let it reduce, then add ¾ cup canned peeled tomatoes, chopped, or some tomato sauce, a few ladles stock, and 1¼ lb fresh or frozen peas. Cover, lower the heat, and cook slowly for about 1 hour. Halfway through the cooking, add ½ cup hot water if the juice is too thick.

Veal Scallops with Ham

Ingredients: *4 veal scallops (about 1 lb) · 4 slices cooked ham · 4 slices Emmenthal cheese · 4 small canned artichokes in oil · ¼ cup butter or margarine · salt · 1 cup dry white wine · 1 cup hot stock*

To garnish: *artichoke hearts · peas · carrots*

Trim the veal slices, and pound well (step 1). Cover ½ of each slice with 1 slice of ham and 1 of cheese (step 2), and 1 artichoke cut into thin slices. Fold the meat and seal the three open sides with toothpicks (step 3). Brown the scallops on all sides over high heat in butter or margarine. Sprinkle with salt. Add the wine, let it reduce, then add the stock. Cover, lower the heat, and cook slowly for 15—20 minutes. Serve garnished with artichoke hearts and a macedoine of peas and carrots.

Veal Scallops with Frankfurter and Cheese Stuffing

Trim 8 small veal scallops and pound them. Put on 4 of them ½ slice Emmenthal cheese, ½ frankfurter (sliced lengthwise) and 1 teaspoon mustard. Cover them with the remaining scallops, and press the edges together to seal them. Dip them in egg beaten with a little salt and breadcrumbs. Let them stand for ½ hour, then brown on all sides over high heat in 4 tablespoons butter or margarine. Cover, lower the heat, and cook slowly until golden.

Veal Scallops with Prosciutto Stuffing

Trim 8 small scallops of veal (about 1 lb) and pound well. Put on each scallop 1 slice prosciutto and 1 sage leaf, sprinkle with lemon juice, season with salt and pepper, then fold it. Close with toothpicks. Cook until golden and cooked through on high heat in oil mixed with butter, or in a moderate oven, as above. Thin slices of fillet of beef can also be used for this recipe.

Cutlets with Cheese Stuffing

Make an incision along the side of 4 veal or pork cutlets, without cutting all the way through. Insert 1 slice Emmenthal cheese and 2 sage leaves. Press the edges of the incision together to seal. Brown the cutlets on both sides over high heat in 4 tablespoons butter or margarine with 2 sage leaves. Season with salt and pepper to taste, cover, lower the heat, and cook for 20—25 minutes.

1

2

3

Saltimbocca Roman Style

Ingredients: *8 small veal scallops (about 1¼ lb) · salt · pepper · 8 slices prosciutto (both the lean and the fat) · flour · ¼ cup butter or margarine · 8 sage leaves · dry white wine*

To garnish: tiny whole potatoes, boiled · butter · parsley

Trim the veal scallops, and pound, making them all roughly the same size. Season with salt and pepper (step 1), and put on each 1 sage leaf. Cover with 1 slice prosciutto (step 2) and fasten with a toothpick (step 3). Dip them lightly in flour. Melt half the butter or margarine in a pan, add the meat slices side by side, increase the heat, and brown on both sides. Continue cooking for a few minutes, until golden and cooked through. Put on a warm serving platter and remove the toothpicks. Add the wine to the cooking juices, and let it reduce on high heat, stirring with a wooden spoon, until it has almost evaporated. Add the remaining butter or margarine, and pour over the saltimbocca. Serve immediately, garnished with tiny whole potatoes tossed in butter and sprinkled with chopped parsley.

Veal Scallops in Piquant Sauce

Trim 8 small veal scallops (about 1¼ lb), pound, and dip in flour. Brown on all sides over high heat in 4 tablespoons butter or margarine. Sprinkle with salt and arrange the scallops on a warm serving platter. Prepare a sauce with 8 anchovy fillets, desalted and mashed with 1 tablespoon capers, chopped parsley, and a little oil and vinegar. Pour the sauce over the scallops.

Sautéed Veal Scallops

Trim 8 small veal scallops (about 1¼ lb) and pound well. Dip them in flour, and brown on all sides over high heat, in 4 tablespoons butter or margarine. Season with salt and pepper to taste, add ¼ cup stock, lower the heat and continue cooking for about 15 minutes. Arrange the meat on a serving platter and keep warm. Remove the pan from the heat, add 2 egg yolks and the juice of 1 lemon, stir well and pour over the meat.

1

2

3

1   2   3

Veal Scallops Viennese Style

Ingredients: *4 large veal scallops (about 1 lb)* · *salt* · *pepper* · *flour* · *1 egg* · *breadcrumbs* · *4 tablespoons butter or margarine* · *4 lemon slices* · *2 olives* · *4 anchovy fillets* · *1 tablespoon capers*

To garnish: *hard-boiled eggs* · *parsley*

Trim the veal and pound well, season with salt and pepper to taste, dip lightly in flour, then in beaten egg (step 1), and in breadcrumbs, pressing well to make them adhere. Brown the scallops, a few minutes on each side, over high heat, in butter or margarine (step 2). Arrange them on a warm serving platter, putting in the center of each 1 peeled lemon slice, 1 anchovy fillet, desalted, rolled around ½ pitted olive, and a few capers (step 3). Garnish the edges of the platter with hard-boiled egg slices and sprigs of parsley and serve immediately.

Veal Cutlets with Sweetbread Stuffing

To prepare the stuffing lightly sauté 4 oz sweetbreads and 4 oz veal in 2 tablespoons butter mixed with chopped parsley and onion. Chop these ingredients and mash them in a mortar (or work them through a sieve) with 1 handful white bread, soaked in stock and squeezed dry. Add 1–2 eggs, 2 tablespoons grated Parmesan cheese, salt and pepper to taste, and mix well. The proportions can be adjusted according to the size of the cutlets. Pound 4 veal cutlets (with bone), season with salt and pepper to taste, and spread the stuffing on both sides of each cutlet.

Dip in beaten egg and in breadcrumbs, and fry in hot oil, or, if preferred, in oil and butter until cooked through. Drain well and serve immediately, garnished with parsley and with lemon quarters.

Veal Cutlets Bolognese Style

Trim the bone off 4 veal cutlets, pound them lightly, season with salt and pepper to taste, dip in flour, then in beaten egg, and finally in breadcrumbs, pressing well to make them adhere. Let them stand for ½ hour, then brown on all sides over high heat in 4 tablespoons butter or margarine. Arrange them in a roasting pan, put on each 1 slice prosciutto, sprinkle with grated Parmesan cheese, dot with butter and put in a very hot oven (475°F) for 2 minutes. Transfer to a warm serving platter, add a few tablespoons of gravy from a roast, or meat extract diluted in hot water, to the cooking juices, and pour over the cutlets.

Cutlets Valdostana Style are also made in this way but fontina (or Gruyère) cheese slices are used instead of Parmesan cheese.

109

Pork

Roast Pork

Ingredients: *2 lb pork loin, boned and rolled ·
2 cloves of garlic · rosemary · 2—3 cloves ·
salt · freshly ground pepper · olive oil*

To garnish: *tiny whole potatoes*

Lard the meat with halved or quartered cloves
of garlic (step 1), rosemary and cloves. Tie it
with string, season with salt and pepper to
taste (step 2), brush with oil, and put it into an
oiled roasting pan. Place in a hot oven (400°F)
and roast for at least 1½ hours, or until the
meat is cooked through and the juices are

no longer pink, turning it over occasionally
with 2 spoons and basting with the cooking
juices. Untie it (step 3), let stand 5—10 minutes,
and slice. Arrange the slices on a warm serving
platter, garnished with tiny whole potatoes,
boiled, tossed in butter and sprinkled with
chopped parsley, and other vegetables according to taste. The dish is equally good when
served cold. Serves 6.

Roast Pork with Orange Sauce

Tie 2 lb boned pork loin with string (see p.111).
Season with salt and pepper to taste. Place
in a buttered roasting pan with 1 slice onion
and 1 celery stalk, cut into thin slices, 1
peeled orange in sections, 1 glass orange
juice, and 1 tablespoon vinegar or 2 tablespoons dry white wine. Put the pan into a
hot oven (400°F) and cook for at least 1½
hours, until the meat is cooked through,

turning it and basting occasionally with the
cooking juices. Remove meat from the pan,
let stand 5—10 minutes, then slice it and place
on a warm serving platter. Serve cooking
juices separately.

Pork Loin with Piquant Sauce

Roll in flour 1 piece pork loin (about 2 lb).
Melt in a pan 2½ tablespoons butter or
margarine with chopped onion and capers to
taste. Add the meat, brown on all sides over
high heat, cover, lower the heat and cook very
slowly for at least 1½ hours, until the meat is
cooked through, turning and adding stock
occasionally. Add salt halfway through the
cooking. When cooked, remove meat from
the pan, let stand 5—10 minutes, then slice and
arrange on a warm serving platter with the
cooking juices and the juice of 1 lemon
poured over. Sprinkle with capers. Serves 4—6.

Crown Roast of Pork

Ingredients: *One 9-rib piece of pork* (carré)

For the stuffing: *4 oz prosciutto or mortadella, chopped · 1 egg · 1 handful white bread, soaked in milk and squeezed dry · a few tablespoons Parmesan cheese · 1 tablespoon French mustard and 1 teaspoon Worcestershire (optional) · chopped parsley · salt · pepper · oil*

To garnish: *tomatoes*

Prepare the *carré* by stripping the meat from the upper part of the bones, and making incisions in the meat between the lower pieces of bone (step 1), or ask the butcher to prepare it. Remove a little meat from the inside and chop it. Shape the ribs into a crown and tie it with string (step 2). Prepare the stuffing in the following manner: mix the chopped pork with the prosciutto, egg, bread, Parmesan cheese, mustard, Worcestershire (if using), parsley, and salt and pepper to taste. Put the mixture, thoroughly blended, inside the crown, and place in an oiled roasting pan. Brush it with oil (step 3) and cap the bone ends with aluminum foil. Place in a hot oven (400°F) and cook for at least 1½ hours, until the meat is cooked through, basting occasionally with the cooking juices. The crown may be filled, if liked, with small potatoes, fried in butter. Garnish with paper frills and tomatoes. Serves 6.

Roast Pork with Prunes

Soak 12 prunes in cold water overnight. Drain. Take 1½ lb pork tenderloin — or any other boneless cut suitable for roasting — and make a deep incision lengthwise into it. Insert the pitted prunes with a wooden spoon handle. Brown the meat on all sides over high heat in 1 tablespoon butter or margarine, season with salt to taste, add ¼ cup stock, cover, lower the heat, and cook for about 1 hour, turning and basting occasionally with the cooking juices, adding more stock if the meat becomes too dry.

The cooking can also be done in the oven at 350°F. Halfway through the cooking add 4 apples, peeled and cored, with a pat of butter in the center.

1

2

3

1   2   3

Spare Ribs Stew

Ingredients: 1¼ lb spare ribs · 4 oz pork rind ·
1 pig's foot · 1 onion · 2 oz salt pork ·
1 tablespoon butter · 3 celery stalks ·
2–3 carrots · 3 tablespoons tomato sauce ·
salt · pepper · 3 or 4 lb cabbage ·
¾ lb sausages

Scrape and scorch the rind and the pig's foot.
Halve the foot lengthwise, and cook in boiling
water for ½ hour, skimming most of the fat.
Drain and cut into pieces. Chop the onion
and salt pork, and brown in butter. Add the
foot, rind, and spare ribs also cut into pieces
(step 1). When browned, add the celery and
carrots, roughly chopped (step 2), the tomato
sauce diluted in a little hot water, and salt and
pepper to taste. After a few minutes add
enough water to cover. Cover the pan, and
cook slowly for 2½–3 hours. Separate the
cabbage leaves, wash, and put in a pan of
boiling water. Drain after 10 minutes. Half
an hour before the cooking is complete, add
the cabbage (step 3), and the sausage cut into

pieces. The cooking juices must be thoroughly
reduced before the dish is served.

Sauerkraut with Frankfurters

Wash thoroughly 3 lb sauerkraut, drain and
squeeze to remove all water. Put in a pan
with plenty of water ½ lb smoked bacon,
½ calf's foot and 6 oz pork rind. Bring to a
boil, then drain. Line the bottom of a pan with
the pork rind, put in half the sauerkraut, the
bacon, ½ lb smoked pork shoulder, the calf's foot,
6 frankfurters, 1 garlic sausage, 1 carrot,
1 small onion stuck with 1 clove, 10 juniper
berries, 1 bouquet garni, made of parsley,
thyme and 1 bay leaf, salt, 2½ tablespoons
butter or margarine, and the remaining
sauerkraut. Add 1 cup dry white wine, and
enough water to cover. Seal the pan with a
double sheet of wax paper or aluminum foil,
and cook very slowly for about 2½ hours.
After ½ hour remove the sausage and the
frankfurters and keep on one side, and after

1½ hours, remove the pork shoulder and the
bacon. Add ¾ lb peeled potatoes, and continue
cooking for ½ hour. Put back everything to
reheat for 10 minutes. By the end of the cooking, the liquid must be almost completely
absorbed. The calf's foot is used only to give
consistency to the stock and is not served
with the sauerkraut, but it can be boned, cut
into strips, and served separately, seasoned
with oil, vinegar, and raw onion slices, if
liked. Serves 4–6.

Variety Meats

Sweetbreads with Mushrooms

Ingredients: 1¼ lb veal sweetbreads · lemon juice or vinegar · pinch of salt · flour · 1 lb fresh mushrooms · 2½ tablespoons butter · ½ small glass brandy · ¼ cup stock · ¼ cup heavy cream

To finish: 1 egg yolk · juice of ½ lemon · chopped parsley · whole button mushrooms (optional)

Soak the sweetbreads in cold salted water for 3 hours with a little lemon juice or vinegar. Rinse them, put them in a pan, and cover with cold water. Add salt and more lemon juice or vinegar. Bring to a boil and cook for 5 minutes, skimming occasionally. Take out the sweetbreads, drain, and rinse again in fresh cold water. Remove the fat, skin and ducts, and let the sweetbreads cool. Slice them (step 1), roll lightly in flour, and brown them on all sides over high heat in the butter. Add the brandy and flame it. Add the mushrooms cut into thin slices (step 2), and, after a moment, add the stock. Lower the heat and cook slowly for 25 minutes. Add the cream, let it thicken on very low heat, then turn off the heat. Add the egg yolk beaten with the lemon juice (step 3), and serve as soon as it has blended with the other ingredients. Sprinkle with chopped parsley, garnish with sprigs of parsley and serve with whole button mushrooms, if liked.

Paupiettes of Brains

Soak 1 lb calf's brains in cold salted water, with the juice of ½ lemon for 2–3 hours. Drain. Cover the brains in stock or water, and simmer for 10–15 minutes until firm, then take them out, drain, and rinse under cold running water. Remove the skins. Dry the brains and let cool. Chop finely and mix with 2 beaten eggs, 2 tablespoons grated Parmesan cheese, and chopped parsley, salt, pepper and grated nutmeg to taste.

Brown the mixture, 1 spoonful at a time, on all sides in melted butter. Serve on a warm platter garnished with parsley sprigs and lemon quarters.

Beef Marrow Paupiettes

Soak 1 lb beef marrow in cold water for 1 hour, drain, and cook in boiling water for 10 minutes. Season with salt towards the end of the cooking. Drain, rinse under cold running water, remove the skins, dry and let cool. Sauté in butter and cut carefully into 3-inch pieces.

Place each piece on 1 slice ham with 2 white truffle slices, and roll the ham. Tie each paupiette with string. Dip in beaten egg and breadcrumbs, and brown them on all sides in golden butter.

1

2

3

Calf's Liver with Onions

Ingredients: *1¼ lb calf's liver, thinly sliced · 2 large onions · 4 tablespoons butter · salt · pepper · flour*

To serve: *lemon quarters*

Cut the onions into thin slices (step 1). Cook them very slowly in half the butter until golden-brown. Season with salt and pepper to taste. Roll the liver slices lightly in flour (step 2). Brown them quickly in the remaining butter in a separate pan, and continue cooking for just a few minutes. Remove from the heat, sprinkle with salt, place on a warm serving platter, arrange the onions around them, and serve immediately with lemon quarters. Calf's Liver Venetian Style is prepared in a slightly

different way: the onions should be cut into somewhat thicker slices and browned in oil on high heat. The liver, cut into small slices or strips, should be put in the same pan as the onions. After 2 or 3 minutes, season with salt and pepper and serve with lemon quarters.

Braised Calf's Liver with Sage

Lard 1¼ lb calf's liver with 4 oz finely diced salt pork (soaked in cold water for 1 hour and drained). Brown lightly, in a high, narrow pan, ¼ cup butter or margarine together with 15 sage leaves, add the liver and sauté it quickly on all sides. Sprinkle with salt, and cover with stock. Cover, and cook slowly for about 2 hours. Ten minutes before the cooking

is completed, add 1 glass milk, and reduce the juices on high heat. Serve the sliced liver with the cooking juices strained through a sieve, accompanied by mashed potatoes.

Calf's Liver with Red Wine

Cut into thin slices 1¼ lb calf's liver. Roll the slices in flour, and brown them quickly in 2 tablespoons butter. Add 1 tablespoon grated onion, cook for 1–2 minutes but do not brown, add 1 glass good red wine, and boil for a few minutes. Blend in a knob of butter, season with salt to taste, then remove the liver slices and arrange them on a warm serving platter. Pour over the cooking juice, and sprinkle with chopped parsley.

1

2

3

1   2   3

Calf's Tongue with Olives

Ingredients: 2 calves' tongues, about 2 lb ·
chopped onion, garlic and parsley ·
4 tablespoons butter or margarine ·
about 1 cup medium-sized green olives ·
stock · salt · pepper

Bring the tongues to a boil in water, rinse
under cold running water and drain. Simmer
in enough water to cover for 1½–2 hours until
tender, then skin (step 1) and slice. Melt the
butter, and sauté on low heat the chopped
onion, garlic and parsley, together with the
olives, pitted or whole according to taste
(step 2). Add the tongue slices (step 3) and 1½
tablespoons stock and continue cooking until
the tongue is well heated and has absorbed
much of the flavor of the other ingredients.

Transfer to a warm serving platter and
serve the tongue with the cooking juices,
surrounded by the olives.

Braised Beef Tongue

Cook 1 beef tongue (about 5 lb) in salted
boiling water for ½ hour. Drain and skin.
Roll strips of bacon or salt pork (soaked in
cold water for 1 hour and drained) in a
mixture of chopped garlic, parsley, salt and
pepper to taste. Lard the tongue with them.
Roll the tongue lightly in flour. Brown in a
large shallow pan ¼ cup butter or margarine.
Add the tongue, 2 onions and 2 carrots, thinly
sliced. Skim the fat, then add 1 cup dry white
wine, and let it reduce by half. Add ½ cup
stock, 1 bouquet garni made of parsley, thyme,
celery and 1 bay leaf, and salt and pepper to
taste. Cover, and continue cooking very slowly
for 2½–3 hours until very tender, adding
more stock as necessary — the juices must be
thick and not fatty. Serve the tongue with the
cooking juices poured over, strained if liked.
Serves 8–10.

Calf's Tongue with Scallions

Bring 2 calves' tongues (about 1¾ lb) to a
boil in salted water, rinse under cold running
water and drain. Simmer in enough water to
cover for 1½–2 hours until tender. Skin them,
dry, and roll lightly in flour. Sauté 1 sliced
onion in ¼ cup butter. Add the tongue and
brown it. Add ½ glass dry white wine, let it
reduce, add ½ lb peeled tomatoes or 1 tablespoon tomato paste diluted in a little stock.
Add ½ cup hot stock, cover, and continue
cooking for 15 minutes. Meanwhile, soak 1 lb
scallions in boiling water. Peel them, put
them in the pan, and continue cooking until
the tongue has absorbed the flavor of the
cooking juices. Slice the tongue and serve with
the reduced cooking juices, garnished with the
scallions.

Lamb

Stuffed Shoulder of Lamb

Ingredients: *1 shoulder of lamb (about 2 lb) ·
4 oz salt pork (soaked in cold water for 1 hour
and drained), or prosciutto ·
a generous measure of fresh rosemary,
parsley and a few celery leaves ·
1 clove of garlic, peeled (optional) · salt ·
pepper · ¼ cup butter or margarine ·
½ glass dry white wine · stock*

To garnish: *macedoine of mixed vegetables*

Chop the salt pork or prosciutto together with
the rosemary, parsley, celery and garlic (if
using). Season with salt and pepper to taste.
Bone the shoulder of lamb (step 1), or ask
your butcher to do it for you. Pound it until as
flat as possible, and cover the inside with the
chopped mixture (step 2), roll it and tie with
string (step 3). Brown it on all sides over high
heat in the butter or margarine, and sprinkle
with salt. Add the white wine, let it reduce,
then add ¼ cup stock. Cover, lower the heat,
and cook for about 1½ hours until tender, adding more stock if the meat becomes dry.
Remove from the pan, let stand for 10 minutes, then remove string and slice the meat.
Arrange on a warm serving platter with the
cooking juices. Garnish with a macedoine of
mixed vegetables.

Carré d'Agneau

Have the butcher prepare a *carré* of lamb with
best end of neck cutlets, cutting through the
base of each cutlet without completely separat-
ing them. Brown over high heat in ¼ cup
butter or margarine on top of the stove, then
put it in a wide buttered ovenproof dish.
Season with salt and pepper to taste, and put
the *carré* in a hot oven (400°F). Cook for at
least 1 hour until the meat is tender, turning it
once. Prepare a mixture of parsley, mint and
garlic, chopped, breadcrumbs, and salt and
pepper to taste. Spread it over the fatty parts of
the lamb, pressing to make it adhere. Pour over
melted butter and gratiné.

Lamb Cutlets with Mashed Potatoes

Prepare mashed potatoes according to taste
with 2 lb potatoes, butter, milk, salt and grated
nutmeg. Brown 8 lamb cutlets in ¼ cup butter
or margarine on both sides over high heat, and
cook for 7–8 minutes, turning once. Season
with salt and pepper to taste. Drain the cutlets
and keep warm. In the fat remaining in the
skillet, brown 4 slices prosciutto or bacon.
Arrange the cutlets and the prosciutto or
bacon over the potatoes on a warm serving
platter, and pour over the cooking juices.

1

2

3

Roast Lamb

Ingredients: *1 leg of lamb (about 3 lb) ·
¼ cup butter or margarine · garlic, rosemary
and parsley · a few tablespoons breadcrumbs ·
salt · pepper*

In an ovenproof casserole brown the leg of
lamb in ¾ of the butter or margarine on all
sides over high heat. Season with salt and
pepper to taste and add the remaining butter
or margarine. Put it in a hot oven (400°F) and
cook for about 1 hour 20 minutes or until
tender (step 1). Chop the garlic, rosemary and
parsley, and mix with the breadcrumbs (step
2). Spread the mixture over the meat (step 3),
and continue cooking for 5–10 minutes, in
the top of the oven, until a golden crust has
formed.

Braised Lamb

Cut into pieces 3 lb lamb meat (neck, shoulder
etc.). Roll the pieces in flour, and brown them
on all sides over high heat in ¼ cup butter or
margarine. Add ½ glass dry white wine, let it
reduce, then add 1 crushed clove of garlic,
1 large onion and 1 carrot cut into slices, 1
clove and 1 bouquet garni made of parsley,
thyme and 1 bay leaf. After 2 minutes add
2 tablespoons tomato paste diluted in 1 cup
water. Season with salt and pepper to taste,
cover, lower the heat and cook slowly for
about 1 hour or until the meat is tender.
Remove the bouquet garni and the garlic
before serving.

Lamb Paupiettes

Mince 1 lb boned lamb shoulder. Mix it with
1–2 handfuls white bread soaked in milk and
squeezed dry, 2–3 tablespoons grated Parmesan or Gruyère cheese, 1 egg, and salt and
pepper to taste. Blend well, shape into a ball
and beat repeatedly against the bottom of the
bowl. Make 4 flat paupiettes – or 8 smaller
ones – and roll them in flour. Brown them on
all sides over high heat in 1 tablespoon butter
or margarine and cook for about 30 minutes,
turning them once. Serve a tomato sauce
separately.

Rabbit

Stuffed Boned Rabbit

Ingredients: *1 rabbit (about 4 lb) ·*
a generous measure rosemary and sage · salt ·
pepper · 6 oz prosciutto (sliced), or salt pork
(soaked in cold water for 1 hour, drained and
sliced) · 1 clove of garlic, peeled ·
¼ cup butter · 2 tablespoons oil ·
2 glasses dry white wine · stock

To garnish: *macedoine of vegetables*

Wash and dry the rabbit. Place it on its back
on a cutting board with the neck towards
you, and make a cut lengthwise along the
breast and belly (step 1). Using a very sharp

1

knife carefully remove all the bones (step 2),
so as to obtain 1 large piece of meat. Mix the
rosemary and sage with salt and pepper to
taste, spread ½ the mixture over the meat,
arrange a layer of prosciutto or salt pork slices
over it, and top with the remainder of the herb
mixture. Roll the meat (step 3), tie it with
string as for any roast meat. Sauté the garlic
in the oil and butter until golden, add the meat
and brown on all sides over high heat.
Remove the garlic. Stir in the white wine, let it
reduce, then add salt to taste and ¼ cup stock.
Lower the heat and cook slowly for 1¼ hours.
When cooked, remove the roll from the pan,
let stand 10 minutes, then remove the string,
slice the meat and arrange on a warm serving
platter with the reduced cooking juices poured
over. Garnish the platter with a macedoine of
vegetables, if liked. The rabbit can also be
cooked in a moderate oven (350°F) for 1½–2
hours, basting the meat occasionally with the
cooking juices. Serves 6–8.

2

Rabbit with Curry Sauce

Wash and dry 1 rabbit (about 2½ lb). Cut into
serving pieces, roll in flour, and brown on all
sides over high heat in 2 tablespoons butter.
In another pan, sauté until golden 1 clove of
garlic, peeled, in 4 tablespoons butter. Remove
the garlic, add 1 medium-sized green apple,
cored and roughly chopped, 1 medium-sized
onion, finely chopped, and ½ teaspoon curry
powder – or more, according to taste. Cook
slowly until the onion is tender, then add 2
tablespoons flour, and salt to taste. Stir constantly, and, after 2 minutes, add 2 cups hot
stock. Add the pieces of rabbit, cover, lower
the heat and cook slowly for 40–45 minutes
or until tender. Serve with the cooking juices
poured over, and boiled rice or pilaff in a
separate dish, if liked.

3

1   2   3

Poultry

Boiled Stuffed Capon

Ingredients: *1 capon (about 5 lb) ·
1 celery stalk · 1 leek · 1 potato ·
¼ lb small onions, peeled and halved · 1 carrot ·
stock*

*For the stuffing: ¼ cup butter or margarine ·
the capon's liver, finely chopped ·
2 oz boned pork loin, finely chopped ·
2 oz prosciutto, finely chopped ·
2 oz sweetbreads or brains (see p.39),
optional · 1 handful white bread, soaked in milk
and squeezed dry · parsley or truffles ·
2 egg yolks · grated Parmesan cheese · salt ·
pepper · grated nutmeg*

Wash and dry the capon (step 1). If you like,
remove the bones from inside the breast,
taking care not to spoil the shape of the bird.
Peel the vegetables and cut into pieces if large.

Prepare the stuffing: sauté lightly in the
butter or margarine the capon's liver, pork
loin, prosciutto, and the sweetbreads or brains,
if using. Add the bread and parsley. (If truffles
are used, cut them into thin slices and add
them later to the chopped mixture.) Put the
mixture in a bowl with the egg yolks, grated
Parmesan cheese, and salt, pepper and nutmeg
to taste, and blend thoroughly. Stuff the capon
with the mixture, sew it with string (steps 2
and 3), wrap it in a clean napkin or cloth, and
tie at both ends. Put it in a pan, cover with
stock and bring slowly to a boil. Skim the
scum, add the vegetables and continue cooking
slowly for about 2 hours, or until the capon is
tender. Remove it from the pan, take it out of
the cloth, and let stand 10 minutes. Remove
string, transfer meat to a warm serving platter,
and surround with the vegetables from the
cooking juices. Serve with a variety of sharp
sauces, according to taste. If liked, the capon
can be carved before serving and reshaped on
the serving platter. The stuffed capon can also
be roasted in a moderate oven (375°F) for 2
hours, instead of being boiled. Serves 6–8.

Capon with Chicken Livers
and Mushrooms

Wash and dry a 5-lb capon. Clean ¾ lb mushrooms, chop them, and sauté for a few minutes
in 1 tablespoon butter, together with 3 sliced
chicken livers. Season with salt and pepper
to taste, add 2 tablespoons hot brandy, bring
to the boil and flame. Remove from the heat
after a few minutes, and mix with 1 handful
white bread, previously soaked in milk and
squeezed dry, 1 egg yolk, grated Parmesan
cheese and chopped parsley to taste. Stuff the
capon with the mixture and proceed as above.

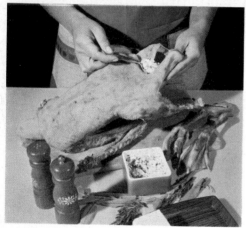

1   2   3

Roast Goose

Ingredients: *1 goose (about 7 lb) ·
¼ cup butter or margarine · sage · rosemary ·
salt · pepper · ½ glass dry white wine*

To garnish: *tiny whole potatoes, boiled ·
parsley sprigs*

Wash and dry the goose. Put inside it 1 tablespoon butter or margarine mixed with chopped
rosemary and sage, and salt to taste (step 1).
Tie with string and sprinkle the outside liberally with salt and pepper (step 2). Dot the
goose with the remaining butter or margarine,
place it in a roasting pan with more chopped
rosemary and sage to taste in a hot oven
(475°F). When brown, baste it with white wine
(step 3), lower the heat to moderate (375°F),
and continue cooking for about 2 hours,
pricking occasionally with a fork to let the fat
escape. When the goose is cooked, remove from
the pan and let stand 10 minutes. Remove

string, transfer to a warm serving platter,
arrange paper frills on legs and garnish with
tiny whole potatoes and parsley sprigs. (Half a
goose can be roasted in the same way: place
it in a lightly buttered roasting pan with the
skin above so that it can be pricked occasionally.) Serves 6–8.

Stuffed Goose Neck

Detach the skin from the neck, turning it
inside out without breaking it, wash, dry, and
tie with string at one end. Soak the liver from
the goose in tepid water for 1 hour, then drain
and chop it. Sauté it in a little butter or
margarine, together with the chopped goose
heart, without letting them brown. Chop ½ lb
raw pork loin. Mix liver, heart and pork with
4 oz sausage meat, 1 handful white bread,
soaked in milk and squeezed dry, 1 slice of
onion (optional), chopped parsley to taste, 2

tablespoons brandy, and plenty of salt and
pepper. Stuff the mixture into the neck skin,
leaving a little space to provide for swelling
during the cooking, and tie the other end. Roll
it with the hand to make it regular, and prick
it all over with a fine needle. Put it in cold
stock, and cook it for about 1 hour. Slice it,
and serve it hot with buttered spinach or
mashed potatoes. Or you may serve it cold,
possibly with aspic and a green salad.

An alternative way of cooking this dish is
to brown the goose neck in goose fat and then
braise it slowly with chopped celery, carrot,
garlic, 1 bay leaf, and stock for about 1 hour.

Chicken Breasts with Cheese Cream

Ingredients: *4 chicken breasts (about 1 lb) · flour · salt · pepper · 2 tablespoons butter or margarine · dry white wine or brandy · stock*

For the Cheese Cream: 4 oz cream cheese · 1 tablespoon butter · 1 tablespoon milk · pepper · truffles or black olives (optional) · peas

Pound lightly the chicken breasts, season with salt and pepper to taste, flour them lightly, and cook them in the butter or margarine on both sides, on high heat, until golden (step 1). Add the white wine or brandy (if using brandy, bring it to a boil and flame it), let it reduce, then add immediately a few tablespoons stock and stir to combine all the cooking juices. Cover and cook slowly for 30–35 minutes.

To prepare the cheese cream, put in a pan the cheese (step 2), butter, milk, and pepper to taste and blend over low heat until creamy. Spread it over the chicken breasts (step 3), and put them under the broiler to brown for a few seconds. Transfer to a warm serving platter and garnish with a few sliced truffles or pitted black olives, if liked, and serve with peas.

Chicken Breasts with Brandy

Melt ¼ cup butter in a skillet. Put in, side by side, 4 chicken breasts (about 1 lb), lightly pounded and floured. Season with salt and pepper to taste Brown them quickly on both sides, on high heat, then cover, lower the heat, and cook slowly for 30–35 minutes. When cooked, arrange them on a warm serving platter, covered with the cooking juices. Heat 1 small glass brandy, flame it, pour over the chicken breasts, and serve immediately.

Stuffed Chicken Breasts

Pound lightly 4 chicken breasts (about 1 lb), and put in the center of each a stuffing prepared in the following manner: mix 3 oz cottage or ricotta cheese with 1 egg yolk, 1 teaspoon chopped parsley, 1 teaspoon grated lemon peel, and salt and pepper to taste. Roll the meat and tie with string. Flour lightly and brown on all sides over high heat in 2 tablespoons butter or margarine. Season with salt and pepper to taste. Add 1 small glass brandy, heated, bring to a boil, flame it, let it reduce, then add ¼ cup hot stock. Cover, lower the heat, and cook slowly for about 30–35 minutes.

1

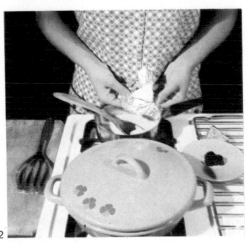

2

3

Stuffed Roast Pigeons

Ingredients: *2 large pigeons · 4 slices salt pork, soaked in cold water for 1 hour and drained, or streaky bacon · 1 tablespoon butter · ½ glass brandy · salt · 1 bay leaf · stock*

For the stuffing: *1 tablespoon butter · livers from the pigeons, minced · 2 oz prosciutto, diced · ½ glass brandy · 1 handful white bread, soaked in milk and squeezed dry · 1 egg yolk · 2 tablespoons grated Parmesan cheese · chopped parsley · salt · pepper*

To serve: *carrots in white sauce*

Wash and dry the pigeons, cutting off the feet (step 1). Prepare the stuffing: sauté lightly in 1 tablespoon butter the minced livers and prosciutto. Add ½ glass brandy, bring to a boil, flame it, and remove from the heat. Mix the livers and prosciutto with the bread, egg yolk, grated Parmesan cheese, and parsley, salt and pepper to taste. Stuff the pigeons with the mixture and sew the openings with string. Place 2 slices salt pork or bacon on the breast of each bird (step 2), tie them with string, and brown on all sides over high heat in the remaining butter. Pour over the remaining brandy (step 3), bring to a boil, flame it, sprinkle with salt, add the bay leaf, cover, lower the heat, and cook for about 1 hour until tender, adding stock if the meat becomes dry. If the pigeons are small, allow 1 per person and double the quantity of stuffing ingredients. When cooked, remove the string, transfer to a warm serving platter and serve surrounded by carrots in a white sauce.

Pigeons with Mushrooms

Wash and dry 2 large pigeons (or 4 small ones). Tie them with string, sprinkle with salt and pepper. Brown them in 1 tablespoon butter, add 1 small glass brandy, bring to a boil, and flame it. Cover, lower the heat, and cook slowly for about ½ hour. Take the birds from the pan, remove string and keep warm. Put in the pan 1 tablespoon chopped onion, ½ lb sliced mushrooms, 6 oz tomatoes, peeled and chopped, 1 bay leaf, and salt and pepper to taste. Cook for 10–15 minutes, put the pigeons back into the pan, and when they are hot, serve them covered with the sauce. Garnish with whole button mushrooms, if liked.

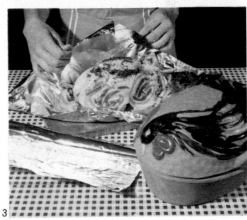

1   2   3

Chicken Cooked in Terracotta

Ingredients: *1 chicken (about 3 lb) ·
8 juniper berries · 1 teaspoon peppercorns ·
leaves of 1 twig rosemary · leaves of 1 twig
sage · salt · 4 oz sliced prosciutto, or salt pork
soaked in water for 1 hour and drained, or
streaky bacon · ¼ cup butter or margarine in
small pieces*

To garnish: *twigs of rosemary*

Clean (step 1), wash and dry the chicken.
Crush the juniper berries and peppercorns in a
mortar and chop them together with the rosemary and sage leaves. Put 1 teaspoon of the
mixture inside the chicken with a pinch of salt
(step 2). Arrange the prosciutto, salt pork or
bacon slices around the chicken on aluminum
foil. Dot with butter or margarine, and spread
the remaining herb mixture over the chicken.
Sprinkle liberally with salt and close the
aluminum foil (step 3). Put the wrapped
chicken in an earthenware dish, cover, and
cook in a hot oven (400°F) for about 2 hours.

Remove the dish from the oven, taking care
not to break it by putting it on a cold surface.
Remove the chicken, take off the aluminum
foil and transfer to a warm serving platter.
Arrange paper frills on the legs and garnish
with twigs of rosemary. Guinea fowl may also
be prepared in this way.

Chicken with Parsley

Wash and dry a 2½-lb chicken. Put in a pan
the chicken neck, leg and wing tips, and
gizzard, together with 1 celery stalk, 1 carrot,
peeled and chopped, 1 onion, peeled and sliced,
and salt and pepper to taste. Cover with water
and simmer 1–2 hours. Strain. Sauté the liver
in ½ tablespoon butter or margarine, then chop
it with a generous handful parsley, and mix
with 1 teaspoon grated lemon peel, ¼ cup
butter, and salt and pepper to taste. Put the
mixture inside the chicken, sew the opening
and tie the bird with string. Sprinkle liberally
with salt and pepper, and brown it on all sides

over high heat in 1 tablespoon butter. Add ¼
cup of the hot stock, cover, lower the heat, and
cook very slowly for about 1 hour or until
tender, adding more stock if the chicken
becomes dry. Remove the chicken from the
pan, take off the string, and keep warm. If the
sauce is too thin, let it reduce on high heat. Add
½ cup light cream, and let the sauce thicken,
without boiling, on moderate heat. Carve the
chicken, arrange on a warm serving platter
and garnish with parsley sprigs. Serve the
sauce in a separate dish.

Stuffed Roast Chicken

Ingredients: *1 chicken (about 3½ lb) · 1 slice cooked ham (about 4 oz) · 1 slice tongue (about 4 oz) · 1 tablespoon pistachio nuts · ¼ cup butter or margarine · 1 small glass brandy*

For the stuffing: ½ lb stewing veal · 4 oz pork loin · 4 oz sausage meat · 2 eggs · ¼ cup grated Parmesan cheese · 1 handful white bread soaked in milk and squeezed dry · salt · pepper · mixed herbs

To garnish: artichoke hearts · green peas · carrots · radish roses (optional)

Wash and dry the chicken, cut off the tips of the wings and legs. Put it on a carving board, breast side down, cut the skin with scissors from the neck to the tail (step 1), and remove the bones, except for the leg bones. Spread it on the board leaving the skin intact.

Prepare the stuffing: chop the veal and the pork loin, and mix in a bowl with the sausage meat, eggs, grated Parmesan cheese, white bread, and salt, pepper and mixed herbs to taste. Blend thoroughly. Cut the ham and tongue into strips. Put ½ the stuffing in the center of the chicken (step 2), sprinkle with ½ the pistachio nuts, and arrange a layer of ½ the ham and tongue strips on top. Cover it with the remainder of the stuffing, and end with a layer of remaining pistachio nuts, ham and tongue. Fold the skin of the chicken over the stuffing, tuck the neck skin inside, and sew carefully together with string (step 3). Tie the chicken with string. Melt the butter or margarine in a roasting pan, put in the chicken, sewed side down, and brown in a moderate oven (350°F). Bring the brandy to a boil in a pan, and flame it. Pour it quickly over the chicken, sprinkle with salt, and cook slowly for 1½–2 hours until tender, basting occasionally with the cooking juices. When cooked, remove from pan, let stand for 10 minutes, then untie and slice it. Arrange on a warm serving platter with paper frills on the legs. Garnish with artichoke hearts sautéed in butter and stuffed with green peas and carrots, and radish roses, if liked. Serve with potatoes mashed in butter and eggs and seasoned with salt, black pepper and grated nutmeg. This dish may also be served cold.

Chicken with Garlic

In a large pan with a tight-fitting lid, mix ½ glass olive oil, 4 celery stalks, chopped, and chopped parsley and salt to taste. Add 4 chicken pieces to the pan, stir, and add 40 unpeeled cloves of garlic and 1½ glasses brandy. Cover the pan and seal it with a paste made of flour and water. Put it in a moderate oven (350°F) for about 1½ hours. Remove garlic before serving.

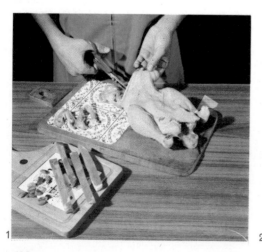

1

2

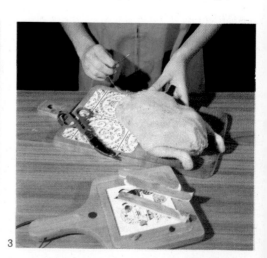

3

Turkey Stuffed with Chestnuts

Ingredients: *1 turkey (about 7 lb) ·
2 slices salt pork soaked in water for 1 hour
and drained, or streaky bacon · ¼ cup butter ·
salt · pepper · ½ glass dry white wine · stock*

*For the stuffing: 1¼ lb roasted chestnuts,
peeled · ¼ cup butter · ½ lb prunes, soaked
according to package directions, and pitted ·
2 large apples · ½ lb sausage meat*

To garnish: *chestnuts · watercress*

Wash and dry the turkey. Prepare the stuffing:
sauté the chestnuts in the butter (step 1) for
10–15 minutes, together with the prunes,
the apples, peeled and cored, and the sausage
meat, stirring occasionally. Put it inside the
turkey (step 2) and sew up the opening with
string. Cover the breast with the salt pork or
bacon slices (step 3) and tie the bird. Put it in
a flameproof casserole with the butter in small
pieces, and brown on all sides over high heat.
Sprinkle liberally with salt and pepper, add the
wine, let it reduce, and add ¼ cup stock. Cover,
lower the heat, and cook for about 2 hours, or
until turkey is tender, basting occasionally
with the cooking juices and adding stock if the
meat becomes too dry. Remove the cover for
the last 10 minutes and finish cooking on high
heat. Remove turkey from pan, transfer to a
warm serving platter, and let stand 10 minutes
before untying and carving. Garnish with
whole cooked chestnuts and watercress, and
decorate turkey legs with paper frills. The
turkey can also be roasted in a moderate oven
(350°F) for 2 hours. Serves 6–8.

Braised Turkey

Cut into pieces 2½ lb turkey meat. Brown it in
¼ cup butter or margarine together with 2 oz
diced salt pork, soaked in cold water for 1 hour
and drained. Add a mixture of chopped celery,
carrot, onion and garlic. Add 1 tablespoon
dried mushrooms, soaked in lukewarm water,
squeezed dry and mashed with 1 tablespoon
flour. Blend well, and, after a few minutes, add
¾ lb tomatoes, peeled and chopped, ¼ cup
stock, 1 bay leaf, and salt and pepper to taste.
Cover, and cook slowly for about 1 hour, adding more stock if necessary.

1

2

3

1   2   3

Game

Duck with Orange

Ingredients: *1 young duck (about 4 lb) · salt · pepper · butter or margarine · 1 glass dry white wine · 4–5 oranges · $\frac{1}{4}$ cup reduced stock · $\frac{1}{2}$ lemon · 2 tablespoons brandy · 1 tablespoon sugar · 1 tablespoon vinegar*

Wash and dry the duck, and tie with string, the legs turned backwards. Sprinkle liberally with salt and pepper, and brush with melted butter or margarine. Brown on all sides over high heat in a buttered pan (step 1), cover, lower the heat and cook for about 45 minutes or until the duck is tender. Baste occasionally with a little white wine. When cooked, take out

and keep warm. Cut into thin strips the rind of 2 oranges (step 2), boil them for a few minutes, drain and refresh in cold running water. Discard excess fat from the cooking juices, mix in the stock gradually, add the juice of 2–3 oranges and the $\frac{1}{2}$ lemon (step 3), the brandy, and a caramel made by dissolving the sugar in the vinegar, then boiling it vigorously with the boiled orange rind. Continue cooking the sauce on low heat for 8–10 minutes until reduced. Remove string from duck, and transfer to a warm serving platter. Pour the sauce over, arranging strips of orange rind decoratively over the breast. Garnish platter with segments from remaining orange, after removing the skin, pith and membrane. Decorate the duck's legs with paper frills.

Rolled Duck with Grand Marnier

Wash and dry a 4-lb duck. Cut it along the back and bone it, being careful not to split

the skin. Cover the inside of the flesh with prosciutto slices and very thin slices of orange, from which the skin, pith and membranes have been removed. Roll the duck and tie with string, like a roast. Brown on all sides over high heat in $\frac{1}{4}$ cup butter or margarine, cover, lower the heat, and cook for about $1\frac{1}{4}$ hours, or until tender. When cooked, take the duck out and keep warm. Discard the excess fat from the cooking juices. Put in another pan $\frac{1}{4}$ cup sugar and 1 tablespoon white vinegar. Heat slowly until sugar dissolves, bring to a boil, and when the sugar begins to caramelize add the juice of 1–2 oranges, 4 tablespoons Grand Marnier, and the grated peel of $\frac{1}{2}$ orange. Continue cooking for 3–4 minutes, then add the cooking juices from the duck, and the rind of 1 orange cut into thin strips, boiled in water for 5 minutes and drained. Remove the string from the duck, slice it, and arrange on a warm serving platter. Pour the sauce over the duck.

Pheasant on Croûtons

Ingredients: *1 pheasant, preferably a hen bird, (about 2½ lb) · 1 bay leaf · 2 juniper berries · 2 slices prosciutto, salt pork or bacon · ¼ cup butter or margarine · salt · pepper · 1 twig rosemary (optional) · ½ glass dry white wine · 1½ tablespoons stock · bread croûtons fried in butter*

Wash and dry the pheasant. Chop the bay leaf and juniper berries together with 2 prosciutto, salt pork or bacon slices and ½ tablespoon butter or margarine. Add salt and pepper to taste. Shape into a ball and place inside the bird (step 1). Sew the opening with string, cover the breast with the remaining prosciutto, salt pork or bacon slices, and tie the bird with string. Brush with melted butter, sprinkle liberally with salt and pepper, put

it in pan with the rosemary, if using, and brown on all sides over high heat. Pour over the wine (step 2), return to heat, let it reduce, and add the stock. Cover, and cook slowly for about 45–50 minutes or until tender, basting occasionally with the cooking juices. The cooking can also be done in a moderate oven (350°F). Arrange the croûtons on a warm serving platter, place the pheasant (whole or carved, according to taste) over the croûtons, and pour over the cooking juices before serving (step 3). Decorate with paper frills.

Pheasant Magyar Style

Wash and dry a 2½-lb pheasant. Chop 1 bay leaf, 1 clove, 1 clove of garlic, peeled, 1 tablespoon parsley and 1 lemon slice (peeled and

without pips). Put the mixture, with salt and pepper to taste, inside the bird, and sew up with string. Cover the breast with a thin slice of fresh pork fat, tie the bird with string, and sprinkle it with Hungarian Tokay wine, or a similar sweet white wine. Sprinkle liberally with salt and pepper, and put it in a casserole with a few slices of onion and mushrooms, then add 1 glass of the wine previously used and 1 glass stock. Put the casserole in a moderate oven (350°F) for 45–50 minutes, basting from time to time with the cooking juices. Drain the pheasant, remove string, cut the bird into serving pieces, and keep it on a warm serving platter. Strain the sauce, removing the excess fat, reduce it on high heat if necessary, stir in 2 tablespoons redcurrant jelly, if liked, and pour over bird.

1

2

3

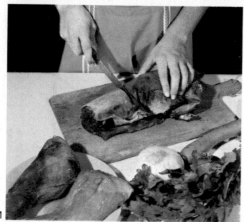

1   2   3

Jugged Hare

Ingredients: *1 hare (about 7 lb) with the blood · 2 tablespoons white wine · 4 oz calf's liver, sliced · 2 oz pork fat · 1 onion, chopped · ¼ cup butter or margarine, or a few tablespoons oil · flour*

For the marinade: *6 cups good, Burgundy-type red wine · 1 celery stalk · 1 carrot, sliced · 2 onions, chopped · 1 small bunch parsley · 1 clove of garlic, crushed · 1 bay leaf · a few leaves thyme, marjoram, sage, rosemary · a few juniper berries · 3–4 peppercorns · 3 cloves · 1 small stick cinnamon · 1 pinch mixed herbs and rock salt*

Wash and dry the hare. Keep the blood in a bowl, mixed with the white wine to prevent coagulation, until blending it with the sauce at the last moment. Cut the hare into serving pieces (step 1), and put them in a bowl together with the liver, heart and lung, and the calf's liver, and pour over the marinade (step 2). Let stand for 24 hours, stirring

occasionally. The next day, brown in a casserole the butter, margarine or oil, pork fat and chopped onion. Drain the pieces of hare (reserving the marinade), dry them, roll lightly in flour, and put them in the casserole. Brown the meat on all sides over high heat, add all the marinade (except the livers), bring to a boil, then cover, lower the heat, and cook for about 2 hours, adding the livers after 1½ hours. If the sauce is too thick, add some stock or hot water. A few minutes before serving take out the pieces of hare, and strain the cooking juices through a sieve (step 3). Return the sauce to the casserole, stir in the blood, add the meat, and as soon as it is hot serve with croûtons fried in butter or a polenta. Serves 10.

Braised Hare

Wash and dry 1 hare (about 7 lb). Cut into serving pieces and rub generously with salt and pepper. Put in a bowl together with ½

cup brandy, 2 tablespoons oil, 1 chopped bay leaf, and ½ onion, finely chopped. Marinate for 2 hours, turning the pieces over occasionally. Chop the hare's liver, place in a bowl and cover with 1 cup good red wine. Brown in a casserole 1 tablespoon butter, ½ chopped onion, and 2 oz salt pork, soaked in cold water for 1 hour, drained and chopped. Add the pieces of hare and the marinade (reserving the liver), passed through a sieve, cover, and cook very slowly for about 1 hour, adding stock if necessary. Add the chopped liver and 1 lb sliced mushrooms, and continue cooking for 1 hour, or less if the hare is tender. Transfer hare to a warm serving platter, thicken the sauce if necessary with a little beurre manié (equal quantities of butter and flour kneaded together), and pour over the hare.

Serve with bread croûtons fried in butter or a polenta. Serves 10.

3

1

2

3

Partridge with Grapes

Ingredients: *2 plump partridges, or 4 smaller ones · 2 (or 4) slices pork fat · butter · salt · pepper · 1 small glass brandy or ½ glass dry white wine · ¼ lb white grapes · stock · 4 bread croûtons fried in butter*

Wash and dry the partridges. Cover the breasts with 1 slice pork fat, and tie them with string, keeping the legs parallel with the bodies (step 1). Brush generously with melted butter, sprinkle with salt and pepper, and cook in a roasting pan in a hot oven (400°F) for about ½ hour, basting from time to time with the cooking juices. Drain them and keep warm. Pour out the fat from the pan, leaving the sediments, and add the brandy or white wine. Dissolve the sediments on low heat, stirring with a wooden spoon. Peel the grapes, remove the pips, and put the grapes in the pan with the partridges (step 2). After a few minutes,

add a few tablespoons stock and 1 tablespoon butter. Reduce the juice over high heat, strain it to separate the grapes, and keep it warm. Garnish the serving platter with the fried croûtons, put in the partridges, after removing string and the grapes (step 3) and serve with the cooking juices in a separate dish.

Partridge Polish Style

Wash and dry 2 partridges. Sauté for a few minutes in a skillet the partridges' livers with 1 tablespoon butter or margarine, 1 chopped scallion, 1 tablespoon chopped parsley, ½ bay leaf, salt and pepper to taste. Remove the bay leaf, and pass the other ingredients through a sieve. Put a little of the mixture inside each bird, and sew up with string. Cover the breasts with slices of salt pork, soaked in cold water for 1 hour and drained, or bacon, according to

taste, and tie the birds with string. Put them in a casserole with 1½ tablespoons stock. Put the casserole in a moderate oven (350°F), and cook for ½ hour, basting from time to time with the cooking juices. You may also cook them on top of the stove, browning them first in butter, and adding stock gradually as required. Take partridges from casserole, remove string and cut the partridges in half. Arrange them on a warm serving platter, pour over the cooking juices and sprinkle with 1 tablespoon breadcrumbs lightly browned in butter. Garnish with lemon quarters and parsley.

1
2
3

Assorted Meat Dishes

Italian Pot-au-feu

Ingredients: 3 quarts water · 1 tablespoon rock salt · 2 lb stewing beef in the slice · 1 carrot, peeled and sliced · 1 onion, peeled and sliced · 1 celery stalk · 1 clove of garlic, crushed · 1 small tomato, quartered (optional) · 1¼ lb stewing veal in the slice · 1 calf's foot · a few potatoes (optional)

Bring the water and rock salt to a boil, add the beef (step 1), and skim the scum (step 2). For a richer stock, put the meat in cold rather than boiling water. Add the vegetables and continue cooking for 3 hours. Add the veal and the calf's foot halfway through the cooking (step 3). Add the potatoes, if liked, ½ hour

before the cooking is completed. Remove meats from pan, slice, and arrange on a warm serving platter. Pour over 1½ tablespoons of the boiling stock. Serve with the vegetables and various sauces to taste, such as ketchup, mustard, green sauce and pickles. You may also add other meats, such as ½ chicken or capon, or garlic sausage cooked separately for 1 hour. Serves 7–8.

Boiled Meat with Tuna Sauce

Cut ¾ lb boiled meat (veal or beef) into thin slices, and arrange them on a shallow platter. Prepare a mayonnaise with 1 egg yolk, ¾ cup

oil, the juice of 1 lemon, and salt and pepper to taste. Mix it with 6 oz tuna fish in oil, 2 anchovy fillets, desalted, and a few capers — all worked through a sieve. Dilute the sauce with a few tablespoons cold stock. Pour it over the meat, and garnish with slices of lemon and red peppers.

Boiled Beef au Gratin

Cut into thin slices, or chop roughly, ¾ lb boiled beef. Put it in a buttered ovenproof dish. Cover with tomato sauce, seasoned with chopped onions and mixed with chopped parsley and basil. Add a layer of mashed potato, and sprinkle with breadcrumbs and grated Gruyère cheese in equal proportions. Dot with butter. Put the dish in a hot oven (400°F) for 15–20 minutes, or until a golden crust has formed. Serve immediately in the same dish.

1   2   3

Fritto Misto

Ingredients: *4 oz chicken · 4 oz veal ·
4 oz pork · 2 oz butter · salt · grated nutmeg ·
2 tablespoons Marsala · 4 oz sweetbreads ·
4 oz chicken livers · 1 thick slice each of
prosciutto and mortadella · 4 oz Gruyère
cheese · hot béchamel sauce prepared with
4 tablespoons butter, ⅔ cup flour, 3 cups milk,
salt and grated nutmeg to taste, with
1 egg yolk added · 2 eggs · breadcrumbs · oil*

To garnish: *parsley sprigs · lemon wedges*

Cut the chicken, veal and pork into 1½-inch
cubes. Brown in 2 tablespoons butter, add salt
and grated nutmeg to taste and the Marsala
and continue cooking. Meanwhile, blanch the
sweetbreads and chicken livers in boiling
water. When they are cold cut them into
cubes of the same size as the meats and add
to the pan. Cut the prosciutto, mortadella and
Gruyère cheese into cubes, add them to the
pan and stir well. When meats are tender
remove all ingredients from pan and string
on small oiled wooden or metal skewers,
alternating the different ingredients. Dip the

skewers in the hot béchamel sauce, put them
on a buttered dish, and let them cool. Roll
them in beaten egg, then in breadcrumbs
(step 1), and fry them in deep hot oil. Drain
them carefully and serve on a warm platter
together with a selection of the meats and
vegetables described below. Garnish with
parsley sprigs and lemon wedges.

Fried Artichokes

Discard the hard outer leaves of 4 artichokes,
quarter them, and let stand for a few minutes
in water and lemon juice. Drain them, dry,
cover in beaten egg, then in breadcrumbs
(step 2) and fry them in hot oil until golden.

Fried Brains and Beef Marrow

Prepare the brains and marrow for cooking, cut
them into pieces, roll them in flour, then in
beaten egg and breadcrumbs, and fry in butter.
You may also dip them in batter, made of
water, flour, grated cheese and egg, and fry
them in hot oil.

Chicken Croquettes

Chop 1 lb cooked chicken together with 2 oz
prosciutto or salami. Prepare a béchamel sauce
with 2 tablespoons butter, 4 tablespoons
flour, ¾ cup milk, salt and nutmeg. Remove the
béchamel sauce from the heat, add the chicken
and prosciutto or salami, 2 tablespoons grated
Parmesan cheese, chopped parsley and 1 egg
yolk. Pour the mixture on a buttered board
and spread it to obtain a 1-inch layer. Let it
cool, cut into pieces, and make into croquette
shapes 2½ inches long and ½ inch in diameter.
Roll them in flour, then in beaten egg and
breadcrumbs (step 3), and brown and cook
them in deep hot oil. Take them out with a
slotted spoon, and drain them on paper towels
as above. Serve with lemon quarters.

Fried Zucchini

Cut zucchini lengthwise in thin slices, dry
them, roll them in flour, then in egg and
breadcrumbs, and fry in deep hot oil. Other
vegetables can also be prepared in this manner.

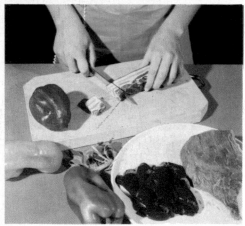

1   2   3

Brochettes Home Style

Ingredients: *10 oz veal · 10 oz calf's liver · 4 oz salt pork in the slice, soaked in cold water for 1 hour and drained · 1 red pepper and 1 green or yellow pepper (fresh or canned) · sage leaves · ¼ cup butter or margarine · salt · pepper · ½ glass dry white wine · stock*

To garnish: *lemon slices · salad (optional)*

Cut the meat, liver, salt pork and peppers in equal pieces. String them with the sage leaves on oiled wooden or metal skewers, alternating the ingredients (step 2). Brown on all sides over high heat in the butter or margarine (step 3). Season with salt and pepper to taste, add the white wine, let it reduce, add the stock, lower the heat and cook slowly or until meats are tender. Serve with the reduced cooking juices. The cooking can also be done under the broiler. Garnish with slices of lemon and salad, if liked.

Veal en Brochette

Cut 1½ lb veal into 1-inch cubes. Marinate them for 1½ hours in a mixture of oil, lemon juice and salt. String on oiled wooden or metal skewers, alternating with sage leaves and diced salt pork, soaked in cold water for 1 hour and drained. Cook on charcoal or under the broiler until meat is tender, turning and basting from time to time with the marinade.

Shish Kebab

Cut 1¼ lb lamb (leg is the most suitable cut for this) into 2-inch cubes. Let them stand for 1½ hours in a marinade prepared in the following manner: mix together 2 tablespoons oil, the juice of 1 lemon, 1 tablespoon chilli powder (or 1 pinch paprika), 1 tablespoon finely chopped onion, 1 mashed clove of garlic, 1 pinch ginger, 1 pinch salt and 1 tea-spoon curry powder. Drain lamb and discard marinade. String the pieces of lamb on long oiled wooden or metal skewers, alternating with pieces of onion, peppers, mushroom caps and halves of tomatoes. Cook over charcoal or under the broiler until lamb is tender, turning and brushing with butter or oil.

Chinese Brochettes

Cut 1½ lb pork (loin, fillet or leg are the most suitable cuts) into 1½-inch cubes. Let them stand for 3 hours in a marinade prepared as follows: mix together 2 tablespoons soy sauce (or Worcestershire), 2 tablespoons dry Marsala, ½ teaspoon sugar and ½ clove of garlic, peeled. Drain pork, reserving the marinade. String the pieces of pork on oiled metal skewers and cook very slowly over charcoal or under the broiler until tender and cooked through, turning and brushing from time to time with the marinade.

Desserts & Drinks

Crêpes Suzette

Ingredients: for the crêpes, *2 eggs · ¾ cup flour · ¼ teaspoon salt · 1 cup milk or water · 1 tablespoon butter, melted · 1 tablespoon Cointreau or Curaçao according to taste · ½ tablespoon sugar · grated peel of ½ orange*

For the sauce: *¼ cup butter at room temperature · ½ cup sugar · the zest of 1 orange · 4 tablespoons Cointreau or Curaçao*

For frying: *2¼ tablespoons butter*

Mix the eggs with the flour and salt in a bowl. Add the milk or water gradually, and the butter. Whip the mixture thoroughly, add the Cointreau or Curaçao, sugar and grated orange peel. Wrap the butter for frying in a piece of cheesecloth. Heat a 6-inch frying pan on high heat, and quickly wipe the wrapped butter over the bottom. Pour 2 tablespoons of the

crêpe mixture into the hot pan, and move it so that the bottom of the pan is spread with a very thin layer of batter (step 1). Turn the crêpe over when the edges become slightly golden and dry, and continue cooking on reduced heat, moving the pan occasionally. Repeat the operation until all the crêpe mixture has been used (about 12 crêpes). Prepare the sauce by beating together the butter, sugar, orange or tangerine zest, orange juice, and Cointreau or Curaçao. Spread a thin layer of sauce over each crêpe. Fold crêpes in flour (step 2), arrange on a warm platter, sprinkle with sugar, pour over the hot Cointreau, and flame while serving (step 3).

Flamed Omelet

Ingredients: *6 eggs · salt · 1 tablespoon butter · 1 pot of jam (flavor according to taste)*

To garnish: *¼ cup confectioners' sugar ·*

4 slices canned pineapple, halved · 8 glacé or maraschino cherries · 1 small glass rum

Beat the eggs with a pinch of salt (step 1). Melt the butter in a heavy frying pan and pour into the beaten eggs. Reheat the pan thoroughly, pour in the eggs, and cook them on high heat (step 2), stirring with a fork or a wooden spoon, until they are completely set. Turn the omelet over, and finish cooking. When the edges are golden, spread the omelet with the jam (step 3), roll it with the help of a spoon, and slide it into a warm oval serving dish. Sprinkle generously with the sugar and, with a red hot skewer, draw a diamond pattern over the surface if desired. Arrange the pineapple slices around the omelet, and place a glacé cherry on each. Bring the rum to the boil, ignite it, and pour it over the omelet. Serve immediately.

1

2

3

Lemon Meringue Pie

Ingredients: for the pastry, *1 cup flour ·
4 tablespoons butter or margarine, cut in very
small pieces · 2–3 tablespoons iced water ·
1 pinch salt*

For the filling. *¼ cup flour · 3 tablespoons
cornstarch · ¾ cup sugar · 3 cups boiling
water · 3 egg yolks · 8 tablespoons lemon
juice · peel of 1 lemon, finely grated ·
1 pinch salt · 1 tablespoon butter*

For the meringue: *3 egg whites ·
1 teaspoon lemon juice · 5 tablespoons sugar*

Make the pastry: sift the flour on a board, make
a well in the center and add the butter or
margarine, the water and salt. Work the dough
very quickly with the fingertips, form into a
ball, cover with wax paper and refrigerate for
at least 20 minutes. Roll out the dough and
use it to line a round 8-inch pie pan. Fold over
the edge all around and pinch between 2
fingers to form a scalloped border (step 1).
Prick the dough with a fork, cover with a
circle of wax paper, then with dried beans or

rice, and bake in a hot oven (400°F) for 20
minutes. Remove the beans or rice and wax
paper, bake the case for another 5 minutes,
then remove from the oven and let cool before
using.

Make the filling: in a pan sift the flour and
cornstarch and add the sugar. Mix in the boiling water a little at a time and cook the mixture,
stirring constantly, over low heat for 15 minutes. Beat the egg yolks lightly in a bowl, add a
few tablespoons of the hot mixture to the bowl
then pour into the pan. Cook the custard over
low heat until it thickens, stirring constantly,
remove from the heat and stir in the lemon
juice and peel, salt and butter. Pour the mixture
into the baked pie case (step 2), and let cool.

Meanwhile, make the meringue: beat the
egg whites with the lemon juice and 2 tablespoons of the sugar until stiff, then fold in the
remaining sugar, beating constantly. Using a
pastry bag fitted with a star nozzle, pipe the
meringue onto the custard and pie crust (step
3). Sprinkle with sugar and bake in a moderate
oven (350°F) for 10–15 minutes or until it is
just golden. Serve cold. Serves 4–6.

Raisin Pie

In a pan mix together 3 tablespoons flour
blended with 4 tablespoons cold water, 1¼
cups raisins, softened in lukewarm water and
dried with a cloth, ¾ cup sugar, 1 pinch salt,
1¾ cups water, 1 level teaspoon each of finely
grated lemon and orange peel, 5½ tablespoons
lemon juice and 8 tablespoons orange juice.
Bring the mixture slowly to a boil and cook for
4–5 minutes or until it thickens. Let cool and
pour into a 9-inch uncooked pie shell made as
above, using 1¼ cups flour, ¼ cup butter or
margarine, 3 tablespoons iced water and 1
pinch salt. With the leftover dough cuttings,
make strips to cover the filling in a lattice
pattern. Bake the pie in a hot oven (400°F) for
10 minutes, lower the heat to moderately hot
(375°F) and continue baking for 30–35
minutes. Serve cold. Serves 4–6.

Cherry Torte

Ingredients: for the sandtorte pastry,
*1½ cups flour · ¾ cup butter or margarine, cut
in small pieces · 4 tablespoons sugar ·
2 egg yolks · 1 tablespoon Marsala ·
peel of 1 lemon, finely grated ·
1 pinch salt*

For the topping: *jam to taste ·
4 oz glacé cherries*

Sift the flour on a board, make a well in the center and add the butter or margarine, the sugar, egg yolks, Marsala, lemon peel and salt. Work the dough quickly, shape into a ball, cover with wax paper and refrigerate for ½ hour. Roll out ⅔ of the dough in a thin sheet and use it to line a round 9-inch buttered pie pan (step 1). With some of the remaining dough make a scalloped border all round. Spread the base of the torte with jam (step 2) and garnish with star and half moon shapes cut from the remaining dough (step 3), and with the cherries.

Bake the torte in a hot oven (400°F) for about 30 minutes until the pastry is golden. Remove from the oven and let cool. This torte is best eaten after 24 hours. Serves 6–8.

Tarte Française

Make the pastry (see p.136) using ¾ cup flour, 3 tablespoons butter, 1–2 tablespoons iced water and 1 pinch salt, and let stand for 20 minutes. Line a round 7-inch pie pan with the dough and prick it with a fork. Peel and core 1 lb apples, halve them and slice them very finely.

Place the apple slices on the dough in a circle, working from the center outwards, sprinkle with sugar and bake in a hot oven (400°F) for about 30 minutes until the pastry is golden and the apples are tender. Brush with apricot jam or other jam to taste and serve hot or cold. Serves 6.

French Apple Tart

Melt 3 tablespoons butter in an 8-inch pie pan or frying pan, add 1 lb apples, peeled and finely sliced, and 2 tablespoons sugar. Sauté the mixture for a few minutes. Prepare pastry as above, using ¾ cup flour, 3 tablespoons butter and 1 pinch salt. Roll out thinly and use it to cover the apple mixture. Bake the tart in a hot oven (400°F) until the pastry is golden and the apples are tender when pierced with a skewer. Serve hot or cold.

1

2

3

Plum Cake

Ingredients: $\frac{1}{2}$ cup butter or margarine, softened · $\frac{1}{2}$ cup sugar · 2 eggs · 1 egg yolk · $\frac{1}{2}$ cup raisins, softened in lukewarm water, and sprinkled with flour · 2 tablespoons candied peel, sliced · 2 tablespoons rum · peel of 1 lemon, finely grated · $\frac{2}{3}$ cup sifted flour

In a bowl beat the butter or margarine with the sugar until the mixture is fluffy (step 1) and add the eggs and egg yolk one at a time, the raisins, candied peel, rum, lemon peel and flour and mix well. Line a plum cake mold with buttered wax paper (step 2), spoon in the mixture (step 3) and bake the cake in a very hot oven (450°F) for 5 minutes. Lower the heat to moderate (350°F) and bake the cake for a further 40 minutes or until a crust has formed on top.

Dundee Cake

Soften $\frac{3}{4}$ cup raisins in lukewarm water. Soak $\frac{3}{4}$ cup almonds in boiling water for a few minutes, drain and peel. Chop half the almonds and split the remaining ones in half. In a large bowl beat $\frac{3}{4}$ cup softened butter or margarine with $\frac{3}{4}$ cup sugar until the mixture is fluffy and add 4 eggs, one at a time, alternating with 1 cup flour sifted with 1 pinch salt. In another bowl mix the raisins, dried with a cloth, $2\frac{1}{2}$ tablespoons candied orange peel, chopped, 1 generous tablespoon flour, the chopped almonds, the finely grated peel of 1 orange, and 1 level teaspoon bicarbonate of soda blended with 1 teaspoon milk. Add this mixture to the butter and sugar mixture. Line a deep 12-inch round cake pan with buttered wax paper, spoon in the mixture and cover with the split almonds in a decorative circular pattern. Bake the cake in a moderate oven (350°F) for about 2 hours, or until cooked (a skewer inserted into the center of the cake should come out clean). Cover the almonds with aluminum foil if they brown. Remove the cake from the oven, let stand 30 minutes, then unmold. Let cool completely on a rack before slicing. Dundee cake always improves if kept before eating.

Panettone

Soften 2 tablespoons raisins in lukewarm water. In a bowl beat 2 egg yolks with 4 tablespoons sugar until the mixture is fluffy and add 4 tablespoons softened butter or margarine, and alternately, a little at a time, $1\frac{1}{4}$ cups flour sifted with 1 tablespoon baking powder, and $\frac{1}{2}$ cup milk. Stir in $\frac{1}{2}$ cup Marsala, the raisins, sprinkled with flour, 2 tablespoons candied peel, cut in thin strips, and 1 tablespoon pine nuts (optional). Fold in 2 egg whites, beaten until stiff. Butter a cake mold, dust with flour, and spoon in the mixture. Bake the cake in a moderate oven (350°F) for about 1 hour or until golden on top. Remove the cake from the oven, let stand 30 minutes, unmold, and let cool on a wire rack.

1   2   3

Apple Strudel

Ingredients: for the pastry, *1¼ cups flour •*
1 egg • 1 tablespoon sugar • 1 pinch salt •
2 tablespoons butter or margarine •
lukewarm water

For the filling: *2 tablespoons raisins •*
2 tablespoons almonds • 1½ lb apples •
3 tablespoons breadcrumbs •
2½ tablespoons butter or margarine •
grated lemon peel • a few tablespoons jam •
4 tablespoons sugar

To finish: *2 tablespoons butter or margarine,*
melted • a few tablespoons confectioners' sugar

Sift the flour on a board, make a well in the
center and add the egg, sugar, salt, the butter
or margarine, melted over very low heat with
1–2 tablespoons water, and enough lukewarm

water to obtain a fairly soft dough. Work the
dough quickly and vigorously, form into a ball,
cover with a cloth and let stand for 30 minutes.
Soak the raisins in lukewarm water for 20
minutes, drain and dry. Soak the almonds in
boiling water for a few minutes, drain, peel and
cut into thin slivers. Peel and core the apples
and slice very finely. Sauté the breadcrumbs in
half the butter or margarine until golden, then
let them stand in the pan. Put the dough on a
large floured cloth, roll out thinly with a
floured rolling pin and spread it gently over the
back of the hands, pulling and stretching it
carefully until it is paper thin and transparent
(step 1). Lay it out flat on the cloth, brush with
the remaining butter or margarine, melted, and
cover with the apple slices, raisins, almonds,
breadcrumbs and lemon peel (step 2). Dot with
spoonfuls of the jam and sugar, leaving a

border of dough all around. Roll up the
strudel using the cloth, being careful not to
touch the dough with the hands (step 3), and
press the edges together so that the filling does
not come out during cooking. Still holding it
by the cloth, put the strudel on a buttered
cookie sheet or a large buttered ovenproof pan,
brush with melted butter or margarine and
bake in a moderate oven (350°F) for 40–50
minutes. Remove from the oven and let stand
for 10 minutes. Transfer to a serving platter
and dust with confectioners' sugar. The
strudel can be served hot or cold.

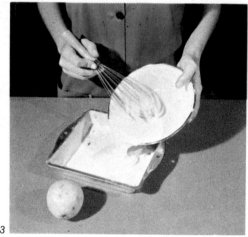

1   2   3

Margherita

Ingredients: *¼ cup butter · 6 eggs · ¾ cup sugar · ½ cup flour · 4 tablespoons cornstarch · 2 teaspoons baking powder (optional) · finely grated peel of 1 lemon · confectioners' sugar*

Melt the butter over very low heat and let cool. Put the egg yolks (reserving the whites) and sugar in a flameproof bowl, put the bowl in a pan containing hot water and beat the mixture with a wire whip until it is light and fluffy and leaves a ribbon trail when the whip is lifted (step 1). Remove the bowl from the pan of hot water and continue beating until the mixture is cold. Mix in a little at a time the flour sifted with the cornstarch and baking powder, if using, the melted butter (discarding the liquid formed during cooling) and the lemon peel. Beat the reserved egg whites until stiff and fold them gently into the mixture (step 2). Butter a square cake pan and dust with flour. Pour in

the mixture (step 3) and bake in a moderate oven (350°F) for about 40 minutes or until cooked (the top will spring back when lightly touched with the fingertip). Dust with confectioners' sugar before serving.

Pan di Spagna

In a bowl standing in a bain-marie or on the top of a double boiler (not touching the water), mix ½ cup sugar with 4 eggs, the finely grated peel of 1 lemon and a pinch of salt. Beat the mixture gently with a wire whip until it begins to swell and leave a ribbon trail, remove the pan from the heat and continue beating until it thickens. Slowly add ¼ cup flour, sifted with 2½ tablespoons potato starch, and 1 tablespoon melted butter. Pour into a deep 10-inch cake pan, lightly buttered and floured, and bake in a moderate oven (350°F) for 20–25 minutes.

Italian Pandoro

In a bowl work ¾ cup butter or margarine, kept at room temperature for 10 minutes. Add 4 egg yolks, reserving the whites, one at a time and beat the mixture until light and fluffy. Stir in 7 tablespoons sugar, 1 tablespoon brandy, a pinch of salt, the juice of ½ lemon, and, a little at a time, ¾ cup each of flour and potato starch, sifted together with ¼ oz vanilla sugar. Beat the mixture for 15 minutes and fold in the egg whites, beaten until stiff, and 1 teaspoon baking powder. Pour the mixture into a deep cake pan, lightly buttered and floured, so that it half fills the mold. Bake the cake in a hot oven (400°F) for about 40 minutes or until cooked (see above), remove from the oven and let stand for 10 minutes. Unmold onto a wire rack and dust the pandoro with confectioners' sugar before serving.

Apple Charlotte

Ingredients: *2½ lb firm apples · ¾ cup butter or margarine · 2 tablespoons potato starch · 4 tablespoons sugar · 1 teaspoon cinnamon · ¼ oz vanilla sugar · 1½ cups apricot jam · 1½ lb white sandwich bread, or ladyfingers*

To serve: *sugar · 1–2 glasses rum*

Peel, core and quarter the apples. Put them in a pan with 2 tablespoons of the butter and cook until puréed, stirring occasionally with a wooden spoon. Add the starch, blended with a little water, the sugar, cinnamon and vanilla sugar and continue cooking the mixture over high heat until it is a thick purée. Stir in 3 tablespoons of the apricot jam and let the mixture cool completely. Trim the crust off the bread slices, cut 6 slices into triangles and halve the other slices. Melt the remaining butter or margarine in a pan and dip the slices quickly into it. Line a high-sided buttered mold or charlotte mold with some of the bread slices, using the triangles for the bottom and overlapping the rectangles around the sides (step 1). Brush the bread slices with the remaining apricot jam, pour in the apple purée (step 2) and cover with a layer of bread slices. Cook the charlotte in a hot oven (400°F) for about 1 hour. Unmold on a warm serving platter and sprinkle with sugar (step 3). Heat the rum, pour it on the charlotte and flame.

Apple Pie Maison

Peel, core and slice 3 apples. Put the slices in a shallow pan with 1 piece cinnamon, crushed, 2½ tablespoons raisins, softened in lukewarm water and dried, and 2 tablespoons water. Cover the pan and cook the mixture over low heat until the apples are tender, shaking the pan occasionally. On a board sift 1½ cups flour with 1 teaspoon baking powder, make a well in the center and add 7 tablespoons butter, cut into small pieces, 7 tablespoons sugar, and 1 egg yolk. Work the dough quickly, form it into a ball, cover with wax paper and refrigerate for ½ hour. Roll out the dough to a 1-inch thickness and cut into two 10-inch circles. Butter a 10-inch high-sided pie pan, line it with one circle, add the cooked apples and cover with the other circle. Cook the pie in a moderate oven (350°F) for 45 minutes or until golden.

1   2   3

Iced Chestnut Cake

Ingredients: *2 lb chestnuts · 3 cups milk · 4 tablespoons sugar · ¼ vanilla bean · pinch of salt · 4 tablespoons softened butter or margarine · 2 tablespoons sweetened cocoa powder · rum · 3 oz macaroons*

To decorate: *2 tablespoons almonds, toasted and chopped · ½ cup whipped cream · marron glacé (optional)*

Peel the chestnuts (step 1), soak in boiling water for 5 minutes and remove the skin with a sharp knife. Bring the milk, sugar, vanilla bean and salt to a boil, remove the vanilla and add the chestnuts. Cook the mixture over low heat for about 1 hour, then work through a sieve and return to the pan. Cook over moderate heat, stirring constantly, until it thickens, remove from the heat and let cool. Stir in the butter or margarine, cocoa, and rum to taste and beat the mixture until all the ingredients are well blended. Line a 9-inch high-sided mold or charlotte mold with dampened cheesecloth, pour in one third of the mixture, add a layer of macaroons soaked in rum (step 2), cover with another third of chestnut mixture, then a layer of macaroons soaked in rum, and finally the remaining chestnut mixture. Refrigerate the cake for a few hours, or overnight, unmold on a serving platter and carefully remove the cheesecloth (step 3).

Press the chopped almonds around the side of the cake and top with whipped cream, and the marron glacé if liked.

Mont Blanc

Prepare 2 lb chestnuts as above and put in a pan with 1 quart hot milk and 1 vanilla bean. Cook the mixture over low heat for about 1 hour, then remove vanilla bean and work through a sieve. Make a syrup by dissolving 1¼ cups sugar and 1 teaspoon vanilla extract in 9 tablespoons water, then boiling until a teaspoon of the mixture dropped in cold water forms a soft ball. Stir the syrup into the chestnut mixture.

Using a pastry bag fitted with a large nozzle, pipe the mixture onto a serving platter, shaping into a dome, and cover with stiffly whipped cream.

1

2

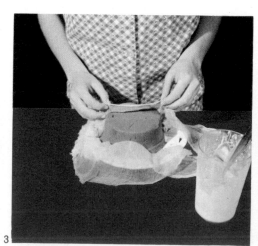

3

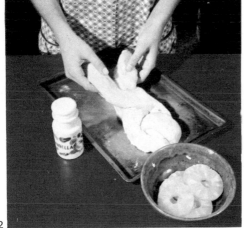

1   2   3

Stuffed Plait

Ingredients: for the pastry, *6–7 tablespoons milk · 2 tablespoons sugar · 1 level teaspoon salt · 2 tablespoons butter or margarine, melted · ½ oz brewer's yeast or baking powder · 2 tablespoons lukewarm water · 1 egg, beaten · 1⅓ cups flour, sifted*

For the filling: *melted butter · 3–4 slices pineapple or other fruit, drained and chopped · a few tablespoons sugar · cinnamon to taste*

To finish: *1 egg yolk, beaten with a little water and sugar · candied peel and glacé cherries*

To make the pastry: heat the milk, add the sugar, salt and butter or margarine and mix until all the ingredients have dissolved together. Let the mixture cool. Mix the yeast or baking powder in the lukewarm water, stir in the milk mixture, add the beaten egg and work in the flour. Work the dough, which should be soft and not too dry, for 10 minutes, put in a buttered bowl, cover with a cloth and let stand in a warm place until it has doubled in volume. Divide the dough into three parts and roll each part into a 15×15 inch rectangle. Brush the rectangles with melted butter and cover with a little pineapple or other fruit (step 1), sugar and cinnamon. Fold in half lengthwise, dampen the edges with water and pinch together securely. On a buttered cookie sheet, lightly dusted with flour, plait the filled strips (step 2). Cover and let stand until plait has doubled in volume. Brush with beaten egg, dot with peel and cherries (step 3), and bake in a moderate oven (350°F) for about 30 minutes.

Kugelhopf

Dissolve ½ oz brewer's yeast or baking powder in 8 tablespoons lukewarm milk. Sift 1½ cups flour into a large bowl, make a well in the center and add the yeast mixture, 4 eggs, lightly beaten with 4 tablespoons sugar, and a little finely grated lemon peel. Mix flour slowly into liquid ingredients and work dough. Cover and let stand until it has doubled in volume. Put on a floured board, flatten and cover with softened butter, cut into small pieces, raisins, softened in lukewarm water and dried, and almonds, peeled and chopped. Work the dough again, put it in a buttered kugelhopf mold and let stand until it has doubled in volume. Bake in a moderate oven (350°F) for about 1 hour. Unmold and dust with confectioners' sugar.

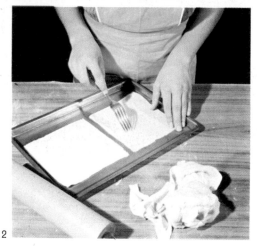

1 2 3

Mille-Feuille

Ingredients: *1¼ lb puff pastry (homemade or frozen)*

For the zabaglione custard: *4 egg yolks · 4 tablespoons sugar · ¾ cup Marsala*

To finish: *confectioners' sugar*

Roll out the puff pastry very thinly between two sheets of wax paper and cut into 4 rectangles 7×13 inches (step 1). Lay the dough on dampened cookie sheets and prick with a fork (step 2) and bake in a very hot oven (425°F) for 10–15 minutes, until golden and crisp. Remove from the oven and let cool. Meanwhile, prepare the custard following the basic zabaglione recipe (see p.39), using the egg yolks, sugar and Marsala, and let cool. Put 1 rectangle of pastry on a serving platter, cover with

custard, cover with another rectangle of pastry and continue in this manner ending with the last pastry rectangle (step 3). Sprinkle with confectioners' sugar before serving.

The zabaglione may be substituted by crème pâtissière (see p.155), flavored with chocolate, or by apple purée. Serves 6.

Pithiviers

Ingredients: *1 lb puff pastry (homemade or frozen)*

For the frangipane cream: *2 egg yolks · 2½ tablespoons sugar · 2¼ tablespoons powdered almonds · 2 tablespoons flour · 1 cup milk*

Prepare the frangipane cream: mix the egg yolks with the sugar, powdered almonds and

flour. Bring 1 cup milk to a boil and stir a little of it into the egg mixture. Stir the mixture for a few minutes, pour in a little more milk then pour the mixture into remaining hot milk.

Heat the cream over low heat, stirring constantly with a wire whip until it begins to boil, boil for a few minutes and let cool. Stir in a few drops almond extract. Roll out the puff pastry and cut into two 8-inch circles, reserving the remaining dough. Lay one of the circles on a dampened cookie sheet, cover with frangipane cream and then with the second circle. Roll out the remaining dough to form a slightly larger circle and use it to cover the cake, sealing the edges together. Brush the pastry with beaten egg and with a sharp knife make light incisions into the dough in a lattice pattern. Bake in a very hot oven (425°F) for about 30 minutes until golden and crisp.

Profiteroles

Ingredients: for the choux pastry, *1 cup water · ½ cup butter or margarine · pinch of salt · ¾ cup sifted flour · 4 eggs*

For the filling: *2 cups heavy cream, whipped · 2 tablespoons sugar*

To serve: *chocolate sauce (see p.158)*

Prepare the pastry: bring the water, butter or margarine and salt to a boil, remove the pan from the heat and pour in the flour all at once, stirring constantly. Return the pan to the heat, stirring constantly, and cook for 5 minutes or until the mixture leaves the sides of the pan. Transfer the mixture to a bowl, let cool and add the eggs one at a time, beating vigorously after each addition. Beat the mixture until it forms small bubbles and is glossy. Using an icing pump or pastry bag fitted with a large plain nozzle, pipe out the mixture in walnut-sized balls onto a dampened cookie sheet, leaving a 1-inch space between the balls (step 1). Bake the profiteroles in a hot oven (400°F) for 20 minutes, without opening the oven door, until insides of profiteroles are empty and dry. Remove them from the oven, take off cookie sheet and prick each one with a skewer to allow steam to escape; let cool on a wire rack. Using a pair of scissors, cut them open on one side and fill with the whipped cream sweetened with the sugar (step 2). Arrange profiteroles in a pyramid shape on a serving platter and cover with chocolate sauce (step 3).

Croquembouche

Defrost frozen puff pastry and roll out into a 15-inch circle, 3 inches thick. Place the circle on dampened wax paper on a cookie sheet, and bake in a very hot oven (425°F) for 15–20 minutes or until golden and crisp. Remove from oven and allow to cool. Prepare choux pastry as for Profiteroles above, using half the quantities. Fill profiteroles with crème pâtissière (see p.155 and halve the quantities). Dissolve ¾ cup sugar slowly in 10 tablespoons water, bring to a boil and cook the mixture until it caramelizes. Remove from heat, dip the profiteroles quickly in the caramel (using cooking tongs) and set them in a pyramid shape on the pastry circle.

Eclairs

Prepare choux pastry as for Profiteroles above. Pipe in 3-inch strips onto a dampened cookie sheet. Brush with beaten egg; bake in hot oven (400°F) for about 25 minutes or until light and golden. Remove the éclairs from the oven, take off cookie sheet and prick each one with a skewer; let cool on a wire rack then cut open on one side. Fill with crème pâtissière (see p.155) flavored with vanilla, chocolate or coffee, or with sweetened whipped cream. Prepare icing: sift ½ cup confectioner's sugar in a bowl and add a few drops lemon juice and enough cold water to obtain a thick but spreading paste. Add a few drops flavoring to taste. Heat the icing in a bain-marie; dip éclairs quickly into icing and leave to set.

1

2

3

1 2 3

Savarin

Ingredients: ½ oz brewer's yeast ·
8 tablespoons lukewarm milk · 1½ cups flour ·
4 eggs · ½ teaspoon salt · 1 tablespoon sugar ·
½ cup softened butter

For the syrup: ¾ cup sugar · 2 cups water ·
10 tablespoons rum, kirsch or other liqueur ·

To finish: ¾ cup apricot jam · 2 tablespoons
sugar · ¾ cup whipped cream, lightly
sweetened · apricots in syrup · glacé cherries

Dissolve the yeast in the warm milk. Sift the
flour into a bowl, make a well in the center and
add the yeast mixture and the eggs, lightly
beaten. Work the flour into the liquid ingredients a little at a time and lift up and beat the
dough, which should be soft and a little sticky,
repeatedly against the sides of the bowl (step 1).

Cover the dough with a light cloth and let stand
in a warm place for about 1 hour or until it has
doubled in volume. Put the dough on a floured
board, flatten it, sprinkle with the salt and
sugar and cover with the butter. Work the
dough for a few moments, lifting it and slapping
it against the sides of the bowl, put in a
buttered savarin mold (step 2), and let stand
until it has doubled in volume. Bake the
savarin in a hot oven (400°F) for 10 minutes,
reduce the heat to moderate (350°F) and continue cooking for about 30 minutes or until
risen and golden. Remove from the oven,
unmold onto a wire rack placed on a plate,
and let cool. Make the syrup: dissolve the sugar
slowly in the water, bring to a boil and cook
over high heat for 5 minutes; remove from the
heat. Stir in the rum or other liqueur, and pour
the syrup on the savarin, spooning it over until

all the syrup has been absorbed. Work the
apricot jam through a sieve, heat with the
sugar until melted and brush over the savarin
(step 3). Fill the center of the savarin with
lightly sweetened whipped cream and surround it with apricot halves, filled with
whipped cream and topped with cherries.

Mirlitons

Make pastry (see p.136) to line 8 tartlet molds,
using ¾ cup flour, 3 tablespoons butter, 1–2
tablespoons iced water and 1 pinch salt. In a
bowl mix 2 eggs with 4 tablespoons apricot
jam, 4 tablespoons almonds, very finely
crushed, 2 tablespoons sugar and 2 tablespoons flour. Spoon the mixture into the tartlet
molds and decorate with almonds. Bake in a
moderate oven (350°F) for 10–15 minutes.

Iced Mocha Cake

Ingredients: for the zabaglione custard,
*4 egg yolks · 4 tablespoons sugar ·
1 cup Marsala*

For the mocha cream: *1¼ cups softened
butter or margarine · ¾ cup confectioners'
sugar · ½ cup strong coffee · 3 egg yolks*

For the filling: *about ¾ lb pan di Spagna (see
p.140), or sponge cake · Marsala*

Prepare the zabaglione custard (see p.155), with
the egg yolks, sugar and Marsala and let cool.
Meanwhile make the mocha cream: beat the
butter or margarine until light and fluffy, beat
in the sugar and add the coffee drop by drop
and the egg yolks one by one. Butter a deep
9-inch round mold and line with some of the
pan di Spagna or sponge cake, cut into slices
and dipped in Marsala. Fill the mold with
alternate layers of mocha cream (step 1),
reserving a little for decoration, pan di Spagna
slices sprinkled with Marsala and zabaglione
custard. End with a layer of pan di Spagna and
cover the cake with a lid and a weight (step 2).
Refrigerate for at least 12 hours, then unmold
carefully onto a serving platter. Dust the sides
of the cake with sifted cocoa powder. Using an
icing pump or a pastry bag fitted with a star
nozzle, pipe out mocha cream rosettes on the
cake (step 3). Serves 8.

Zuppa Inglese

Prepare a crème pâtissière (see p.155) and let
cool. Stir in peeled chopped pine nuts and
almonds, and raisins softened in lukewarm
water and dried, to taste, and a few small
pieces of candied peel. Divide the cream in two
and add 1 tablespoon cocoa powder to one half.
Make a fruit syrup: work 3–4 tablespoons
apricot or peach jam through a sieve and dilute
with a little Cognac, mixing well. In an ovenproof metal dish, make alternate layers of plain
crème pâtissière, fruit syrup and cocoa crème
pâtissière, using slices of pan di Spagna,
sprinkled with liqueur to taste, between each
different layer and at the top and bottom of the
mold. Beat 4 egg whites until stiff and beat in
two tablespoons sugar. Spread or pipe the
mixture all over the cake and bake in a hot
oven (400°F) for a few minutes. Serves 6–8.

1   2   3

Saint-Honoré

Ingredients: *for the base, 4 tablespoons butter or margarine, melted and cooled · 6 eggs, separated · 6½ tablespoons sugar · ¾ cup flour · ¼ oz vanilla sugar · 1 teaspoon baking powder · maraschino · crème pâtissière (see p.155 and halve quantities) · 1 cup whipped cream · pan di Spagna (see p.140) · 6–8 profiteroles (see p.145) · zabaglione (see p.155)*

For the Saint-Honoré cream: ½ oz gelatin · 2 egg yolks · ½ cup sugar · 2 tablespoons flour · 1 cup milk · ¼ oz vanilla sugar · 3 egg whites · 1½ cups whipped cream · 2 teaspoons cocoa powder

For the caramel: 3 tablespoons sugar · water

Make the pastry base: melt the butter or margarine over moderate heat and let cool. In a bowl beat the egg yolks, reserving the whites, with the sugar for 15 minutes and add, a little at a time, the flour sifted with the vanilla sugar and baking powder. Fold the egg whites, beaten until stiff, and the melted fat gently into the mixture with a spatula. Spoon the mixture into a 12-inch cake pan, buttered and dusted with flour (step 1), and cook in a moderate oven (350°F) for 35–40 minutes.

Meanwhile, make the crème pâtissière, profiteroles (step 2), and zabaglione. Prepare the Saint-Honoré cream: soften the gelatin in cold water. Beat the egg yolks with the sugar and stir in the flour and milk. Cook the cream, stirring constantly, over very low heat until it thickens but does not boil. Stir in the gelatin, remove from the heat, add the vanilla sugar and fold in the egg whites, beaten until stiff. Let cool and fold in ⅔ of the whipped cream. Divide the mixture into two parts and stir the sifted cocoa into one half. Slice the cake into 2 or 3 layers, sprinkle them generously with maraschino liqueur and cover with crème patissière, mixed with some of the cream. Brush cake with remaining whipped cream and press pan di Spagna against it. Using a pastry bag fitted with a large nozzle, make large rosettes of plain Saint-Honoré cream on top of cake, alternating with chocolate Saint-Honoré cream. Fill profiteroles with zabaglione, dip in caramel, made by dissolving the sugar slowly in the water, then cooking until golden, and set around top of cake (step 3). Serves 6–8.

Chocolate Cake

Ingredients: *3 eggs, separated · ¾ cup sugar · 4 tablespoons butter or margarine, melted · 5 tablespoons potato starch · 5 tablespoons flour · 5 tablespoons cocoa powder · ¼ oz baking powder · ¼ oz vanilla sugar · ¼ cup milk · 1 pinch salt*

For the icing: 2 egg whites · 1½ cups sugar · ¼ oz vanilla sugar · 6 tablespoons water

In a bowl beat the egg yolks, reserving the whites, with the sugar, add the butter or margarine, the starch sifted with the flour, cocoa, baking powder, vanilla sugar, milk and salt and fold in the egg whites, beaten until stiff. Pour the mixture into a deep 12-inch cake mold, buttered and dusted with flour, and bake in a moderate oven (350°F) for 45 minutes or until cooked (when a skewer inserted in the center comes out clean). Remove from the oven, let cool and slice into 2 or 3 layers (step 1).

Make the icing: put the egg whites, sugar, vanilla sugar and water in a bain-marie of boiling water or in the top of a double boiler and beat the mixture with an electric or rotary beater for 7–8 minutes or until stiff (step 2). Ice the top of each layer of the cake immediately and thickly, reassemble cake, making little peaks on the top layer with a fork (step 3). Let the cake stand for a few hours before serving.

Butter Icing

Sift ¾ cup confectioners' sugar with ¼ oz vanilla sugar, add 4 tablespoons butter or margarine at room temperature and 3 tablespoons milk or cream and beat the mixture until fluffy. The icing may be used as it is or may be flavored with chocolate, melted in a bain-marie or in the top of a double boiler, or with lemon or orange juice instead of milk and vanilla sugar.

Quick White Icing

In a bowl put 2 tablespoons hot milk, add 1 knob of butter and stir it until melted. Stir in ¾ cup confectioners' sugar, a little at a time, until thick enough to spread. Add a few drops of rum or vanilla extract to taste. The icing may be colored with fruit juice or commercial coloring, if desired.

Coffee Icing

Make the white icing as for the chocolate cake above, halving the quantities, and adding some very strong diluted instant coffee instead of water.

Chocolate Icing

Make a white icing as above, halving the quantities. Stir in 2 tablespoons chocolate, melted in a bain-marie or in the top of a double boiler.

1   2   3

Zuccotto

Ingredients: *6 oz pan di Spagna (see p.140) or sponge cake, sliced into rectangles · liqueur to taste · 2 cups heavy cream · 3 tablespoons confectioners' sugar · ½ oz gelatin, softened in a little warm water · 4 tablespoons candied peel, cut into small pieces · 4 tablespoons chocolate, cut into small pieces · 2 tablespoons cocoa*

For the chocolate syrup: 1 tablespoon butter · 1 heaped tablespoon unsweetened cocoa powder · 2½ tablespoons water · 4 tablespoons sugar

Make the chocolate syrup: heat the butter over low heat, add the cocoa and stir until well blended. Add the water and sugar and cook the syrup, stirring constantly, for 3–4 minutes. Dip the pan di Spagna slices in the liqueur and use them to line a 2-quart bowl (step 1) reserving some to cover. Whip the cream until stiff and fold in the sugar and gelatin gently. Divide the whipped cream into two parts and stir the chocolate syrup gently and gradually into one half (step 2). Pour the chocolate cream into the lined bowl, sprinkle with half the candied peel and chocolate pieces and pour in gently the remaining whipped cream, mixed with the remaining fruit and chocolate (step 3). Cover with pan di Spagna slices and refrigerate the zuccotto for at least 4–5 hours. Unmold and decorate to taste. Serves 6.

Iced Raspberry Mold

Soften 1 oz gelatin in a little cold water. Stir the gelatin into 2 cups boiling water, melt, stirring constantly, and let cool. Work 1 lb raspberries through a fine sieve and through a cheese-cloth. Stir in the juice of 1 lemon and 1 cup sugar. Stir the gelatin mixture into the fruit syrup, pour the mixture into a high-sided round mold and refrigerate 2 or 3 hours. Unmold before serving. Strawberries, blueberries, red or black currants and cherries can also be used. Serves 6.

Magic Square

In a bowl beat 6 egg yolks with ¾ cup confectioners' sugar until the mixture is light and fluffy. Stir in ¾ lb chocolate, melted with 3 tablespoons milk in a bain-marie or in the top of a double boiler, and ¾ cup butter or margarine at room temperature, and fold in 6 egg whites, beaten until stiff. Stir the mixture until well blended and creamy. Line a 10-inch square mold with a slightly dampened cheese-cloth and place a layer of ladyfingers sprinkled with rum on the bottom. Pour in half the chocolate cream, place another layer of lady-fingers on top, then add another layer of cream and end with a layer of ladyfingers, sprinkled with rum. Refrigerate the dessert for at least 12 hours, unmold onto a serving platter and remove the cheesecloth just before serving.

Decorate the sides with ladyfingers and the top with whipped cream if liked.

Tropical Cake

Ingredients: for the cake, $\frac{1}{4}$ cup butter •
6 eggs • $6\frac{1}{2}$ tablespoons sugar • $\frac{1}{2}$ cup flour •
6 tablespoons cornstarch • 2 teaspoons baking
powder (optional) • finely grated peel of 1 lemon

For the filling: 6 ripe bananas • 3 oranges •
4 single measures rum or Cognac •
4–5 tablespoons confectioners' sugar •
1 lb walnuts • $1\frac{1}{2}$ cups heavy cream, whipped

Make the cake following the recipe for
Margherita (see p.140). Pour into a deep cake
pan, buttered and lightly dusted with flour,
and cook in a moderate oven (350°F) for about
40 minutes or until cooked (the top will spring
back when lightly touched with the fingertip).
Remove from the oven, unmold onto a wire
rack and let cool. Meanwhile, make the filling:
peel 5 bananas, slice them and put in a bowl
with the juice of 1 orange, 2 measures rum
or Cognac and 2 tablespoons confectioners'
sugar for at least 1 hour. Shell the walnuts and
chop coarsely, reserving about 16 halves for
the decoration. Mix the juice of the remaining
oranges with the remaining rum. Slice the
cake into three layers, put the first layer on a
round serving platter and soak with some of
the orange juice and rum mixture (step 1).
Cover with $\frac{1}{3}$ of the whipped cream, add a
layer of half the drained banana slices and
sprinkle with $\frac{1}{2}$ the chopped walnuts. Repeat
these layers once more (step 2), topping them
with the third layer of cake, soaked in orange
juice and rum. Cover with whipped cream, add
rings of banana slices (step 3), and walnuts.

Candied Fruit Cake

In a bowl beat 5 egg yolks with $\frac{3}{4}$ cup sugar
until the mixture is fluffy and stir in $6\frac{1}{2}$ tablespoons peeled almonds, finely chopped, 4
tablespoons raisins, softened in lukewarm
water and dried, 4 tablespoons candied peel
and glacé cherries, cut into thin strips,
$\frac{1}{4}$ oz vanilla sugar, $\frac{1}{2}$ teaspoon baking powder,
5 oz crisp sweet biscuits, pounded finely and
6 tablespoons rum. Fold in 5 egg whites, whipped. Pour into a buttered 10-inch cake pan
and bake in a moderate oven (350°F) for about
1 hour. Unmold and slice into 3 layers. Sprinkle
each layer with rum, cover with heavy cream
and reassemble cake.

1   2   3

Strawberry Bombe

Ingredients: *4 cups vanilla ice cream · 2 cups strawberry ice cream*

To serve: *¼ lb strawberries · a few tablespoons kirsch · sugar*

Put a 3-lb bombe mold with a lid into the freezer or freezing compartment of the refrigerator until very cold, remove and line with 1 inch of vanilla ice cream (step 1). If the ice cream softens, return the mold to the freezer for a few minutes. Fill the mold with strawberry ice cream, using a spoon and patting down tightly so that there are no air pockets (step 2), and cover the top with a piece of buttered wax paper. Add the bombe lid (step 3) and seal the top by covering with a thin layer of butter. Freeze the mold for 3–4 hours. Dip the mold quickly in hot water, overturn on a serving platter. If liked, surround the bombe with strawberries, soaked in kirsch and sugar. Serve immediately. Serves 8–10.

Pineapple Bombe

Use lemon ice cream or sherbet instead of vanilla ice cream and fill the center with pineapple ice cream.

Pineapple and Orange Bombe

Use pineapple ice cream instead of vanilla ice cream and fill the center with orange sherbet.

Raspberry Bombe

Use pistachio ice cream instead of vanilla ice cream and fill the center with raspberry sherbet.

Hazelnut Bombe

Use orange sherbet instead of vanilla ice cream and fill with hazelnut ice cream.

Chocolate Parfait

Proceed as for Coffee Parfait but instead of the coffee stir in 2 tablespoons chocolate, melted with 2 tablespoons milk. Cool the cream, stirring constantly, over crushed ice and fold in 1 cup whipped cream. Pour the mixture into a wetted mold, close securely and freeze.

Coffee Parfait

In a small pan bring ¾ cup sugar and 3 tablespoons water to a boil and cook over low heat for 8–10 minutes or until the mixture forms a thread from a teaspoon dipped into it. Remove from the heat, stir in 4 egg yolks beaten with 1 teaspoon water, a little at a time, and return to the heat. Cook the cream over low heat, stirring constantly, until it thickens but does not boil and stir in 2 teaspoons instant coffee diluted in 1 teaspoon warm water. Strain the cream through a sieve and put in a bowl placed into another bowl of crushed ice. Stir until cool, fold in 1 cup whipped cream and pour the mixture into a wetted mold. Cover and freeze. Unmold by dipping quickly in hot water.

1

2

3

Striped Bavaroise

Ingredients: *2 packages vanilla pudding · 1 package chocolate pudding · 1 package strawberry pudding*

To decorate: *mixed fruit*

Prepare the puddings following package instructions (step 1). Do not allow to set. Pour half the vanilla pudding into a mold, moistened with water or liqueur, and refrigerate the mold until the mixture is set. Add the chocolate pudding (step 2), refrigerate the mold until set, add the remaining vanilla pudding and refrigerate the mold until set. End with the strawberry pudding and refrigerate the mold for a few hours. Unmold on a serving platter (step 3) and surround with mixed fruit. Serves 8.

Apricot Coupe

Prepare 1 package vanilla pudding following the instructions on the package. Stir in canned apricots to taste, drained and coarsely chopped. Line 4 Champagne glasses or tall glasses with sliced pan di Spagna (see p.140) or ladyfingers, spoon in the pudding and refrigerate until set. Before serving, decorate each with 1 glacé cherry surrounded by piped whipped cream.

Banana Coupe

Prepare 1 package vanilla pudding following the instructions on the package, or a crème pâtissière (see p.155). Line 4 Champagne or tall glasses with banana slices, macerated in liqueur and sugar to taste, pour in the pudding and refrigerate until set. Garnish with whipped cream, banana slices and chopped almonds before serving.

Fruit Coupe

Prepare a crème pâtissière (see p.155), adding grated orange peel instead of lemon peel, and 2 tablespoons curaçao or orange juice. Macerate strawberries or raspberries in a little curaçao and sugar. Fill 4 tall glasses with alternate layers of crème pâtissière and prepared fruit, ending with a layer of crème pâtissière. Top with whipped cream and fruit.

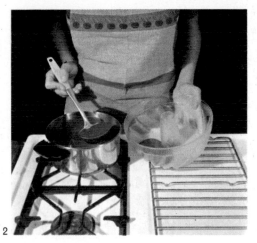

1   2   3

1   2   3

Chocolate Meringue Cups

Ingredients: *36 small meringues, commercial or homemade (see p.168) · 9 tablespoons very strong diluted instant coffee · 1 tablespoon butter or margarine · 5 oz bitter chocolate, cut into pieces · 2 cups heavy cream · 1 heaped table-spoon confectioners' sugar*

In a small pan put the chocolate, cut into pieces, butter or margarine and coffee, and cook the mixture, stirring constantly, until the chocolate is melted (step 1). Keep the chocolate sauce warm in a bain-marie or in the top of a double boiler. Whip the cream until stiff and stir in the confectioners' sugar. Put 4 meringues in each serving dish or glass, pour in $\frac{3}{4}$ of the chocolate sauce (step 2), add 2 more meringues and cover with whipped cream. Pour the remaining chocolate sauce over (step 3). Serves 6.

Romanov Cups

Wash and hull 4 cups strawberries, drain and macerate in 1 cup Grand Marnier mixed with $\frac{1}{2}$ cup sugar. Divide them between 6 serving dishes and cover with $1\frac{1}{4}$ cups heavy cream, whipped with confectioners' sugar. Serves 6.

Coconut Cups

Grate 1 lb fresh coconut into a bowl and stir in 1 tablespoon unsweetened cocoa powder, 2 tablespoons grated bitter chocolate and 4–5 tablespoons aniseed liqueur or other liqueur to taste. Add 2 tablespoons chocolate melted with 3 tablespoons honey in a bain-marie or in the top of a double boiler, and fold in 1 cup whipped cream. Divide between serving dishes and decorate with whipped cream.

Nutty Fruit Cups

Toast 3 oz hazelnuts in the oven for a few minutes, peel and chop. Dice 2 pineapple slices and 1 banana and macerate in maraschino. Whip $1\frac{1}{2}$ cups heavy cream until stiff, stir in 2 tablespoons confectioners' sugar, sifted with $\frac{1}{4}$ oz vanilla sugar, and gently fold in the nuts and fruit in the liqueur. Divide the mixture equally between 4 serving dishes or glasses, garnish with a few pieces pineapple and 1 cherry and refrigerate.

Crème Caramel

Ingredients: *2 cups milk · ½ vanilla bean, or 1 piece lemon peel · 5 eggs · ½ cup sugar*

For the caramel: *3–4 tablespoons sugar*

Bring the milk with the vanilla bean or lemon peel to a boil, remove from the heat and discard the vanilla. In a bowl beat the eggs with the sugar and pour in the hot milk a little at a time, stirring constantly. Melt the sugar for the caramel in a deep metal mold over moderate heat, cook until it starts to turn deep golden, remove from the heat and tilt and rotate the mold until the caramel coats all sides (step 1). Strain the cream into the mold (step 2), half-covering the mold so that the steam can escape, and bake it in a bain-marie with very hot but not boiling water, on top of the stove (step 3), or, preferably, in a moderately hot oven

(375°F) for 40–50 minutes until set. Remove the mold, let cool and unmold on a serving platter. Refrigerate before serving.

Zabaglione

In a bowl, using a wooden spoon, beat 4 egg yolks with 4 tablespoons sugar for about 15 minutes and stir in 1 cup Marsala, a little at a time. Cook the zabaglione, stirring constantly, over moderate heat or in a bain-marie until it thickens, without letting it boil. Remove the zabaglione and serve hot or cold or use in other recipes.

Custard Pots

Beat 10 eggs with 1 cup sugar until the mixture is fluffy and stir in 1 quart milk, a little at a

time. Add a few drops almond or vanilla extract, or finely grated lemon or orange peel to taste. Divide the mixture equally between individual dishes and cook in a bain-marie as above until set. Serve in the dishes without unmolding.

Crème Pâtissière

In a bowl beat 4 egg yolks with 4 tablespoons sugar for about 15 minutes, add 3–4 tablespoons flour and stir in 2 cups lukewarm milk, a little at a time. Add a little lemon peel and 1 tablespoon butter or margarine and cook the cream, stirring constantly, until it thickens, without letting it boil. Remove the lemon peel before serving. Coffee or chocolate may be added to vary the flavor.

Vanilla Ice Cream

Ingredients: *4 egg yolks · ¾ cup sugar · 1 cup heavy cream · 2 cups milk · ½ vanilla bean*

In a bowl beat the egg yolks with the sugar vigorously and stir in the cream, milk and vanilla. Pour the mixture in a pan and cook, stirring constantly, over low heat until it thickens, without letting it boil (step 1). Remove the cream from the heat, transfer to a bowl, remove the vanilla bean and let cool, stirring occasionally to avoid the formation of a skin. Pour the cream into an ice cream churn or beat vigorously and pour into a freezer or ice tray (step 2). Freeze, setting the temperature at the coldest point, until hard, turn it out into a chilled bowl and beat vigorously until foamy. Return to the freezer tray and freeze until solid.

Chocolate Ice Cream

Follow the above recipe, adding 4 oz chocolate, melted with 2 tablespoons milk in a bain-marie or in the top of a double boiler, to the beaten eggs before stirring in the cream and milk. Serve the ice cream with an ice cream scoop (step 3) in Champagne glasses with different flavored ice creams.

Coffee Ice Cream

In a small pan bring 2 cups water to a boil, stir in 2 tablespoons instant coffee powder, remove the pan from the heat, cover, let stand for 30 minutes, then strain. Beat 4 egg yolks with ¾ cup sugar vigorously, stir in 1 cup boiling milk, a little at a time, and add the coffee. Cook the mixture, stirring constantly, over moderate heat until it thickens, without letting it boil. Remove the cream from the heat and let cool, stirring occasionally to avoid the formation of a skin. Pour into an ice cream churn or into an ice tray and proceed as above.

Strawberry Ice Cream

Heat 1 cup cream, add ¾ cup sugar and stir the mixture until the sugar is melted. Let the mixture cool and add 3 cups heavy cream, ¼ oz vanilla sugar and 1 lb strawberries, washed, mashed with a fork and lightly sweetened. Pour the mixture into an ice cream churn or an ice tray and proceed as above.

Fruit Ices or Sherbets

Boil 2 cups water with 1½ cups sugar for 5 minutes, strain the syrup through a fine cloth and let cool. Work ½ lb ripe fruit (raspberries, peaches, apricots, strawberries or bananas) through a fine sieve, stir in the juice of 1 orange and 1 lemon, a little lemon peel, and the syrup and let the mixture stand for ½ hour. Strain the mixture through a fine cloth, pour into an ice cream churn and proceed as above.

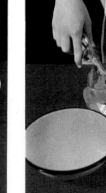

1   2   3

1   2   3

Baked Alaska

Ingredients: *1 rectangle pan di Spagna (see p.140) or sponge cake · 4 egg whites · 4 tablespoons sugar · 2 lb vanilla ice cream in brick form*

Put the pan di Spagna or sponge cake on a metal tray and sprinkle with liqueur to taste (step 1). Beat the egg whites with ¾ of the sugar until they form very stiff peaks. Put the very cold ice cream on the pastry (step 2), leaving a 1-inch border of pan di Spagna or sponge cake all around, and using an icing pump or a pastry bag fitted with a large nozzle, quickly pipe out the meringue thickly, completely covering both cake and ice cream (step 3). Sprinkle with remaining sugar and bake in a very hot oven (450°F) for a few minutes or until the meringue is golden. Serves 8.

Orange Omelet Soufflé

Beat 6 egg yolks with 1 cup sugar until the mixture is thick, stir in the peel of 2 oranges, cut into thin strips, and fold in 8 egg whites, beaten until very stiff. Pile the mixture onto an oval metal platter, buttered and sprinkled with sugar, shaping into a 'mound' with a spatula. Bake the omelet in a moderate oven (350°F) for 20–25 minutes. A few minutes before taking it from the oven, glaze the top by sprinkling it with confectioners' sugar.

Oranges Soufflées

Using a very sharp knife, halve 4 oranges and remove the fruit very gently, keeping the orange shells intact. Reserve the fruit for another recipe and keep the orange shells in the freezing compartment of the refrigerator until very cold. Prepare a meringue by beating 3 egg whites with 4 tablespoons sugar and 1 oz vanilla sugar until very stiff. Fill the orange shells with very cold orange sherbet and cover the sherbet very quickly with the meringue mixture.

Bake the oranges in a very hot oven (450°F) for a few minutes or until the meringue is golden and crisp, and serve immediately on individual plates.

1　　　　2　　　　3

Vanilla Sauce

Ingredients: *1 cup milk · 1 cup light cream · ½ vanilla bean · 4 egg yolks · 4 tablespoons sugar · ½ teaspoon flour*

Heat the milk and cream with the vanilla bean over very low heat in a bain-marie or the top of a double boiler. In a bowl beat the egg yolks with the sugar and flour until the mixture is light and fluffy and stir in the hot milk quickly (step 1). Put the mixture in a bain-marie or in the top of a double boiler and cook, stirring constantly, until it has thickened (step 2). Strain the sauce through a fine sieve and serve immediately, or let cool, stirring occasionally to prevent a skin forming.

Chocolate Sauce

Melt 2 tablespoons grated chocolate with 2 tablespoons sugar and 2½ tablespoons water in a bain-marie or in the top of a double boiler and stir the mixture into a vanilla sauce made as above.

Apricot Sauce

Soak 1 cup dried apricots in water overnight, drain and put in a pan with enough water to cover. Cook over moderate heat until tender, work through a sieve and return them to the heat with 4 tablespoons sugar. Cook the sauce until the sugar is melted, remove from the heat and stir in 2 tablespoons rum, if the sauce is to be served hot, or 2 tablespoons kirsch, if cold. The sauce may also be prepared in the following manner: work 1 jar apricot jam through a sieve, add 3–4 tablespoons water and 2 tablespoons sugar and heat the mixture. Add kirsch or Cognac to taste.

Banana Sauce

Peel 2 small ripe bananas, work through a sieve and add 4 tablespoons sugar, and 2 tablespoons kirsch. Bring the mixture to a boil over very low heat and let cool. Refrigerate and fold in whipped cream before serving.

Orange Sauce

In the top of a double boiler blend ½ cup sugar with 2 tablespoons cornstarch, add 4 tablespoons boiling water and stir the mixture until it is transparent. Add 1 small piece orange peel and cook the mixture for 5–6 minutes. Remove the sauce from the heat, strain it slowly into 2 beaten egg yolks and let cool. Stir in 1 tablespoon lemon juice, 6–8 tablespoons orange juice and 1 tablespoon kirsch and refrigerate.

Coffee Sauce

Prepare vanilla sauce as above substituting 4–5 tablespoons very strong diluted instant coffee for the vanilla.

Whipped Cream Sauce

Prepare vanilla sauce as above, halving the quantities, fold in 4 tablespoons whipped cream (step 3), and stir in liqueur to taste.

Liqueur Soufflé

Ingredients: *2 tablespoons butter or margarine · 2 tablespoons flour · 1 cup milk · 1 pinch salt · 3 tablespoons sugar · 3 tablespoons liqueur to taste · 3 tablespoons cornstarch · 4 egg yolks · 4 egg whites, whipped with lemon juice and a little salt until very stiff*

Melt the butter or margarine, add the flour and cook the mixture, stirring constantly, until it starts to brown. Add the milk all at once, bring the mixture to a boil and stir in the salt. Turn off the heat, stir in the sugar, liqueur, cornstarch and the egg yolks one at a time and fold in the egg whites (step 1). Butter a soufflé mold, dust with sugar (step 2), and pour in the mixture (step 3). Bake the soufflé in a hot oven (400°F) for 20 minutes.

Chestnut Soufflé

Work 1¼ cups marrons glacés through a sieve. Melt 2 tablespoons butter or margarine, add 4 tablespoons flour and 1 cup milk all at once and stir in 1 pinch salt. Cook the mixture, stirring constantly, for 8 minutes, and let cool. Blend in the puréed marrons glacés and 4 beaten egg yolks and fold in 4–5 egg whites, beaten until very stiff. Pour the mixture into a buttered soufflé mold, dusted with sugar, bake in a very hot oven (425°F) for 15 minutes, lower the heat to 400°F and continue baking for 30–35 minutes, without opening the oven. Serve immediately. Serves 4–5.

Cherry Soufflé

Cook about ¾ cup pitted cherries in a syrup made by cooking 4 tablespoons sugar in 3 tablespoons water, or use 4 tablespoons thick cherry jam. Heat ½ cup milk in a pan. In a bowl blend 1 level tablespoon sugar and 1½ tablespoons cornstarch in 2 tablespoons cold milk, add this mixture to the warm milk a little at a time and cook the cream, stirring constantly, over low heat until it thickens. Remove the pan from the heat, strain the cream through a sieve and stir in 3 beaten egg yolks. Add the cooked cherries or the jam and 1 tablespoon kirsch, and fold in 3 egg whites, beaten until stiff. Pour the mixture into a buttered soufflé mold, dusted with sugar, and bake in a moderate oven (350°F) for about 30 minutes or until the soufflé is well puffed and golden. Serve immediately with vanilla sauce (see p.158).

Ice Cream with Liqueur

Prepare 2 cups ice cream to taste (see p.156), and divide into 4 Champagne glasses or individual serving dishes. Add liqueur to taste. Some good combination are: vanilla ice cream with whisky, Cognac or crème de cacao; coffee ice cream with crème de menthe; peach ice cream with cherry brandy; raspberry or strawberry ice cream with kirsch.

Cold Orange Soufflé

Ingredients: *8 eggs, separated · 1 cup sugar · 2 tablespoons finely grated orange peel · 1 tablespoon finely grated lemon peel · 15 tablespoons orange juice · 5 tablespoons lemon juice · 1 pinch of salt · 2 tablespoons gelatin, softened in a little lukewarm water · 2 cups heavy cream*

To decorate: *orange quarters · cherries in syrup*

In a bowl beat the egg yolks, reserving the whites, with 4 tablespoons of the sugar, the orange and lemon peel, orange and lemon juice and salt until the mixture is fluffy, stir in the gelatin and cook the mixture, stirring constantly, in a bain-marie of hot but not boiling water until it thickens (step 1). Remove from the bain-marie and let cool, stirring constantly. Beat the reserved egg whites until stiff, beat in the remaining sugar and fold in the heavy cream, whipped until stiff, and the cooked cream very gently. Cut a 15-inch wide strip of aluminum foil or wax paper, fold it in 3 lengthwise and tie securely with Scotch tape or string around the top edge of a large soufflé mold, to come about 2 inches above the edge (step 2). Brush the mold and foil or paper with oil, fill the mold with the mixture and refrigerate for 3–4 hours. Remove the paper gently (step 3), decorate the top with orange quarters and cherries to taste and serve. Serves 8–10.

Vanilla Bavaroise

Soften 1 tablespoon gelatin in a little water. In a bowl beat 4 egg yolks with 4 tablespoons sugar until the mixture is fluffy and stir in 1 cup milk, heated with ½ vanilla bean. Add the gelatin and cook the cream, stirring constantly, over very low heat until it thickens. Remove from the heat, discard the vanilla bean and let cool, stirring occasionally to avoid the formation of a skin on the surface. Beat 1 cup heavy cream until stiff and fold it into the cooked cream. Pour the cream into a wetted mold, chill for 4–5 hours, dip quickly into boiling water and unmold onto a serving platter. Surround with rosettes of whipped cream and fruit, macerated in sugar and liqueur. Serves 4–6.

Cold Chestnut Soufflé

In a bowl beat 4 eggs, 3 egg yolks and ½ cup sugar until the mixture is very thick and light in color. Soften 2 tablespoons gelatin in 6 tablespoons rum and dissolve over hot water. Stir the gelatin mixture into the beaten eggs, add 1 cup sweetened chestnut purée and fold in 1 cup heavy cream, beaten until stiff. Prepare a soufflé mold as above, and brush the paper and the mold with oil. Pour in the mixture and refrigerate. Remove paper and decorate with whipped cream and marrons glacés. Serves 6.

1

2

3

1   2   3

Pineapple with Fruit

Ingredients: *1 fresh pineapple with its leaves ·
1 small glass kirsch · 4 tablespoons
confectioners' sugar · ½ lb strawberries or
raspberries, fresh or frozen · the juice of
1 orange or 1 lemon · 4 tablespoons heavy
cream · ¼ oz vanilla sugar · candied peel, cut
in thin strips*

Halve the pineapple lengthwise and remove
the pulp with a sharp knife (step 1), discarding
the hard part in the middle. Dice the pulp and
macerate in the kirsch and sugar for 45 minutes. If using fresh fruit, wash quickly, halve if
necessary and macerate in a bowl with the
orange or lemon juice. Whip the cream until
stiff, stir in the vanilla sugar and chill. Mix the
strawberries or raspberries, reserving a few
for decoration, with the pineapple pulp and
divide the fruit mixture between the two
pineapple halves (step 2). Using an icing pump
or a pastry bag fitted with a large nozzle,
decorate the pineapple with the whipped
cream (step 3), add the reserved berries and
the peel, cut into thin strips, and chill before
serving.

Stuffed Peaches

Wash and dry 4 large yellow peaches, halve
and discard the pit. Using a teaspoon, remove
a little of the pulp from each half, forming a
hollow. In a bowl, mix the chopped pulp with
2½ oz macaroons, liqueur to taste, 1 egg yolk, 2
tablespoons sugar, 1 oz almonds, peeled and
finely chopped, and 1 tablespoon butter or
margarine. Fill the peach halves with the
mixture, dot with butter and put on a
generously buttered cookie sheet. Cook the
peaches in a hot oven (400°F) for 45 minutes,
transfer to a serving platter and dust with
confectioners' sugar. Decorate with peeled
almonds if liked.

Pears Marli

Prepare 2 cups vanilla ice cream (see p.156),
and divide equally between 4 Champagne
glasses or crystal cups. Stick together 8 drained
canned pear halves in pairs by putting crushed
marrons glacés or thick crème pâtissière (see
p.155) between each pair and put 1 reassembled
pear in each glass. Cover with whipped cream.
Decorate with grated chocolate and cherries.

Peach Melba

Poach 4 large yellow peaches in 2 cups water
and ½ cup sugar for 15 minutes. Peel the
peaches, halve, remove the pit, and chill.
Put 1 large scoop vanilla ice cream in each
individual dish, top with two peach halves
and cover with 2 cups fruit syrup (raspberry,
blackcurrant or redcurrant). Sprinkle with
almonds and decorate with whipped cream.

1

2

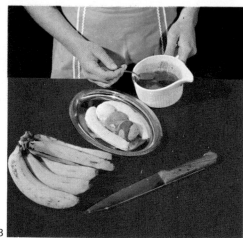

3

Banana Split

Ingredients for each serving: *1 banana ·
1 scoop each of vanilla ice cream, chocolate ice
cream and strawberry ice cream · 2 tablespoons
chocolate · 2—3 tablespoons milk*

To decorate: *whipped cream ·
2 tablespoons chopped walnuts*

Peel and halve the banana lengthwise (step 1)
and place the halves along the edge of a small
oval platter. Place the ice cream scoops in the
middle (step 2) and cover with the chocolate,
melted with the milk in a bain-marie or in the
top of a double boiler (step 3). Decorate with
piped rosettes of whipped cream, sprinkle with
chopped nuts and serve immediately. To make

a richer dessert, cover the vanilla scoop with
jam, the chocolate with melted chocolate and
the strawberry with fruit syrup.

Apple Clafoutis

Sift ½ cup flour into a bowl, make a well in the
center and add 3 eggs, 2 tablespoons sugar,
1 pinch of salt, 1 cup milk, 3 tablespoons
melted butter and 1 tablespoon baking powder.
Work the ingredients together quickly and
thoroughly. Stir in 10 oz apples, peeled, cored
and cut into very thin slices. Pour the mixture
into a buttered pie pan and bake in a moderate
oven (350°F) until golden-brown and the
apples are cooked through.

Cherry Clafoutis

Pit 10 oz Bing cherries and macerate in a little
kirsch. Sift ½ cup flour into a bowl, make a well
in the center and add 3 egg yolks, 2 tablespoons sugar, 1 pinch salt, 1 cup milk, 3
tablespoons melted butter and 1 tablespoon
baking powder. Work the ingredients together
thoroughly and beat the mixture until it has
the consistency of pancake batter. Whip 3 egg
whites until stiff and fold gently into the batter.
Butter a high-sided pie pan, pour in a layer of
batter, add a layer of cherries, and end with a
layer of batter and a layer of cherries. Bake
in a moderate oven (350°F) until golden-
brown and the cherries are soft.

Flamed Bananas

Ingredients: *4 bananas · 6 tablespoons sugar · flour · 1–2 eggs, beaten · 2 tablespoons butter or margarine · ½ glass kirsch or Cognac*

Peel the bananas, halve lengthwise and sprinkle with sugar. Dip in flour (step 1), in the beaten egg and again in flour and sauté lightly in the butter until golden on both sides (step 2). Place the bananas on a warmed platter, with candied cherries, sprinkle with the remaining sugar (step 3) and pour the hot kirsch or Cognac over them. Flame the kirsch and serve immediately.

Banana Delight

Peel 4 large bananas, halve lengthwise and place in a buttered ovenproof dish. Sprinkle them with 2½ tablespoons sugar, mixed with 8 tablespoons orange or lemon juice or liqueur to taste, and 1 tablespoon butter in small pieces, and cover with a ½-inch thick layer of grated coconut. Bake the bananas in a hot oven (400°F) for 10 minutes or until golden on top. Serve like this or with a vanilla or orange sauce (see p.158).

Banana Pudding

Peel 6 ripe bananas, mash with a fork and mix with 2 tablespoons rum, 1 beaten egg, 2½ tablespoons melted butter or margarine, 1 pinch each of cinnamon and grated nutmeg and 2 tablespoons flour, sifted with 1 teaspoon baking powder. Pour the mixture in a buttered mold, sprinkled with sugar, and cook in a bain-marie on top of the stove or in the oven for about 1 hour or until set. Serve cold decorated with whipped cream and glacé cherries if liked.

Banana Beignets

Prepare the batter: in a bowl mix ½ cup sifted flour with 2 tablespoons sugar, 1 tablespoon melted butter or margarine, 1 pinch salt and about 4 tablespoons hot water. Add 2 tablespoons brandy or rum and 1 beaten egg yolk and let the batter stand for 1–2 hours. Peel 8 small bananas or 6 large ones, halve lengthwise and cut the halves into 2 or 3 pieces, depending on size of bananas. Fold 1 egg white, beaten until stiff, into the batter, dip the banana pieces into the mixture a few at a time and fry in hot deep oil until golden on all sides. Drain the beignets on absorbent paper, sprinkle with confectioners' sugar and serve hot or cold. Serves 4–6.

Melon with Macedoine of Fruit

Ingredients: *2 medium-sized melons or 4 small ones*

For the macedoine: *peaches, oranges, apples, pears, bananas, strawberries, cherries · liqueur · sugar*

Peel the fruit, discard the pits, dice (step 1), add the liqueur and sugar to taste and chill the mixture. Chill the melons until ready to use. Halve the melons, discard the seeds, remove a little of the pulp from each half with a melon ball cutter (step 2), and add the melon balls to the macedoine. Divide the macedoine equally between the melons (step 3), garnish with a strawberry or mint leaves and serve immediately.

The macedoine may be served in individual dishes if liked.

Melon Fantasia

Peel and halve 1 melon, remove the seeds and cube the pulp. Put the melon cubes into a glass serving dish, sprinkle with a few tablespoons sugar and chill for a few hours. Sprinkle the fruit with brandy, lemon juice, raisins, softened in brandy, and chopped walnuts.

Melon with Port

Cut and reserve a small slice from the top of 1 large cantaloup melon. Using a teaspoon, remove and discard the seeds and add sugar to taste and 1–1½ cups port, Madeira or Marsala. Return the top to the melon and chill for at least 2 hours. Remove the melon from the refrigerator, remove the pulp with a spoon and serve with a little of the wine.

Melon Cups

Remove the seeds from 1 cantaloup melon and ½ watermelon and scoop out the pulp in balls with a melon ball cutter, putting each type of melon into a separate bowl. Cut canned pineapple slices into cubes and put in a separate bowl. Mix the pineapple juice with orange juice, lemon juice and sugar to taste, and divide the mixture between the three melon cups. Chill the bowls for a few hours and divide their contents equally between 4 Champagne glasses or individual serving dishes. Decorate with whipped cream.

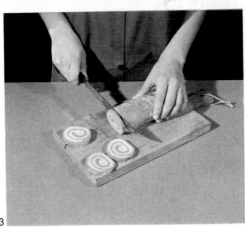

1 2 3

Petits Fours

Ingredients: *¼ cup butter or margarine at room temperature · 3 tablespoons confectioners' sugar · ¼ oz vanilla sugar · 1 egg yolk · 1 cup sifted flour · 1 pinch salt · a few drops red food coloring or a few tablespoons unsweetened cocoa powder*

To finish: 1 egg white · 2 tablespoons water · sugar crystals

In a bowl work the butter or margarine with the sugar, vanilla sugar and egg yolk, work in the flour and the salt until the mixture is smooth and divide into two. Add the food coloring or cocoa powder to one half (step 1). Form the dough into two balls, cover with wax paper and let stand in the refrigerator for 30 minutes. Remove the plain dough from the refrigerator, work it for a few minutes, put on a board, covered with a floured cloth, and roll out, not too thinly, into a rectangle. Roll out the colored dough in the same manner, put the plain dough on top of it (step 2), and

roll up the layers together. Cover the roll in wax paper, return to the refrigerator for 1 hour and cut into slices (step 3). Place the slices on a lightly buttered cookie sheet and bake the cookies in a hot oven (400°F) for about 10 minutes. Remove from the oven, brush with the egg white mixed with the water, and sprinkle with sugar crystals. Let cool on a wire rack.

Cherry and Pine Nut Cookies

On a board sift 1 cup flour with 1 teaspoon baking powder, make a well in the center and add 3 tablespoons sugar, 2 egg yolks, ½ cup butter in small pieces and a little finely grated lemon peel. Work the ingredients together quickly, shape the dough into a ball, cover with wax paper and let stand in the refrigerator for 30 minutes. Soak 30 pine nuts in boiling water, drain and peel. Halve 15 candied cherries. Cut the dough into walnut-sized balls, make a slight hollow in the center of the balls and dip

them in beaten egg white. Place on a buttered cookie sheet, cover half of them with pine nuts, the other half with cherry halves and cook in a hot oven (400°F) for about 20 minutes or until crisp and golden-brown. Remove from the oven and let cool on a wire rack. Makes 60 cookies.

Almond Cookies

In a bowl beat 4 eggs with 4 tablespoons sugar until the mixture is fluffy and stir in 1½ cups flour, sifted with a pinch each of bicarbonate of soda and cream of tartar, and 3 oz almonds, peeled and chopped. Work the ingredients together until the mixture is smooth, shape into a roll and place on a buttered cookie sheet, dusted with flour. Cook the roll in a moderate oven (350°F) for 20–30 minutes, let cool and cut into slices. Decorate each slice with peeled almonds, dipped in egg white, and return the cookies to the oven until crisp and golden-brown.

Sicilian Cannoli

Ingredients: for the dough, *¾ cup flour ·
1 tablespoon sugar · 2 tablespoons
confectioners' sugar · 1 tablespoon unsweetened
cocoa powder · ½ teaspoon instant coffee
powder · 1 tablespoon butter or margarine, in
small pieces · ¼ cup dry white wine · 1 egg white*

For the filling: *1 cup ricotta or cream cheese ·
¾ cup confectioners' sugar · liqueur to taste ·
1 tablespoon candied peel, chopped · 2 oz glacé
cherries, chopped · powdered chocolate*

To finish: *oil for frying · confectioners' sugar*

Make the dough: on a board sift the flour, sugar,
confectioners' sugar, cocoa and coffee, make a
well in the center and add the butter or
margarine and the white wine. Work the
ingredients quickly and thoroughly, shape the
dough into a ball, cover with wax paper and
let stand in the refrigerator for about 1 hour.
Meanwhile, make the filling: in a bowl blend
the cheese with the sugar and liqueur, work the
mixture through a sieve, then stir in the
candied peel and glacé cherries, reserving a
few cherries for decoration. Divide the mixture
into two parts, add the powdered chocolate to
one and chill both mixtures. Butter cannoli,
cream horn or tube molds 10 inches long by
1 inch wide. Roll out the dough thinly and
cut into 4-inch squares. Put a mold diagonally
in the center of each square (step 1), roll up
the dough around the tube and press the dough
together, brushing with a little egg white. Heat
the oil, and cook the cannoli (step 2). Drain
and let cool. Remove the molds and let the
cannoli cool. Fill half with plain cream and
half with chocolate cream (step 3), add a
cherry to each end and dust with confectioners'
sugar. Serves 6.

Epiphany Cake

Dissolve ½ tablespoon fresh brewer's yeast in a
few drops lukewarm water in a bowl. Add 2
eggs and 1 cup sifted flour and mix the ingredients quickly and thoroughly. Heat 2 tablespoons butter in a small pan with the juice and
finely grated peel of 1 orange, the juice and
finely grated peel of ½ lemon and a few drops
orange flower extract. Pour the mixture drop
by drop into the dough and continue working
and pounding the dough until elastic. Shape the
dough into a ball, cover and let stand in a warm
place until it doubles in volume. Pound for a
few minutes with lightly floured hands, shape
into a ball, cover and let stand in a cool place
until it has again doubled in volume. Put it on
a floured board, work for a few minutes, shape
into a ball, make a hole in the middle and widen
it to form a crown. Let stand until it has again
doubled in volume, brush with beaten egg yolk
and bake in the lowest part of a hot oven
(400°F) for about 25 minutes.

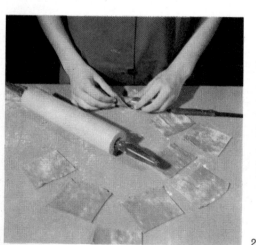

1

2

3

Stuffed Dates, Prunes and Walnuts

Ingredients: *6 oz dates · marzipan (in 3 different colors, if liked), or almond paste · 6 oz prunes · 6 oz shelled walnuts, halved*

For the syrup: 1½ cups sugar · 10–11 tablespoons water · 1 pinch cream of tartar

Make an incision into the sides of the dates, discard the pits (step 1) and fill with a little pink marzipan (if using colored marzipans), or almond paste. Fill the prunes in the same manner, using green marzipan (step 2) and sandwich the walnut halves together, two by two, by putting a little plain marzipan between the 2 halves. Make the syrup: in a small pan cook the sugar, water and cream of tartar over moderate heat until a little of the mixture dropped in cold water forms crunchy threads. Remove the pan from the heat, dip in cold water to stop the cooking and place on a pan of hot water to keep the mixture liquid. Using a slotted spoon, toothpicks or metal skewers, dip the stuffed fruit, one at a time, into the syrup (step 3), place on an oiled wire rack and let cool.

Nougat

Soak 1½ cups almonds in boiling water for a few minutes, drain, peel and cut into thin strips or chop. In a pan heat 1½ cups sugar with a knob of butter over moderate heat, cook the mixture, stirring slowly, until the sugar is melted, and add the almonds. Cook the mixture until golden, remove from the heat and pour on a marble slab or tin, dampened with oil. Using a whole lemon, flatten the mixture quickly to a ½-inch thickness and score with a knife into squares so that it will break easily. Let cool completely. Keep in sealed jars.

Candied Orange Peel

Cut the skin of a few oranges in quarters and soak the quarters in cold water for 3 days, changing the water twice a day. Drain the quarters, cook in boiling water for 15–20 minutes, drain and cut into very thin strips discarding the white part of the skin. Weigh the strips and put them in a small pan with an equal weight of sugar and just enough water to moisten the sugar. Cook the mixture until the sugar starts to turn golden and is almost completely absorbed. The mixture should be syrup-like but not granular. Put the strips on a marble slab or a plate, separate them and let cool.

1

2

3

Drinks

Mixing cocktails is very much a matter of individual preference. Here are some suggestions to follow or to use as a basis for your own experimentation; the strengths of the cocktails can be increased according to taste.

Rum Cocktail

Fill ⅓ of a shaker with ice, add 1 part lemon juice, 4 parts rum (steps 1 and 2), ½ teaspoon sugar (optional), and 2–3 dashes of grenadine. Shake vigorously and strain the drink into the glasses (step 3). This cocktail may also be prepared in a mixer and served on the rocks.

Atomic Bomb

In each glass put 1 sugar cube, a dash of Angostura, 2 parts Scotch, 1 part Aperol (optional), 1 part Cognac and the juice of ¼ orange. Do not mix. Serve with ice and a slice of orange. If prepared in a shaker, put the sugar and Angostura in each glass separately.

Brandy Cocktail

Fill ½ a shaker with ice, add 1 part lemon juice, 2 parts curaçao, 8 parts brandy and 2 dashes of Angostura. Shake well and serve.

Teacher's Cocktail

In a mixer put 1 part vodka, 1 part gin and 1 teaspoon dry vermouth. Mix well and pour in a glass containing ice and 1 olive.

Pernod Cocktail

Fill ¼ of a mixer with ice, add 1 part dry vermouth, 1 part sweet vermouth and 1 part Pernod. Mix well and serve in frosted glasses.

Screwdriver

Fill ⅓ of a shaker with crushed ice and add 1 part orange juice and 1 part vodka. Shake vigorously and serve.

Old-fashioned

In a low glass crush 1 sugar cube with 1 teaspoon water and 1 dash Angostura. Fill ⅓ of the glass with crushed ice, add a measure of Scotch and mix well. Serve with a maraschino cherry and a twist of orange or lemon on the edge of the glass.

Whisky Sour

Fill ⅓ of a shaker with crushed ice, add 1 teaspoon sugar for each glass, 2 parts lemon juice and 8 parts bourbon. Shake vigorously and serve in chilled glasses, garnished with 1 maraschino cherry and a twist of orange or lemon on the edge of the glass.

Negroni

Fill a mixer with ⅓ ice, add 1 part Campari bitters, 1 part dry gin and 1 part red vermouth. Mix well, pour and add 1 slice of orange.

Manhattan

Fill ⅓ of a mixer with crushed ice, add 1 part sweet vermouth, 2 parts Scotch and 1 dash Angostura. Mix well and strain the cocktail into chilled glasses, each containing a maraschino cherry.

Dry Martini

Fill ⅓ of a mixer with ice, add 2 parts gin and 1 part dry vermouth. Mix well and pour into chilled glasses. Add a little lemon peel, 1 cube of ice and 1 green olive on a toothpick to each glass.

Alexander

After collecting all the necessary cocktail utensils together, fill ⅓ of a shaker with ice, add 1 part crème de cacao, 1 part cream and 2 parts gin or Cognac, shake well and serve immediately.

1

2

3

1   2   3

Sweet-and-Sour Drink

Ingredients: *2 cups grapefruit juice ·
3 tablespoons lemon juice · sugar ·
2 cups ginger ale · ice cubes*

Blend the grapefruit and lemon juice together
in a jug (step 1) and refrigerate for a few hours.
Frost the glasses by dipping the rims in lemon
juice and then in sugar (step 2) and chilling
them. Mix the fruit juices with ginger ale and
pour into the glasses, over ice cubes and sugar.

Lemonade with Rosemary

Bring 1 quart water, ¾ cup sugar, 2 tablespoons
lemon juice and 1 teaspoon fresh rosemary
leaves to a boil and cook the mixture for 6
minutes. Strain the liquid, let cool and add 8
tablespoons lemon juice. Refrigerate the liquid
for a few hours and serve in tall glasses with 1
lemon slice and a twig of rosemary in each
glass. Serves 4–6.

Apricot and Orange Drink

In a jug mix 2 cans or bottles apricot juice with
2 cans or bottles orange juice and add the
juice of 2 lemons or of 1 grapefruit and a few
mint leaves, if desired. Refrigerate the jug for a
few hours and serve the drink over ice cubes
in frosted glasses.

Spicy Tomato Juice

In a jug mix 1 quart tomato juice with 2 teaspoons tomato ketchup, a few drops Worcestershire, the juice of ½ lemon or more to
taste and salt and pepper. Refrigerate before
serving or serve over ice cubes.

Summer Drink

In a jug mix ½ glass pineapple juice with ½ cup
grapefruit juice, the juice of 1 orange and 4

teaspoons sugar. Refrigerate the jug for a few
hours and add 1 cup mineral or soda water.
Serve immediately with 1 lemon or orange
slice in each glass. The measurements can be
adjusted to taste.

Pink Drink

In a jug blend 1 cup tomato juice with 1¼ cups
orange juice and the juice of 1 lemon. Refrigerate for a few hours and serve over ice cubes.
Add ½ slice orange or lemon to each glass.

Mixed Fruit Drink

In a jug mix the juice of 4 oranges and 2 lemons,
1 can or bottle pear juice, 1 can or bottle apricot
juice and 1 teaspoon raspberry syrup and
refrigerate the mixture for a few hours. Mix
again and pour the drink over ice cubes. Add
1 orange slice to each glass.

Gourmet Coffee

Ingredients: *¾ cup chocolate · 2 tablespoons water · 1 pinch cinnamon · 4 small cups hot strong black coffee · crushed ice · sugar cubes · whipped or light cream*

Melt the chocolate in a bain-marie or in the top of a double boiler with the water. Add the cinnamon, and the hot coffee, a little at a time (step 1). Fill 4 tall glasses with crushed ice, add the chocolate mixture and more coffee if necessary, to fill the glass (step 2) and sugar to taste and serve with whipped cream on top (step 3) or light cream separately.

Coffee Delight

Mix 1 tablespoon instant coffee powder with 2 tablespoons hot water, add ¾ cup cold water and refrigerate the mixture until very cold. Stir in 1 cup commercially prepared or homemade coffee ice cream (see p.156), whipped until soft. Pour the mixture in tall chilled glasses, add a little whipped cream on top and serve immediately.

Sugared Coffee

Make 6 small cups of strong black coffee. In a bowl put 1 teaspoon or more sugar per person, add 4 teaspoons coffee and beat the mixture until frothy. Divide the mixture equally between 4 cups and add the hot coffee. A light froth will form on the top.

Iced Tea Cubes

Prepare tea to taste, add sugar and lemon juice to taste and let cool in an ice cube tray with maraschino cherries in some of the cubes, pieces of pineapple in others, mint leaves in others. Freeze the tray until solid, take out the cubes and serve in individual glasses.

Mint Tea

Put 6 teaspoons orange Pekoe tea in a teapot, add 4 cups boiling water and let stand for 10 minutes. Fill 4 tall glasses ⅔ full with tea, add fresh mint leaves and pour in more tea. Serve lemon slices and sugar separately, or, add sugar while the tea is still hot, refrigerate until very cold and serve with ice cubes and lemon slices.

Hot Tea with Rum

In each tall glass put equal measures of rum and strong black tea and sugar to taste. Top with hot water boiled with cloves.

Iced Tea with Peaches

In a jug put 2–3 ripe peaches, peeled, pitted, cubed, sugared and mixed with lemon juice. Add strong hot tea, cool, and then refrigerate.

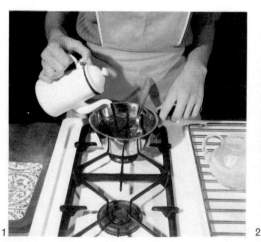

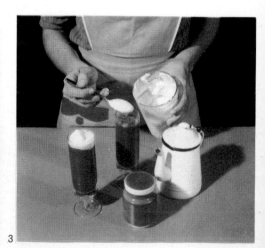

1   2   3

Hot Spicy Chocolate

Ingredients: *4 tablespoons unsweetened cocoa powder, sifted · 3 tablespoons sugar · 1 pinch salt · 3 tablespoons water · 6 cloves · 3 cups milk · 1 cup heavy cream · 4 cinnamon sticks*

In a pan put the cocoa, sugar, salt, water and cloves. Bring the mixture to a boil (step 1), stirring constantly, and cook for 2–3 minutes. Add the milk and ½ the cream (step 2), and heat, stirring constantly. Spoon into 4 mugs, discarding cloves (step 3), and add 1 cinnamon stick and a little whipped cream.

Hot Chocolate Chiquita

Melt 2½ tablespoons chocolate in a bain-marie or in the top of a double boiler, add 2 table-spoons sugar, a few drops vanilla extract, 2 teaspoons instant coffee powder and 4 table-spoons water and cook the mixture for a few minutes. Add 2 cups each of hot water and hot milk and heat the mixture, stirring constantly, without boiling. Serve the chocolate in mugs, topped with whipped cream and cinnamon.

French Chocolate

Melt 4 oz chocolate with 4 tablespoons water in a bain-marie or in the top of a double boiler. Remove the chocolate from the heat and beat vigorously until thickened. Stir in ½ cup water and divide the mixture equally between 4 mugs. Add 1 quart hot milk, stirring constantly and top each mug with whipped cream and powdered cinnamon. Serve immediately.

Spanish Chocolate

Melt 2 tablespoons chocolate with 1 teaspoon butter in a bain-marie or in the top of a double boiler. Add 3 tablespoons sugar, 1 pinch grated nutmeg, 1 pinch cinnamon and ¾ cup hot black coffee a little at a time. Bring the mixture to a boil and cook for 2–3 minutes. Remove from the heat and let cool. Divide it equally between 5–6 tall glasses and fill up with cold milk.

1

2

3

Uncle Tom's Eggnog

Ingredients: *3 eggs, separated · 3 tablespoons sugar · 5 tablespoons bourbon · 5 tablespoons brandy · 1 tablespoon rum · 1 cup milk · 1 cup heavy cream · grated nutmeg*

Beat the egg yolks with a wire whip until they are pale yellow (step 1). Add the sugar, a little at a time, beating constantly. Stir in the bourbon, brandy and rum and refrigerate the mixture for a few hours. Just before serving, remove from the refrigerator, stir in the milk and fold in the cream and the egg whites, both whipped until stiff (step 2). Serve the eggnog in punch cups, sprinkled with grated nutmeg (step 3). Serves 10–12.

Orange Eggnog

Separate 2 eggs, reserving the whites, and beat the yolks with a wire whip until they are pale yellow. Beat in ½ cup orange juice and 1¼ cups cold milk a little at a time. Beat the egg whites until stiff and add 4 tablespoons sugar and ½ cup orange juice, one tablespoon at a time. Fold the egg white mixture carefully into the eggnog.

Divide the eggnog equally between 4 tall glasses and sprinkle with finely grated orange peel.

Tom-and-Jerry

Separate 4 eggs, reserving the whites, and beat the yolks with a wire whip until they are pale yellow. Add 4 teaspoons sugar, 2 teaspoons mixed spice and 4 measures white rum and continue beating the mixture thoroughly until it is creamy.

Fold in the 4 egg whites, whipped until stiff, and add 2 small glasses brandy. Pour the mixture in 4 mugs, fill with hot milk and sprinkle with grated nutmeg.

Vin Brûlé

In a pan put 2½ tablespoons sugar, the peel of ½ lemon, 1 piece cinnamon, 1 clove and ½ bottle good red wine. Bring the mixture to a boil, flame the wine and strain immediately into glasses, preferably with metal glass holders, or into warm cups.

Tea Punch with Rum

In each glass put 1 teaspoon each of lemon juice and sugar, 1½ measures rum and a small sliver lemon peel. Fill with hot tea and serve.

Coffee Punch

In 4 glasses, preferably with metal glass holders, put a few grains sugar, 1 small sliver orange peel, hot black coffee and brandy. Mix well.

1

2

3

1

2

3

Tutti-Frutti Cream

Ingredients: *1 apple · 1 pear, or peach · 1 banana · 1 orange · 2 apricots, fresh or canned · 2 tablespoons sugar, or more to taste · 1 cup milk · 3 cubes crushed ice*

Peel, pit and slice the fruit (step 1) and put in a blender with the sugar, milk and ice (step 2). Set the blender on high speed for 2 minutes and pour the cream in glasses (step 3).

Pineapple Cream

In a blender put 4 slices fresh or canned pineapple, 2 peeled and sliced bananas, the juice of 2 oranges, preferably blood oranges, the juice of 1 lemon, and a cold syrup, made by dissolving 4 tablespoons sugar in 1 cup water, then boiling until quite thick. Set the blender on high speed for 2 minutes then pour the cream over crushed ice cubes in tall glasses and decorate with pineapple slices.

Apricot Cream

Peel and pit 4 apricots and 1 orange, and peel 1 banana. Slice the fruit and put in a blender with 1 cup milk, 2 tablespoons or more sugar to taste and 3 cubes crushed ice. Set the blender on high speed for 2 minutes and pour into glasses.

Apple Cream

Peel, core and slice 2 apples, and peel and slice 1 banana and put them in a blender with 2 tablespoons sugar, 2 cubes crushed ice and 1 cup milk. Set the blender on high speed for 2 minutes, then pour into tall glasses.

Orange Cream

In a blender put the juice of 4 oranges and 1 lemon, the finely grated peel of ½ orange, 1 apple, peeled, cored and sliced, 1 small glass kirsch or other liqueur to taste, 2 tablespoons sugar and 6–8 cubes crushed ice. Set the blender on high speed for 2 minutes, then pour into glasses.

Melon Cream

Peel 1 small melon, discard the seeds, slice and put in a blender. Add 3–4 tablespoons sugar, the juice of 1 lemon, 2 tablespoons liqueur to taste, 1 cup dry white wine and 3 cubes crushed ice. Blend and serve as above.

Pear Cream

Peel, core and slice 2 pears, peel and slice 1 banana and put them in a blender with 4–5 tablespoons grenadine or the juice of 1 blood orange, 1 cup milk and 2 cubes crushed ice. Blend and serve as above.

Sangria

Ingredients: *2 cups red wine · 1 cup Malaga wine · ½ glass Cognac · 1 tablespoon sugar · 1 pinch of cinnamon · 1 pinch of grated nutmeg · 2 oranges · 1 lemon · 2 cups peaches, or 2 bananas*

In a large jug pour the wines and the Cognac (step 1), add the sugar, cinnamon and grated nutmeg. Slice the oranges and lemon and peel and dice the peaches or bananas (step 2). Add the fruit to the wine mixture (step 3) and let macerate for 2 hours at room temperature. Refrigerate the mixture for at least ½ day. Serve the sangria very cold with ice cubes and soda water. The quantities of sugar, cinnamon and grated nutmeg may be adjusted according to taste.

Apple Tonic

In a mixer put 2 parts cider or apple juice, 1 part tonic water and 1 part ice cold soda water. Mix well and serve with ice cubes.

Cuba Libre

Put 1 measure white rum in each tall glass and add ice cubes and Coca-Cola.

Gin and Tonic

Put 1 measure gin in each tall glass, add 1 slice lemon and a few ice cubes and fill with tonic water.

Light Drink

In a mixer put 1 measure each of gin and bitters, the juice of ½ lemon and ½ small bottle tonic or soda water for each person. Mix well and serve in a tall glass with ice cubes.

Mint Julep

In each tall, chilled glass put 1 teaspoon each of sugar and water, and 4 mint leaves. Stir with a teaspoon until the sugar is melted. Fill the glasses with crushed ice, add 1 measure bourbon and stir rapidly for a few minutes. Add enough bourbon to fill the glass. Dip a fresh mint sprig in confectioner's sugar and use to decorate the glass. Serve with a straw.

Country Inn Milk

In a punch bowl pour 1 bottle good red wine, ¼ cup plum brandy and 1 dash Angostura. Mix well and serve at room temperature in punch cups. Serves 6.

This drink is particularly good with roasted chestnuts.

Tom Collins

Fill ⅓ of a shaker with ice, add 1 tablespoon sugar syrup (sugar dissolved in water, then boiled), the juice of ½ lemon and 1 measure gin for each person. Shake vigorously and serve in tall glasses. Add ice cubes and enough soda water to fill glasses.

1

2

3